The Time Worksh

The Time Workshops

Abrielle Jones

B.Sc. (Hons.)

Published by
TIMESLIP BOOKS

Copyright © 2007 Abbrielle Jones
Published in 2007 by
Timeslip Books
Cwmiorwg, Gwynfe, Llangadog
Carmarthenshire, SA19 9PT
e-mail: timeslipbooks@yahoo.co.uk

A CIP catalogue record for this book is
available from the British Library.

ISBN 978-0-9539031-1-5

Printed and bound in Wales by
Dinefwr Press Ltd.
Rawlings Road, Llandybie,
Carmarthenshire, SA18 3YD.

Acknowledgements

My sincere thanks go to all of those appearing in this book, and to those who made the Time Workshops possible, on all the many planes of existence.

To Spirit for their close supervision of my activities and their guidance in all aspects of my life.

To Stanley-Ti Ming whose persistence, humour and patience presented the wisdom of the workshops in his-their own inimitable way.

To Betty whose lifelong friendship with me now continues from over the other side of life, and whose presence and love I continue to feel.

To June for her friendship and support over the many years of our acquaintance, and for her trust and humour.

To Cynthia for taking care of practicalities and for her many years of friendship and support.

In remembrance of Hugh for his love and affection.

To Laurence and Samantha for being my natural mirrors.

Contents

Introduction

Strange people interest me because they are different from the norm. I want to know what makes them tick. Conversations with them are more interesting than TV, sport, cars, the weather or the news. Stanley (at that time) didn't have a TV or a car. He didn't like sport, read newspapers or discuss the weather. That he was a brilliant psychic I found out from our first meeting and his mystery kept me intrigued for many years, before he finally admitted the truth about himself.

'Well alright, if you really want to know, I'm a Time Master.'

It was not the answer I was expecting.

'You're a what? You've been reading too much sci-fi,' was my reaction to the news. 'I suppose you've got a Time Ship around here somewhere.'

'No, I'm not that kind of Time Master,' he replied, somewhat offended. 'I'm a Master of Time. It's got nothing to do with Jules Verne.'

'You're weird, you know.'

Surprisingly, he agreed to this.

'Yes I am. I follow the Way of the Wyrd, that's W-Y-R-D, the ancient path of the wise.'

'Oh, so now you're a wise Time Master?' I shrugged despairingly.

'Are you trying to wind me up?'

'No,' he shook his head, with a somewhat bewildered expression as if the thought had never crossed his mind. Upon reflection, it probably hadn't.

'But you are joking?'

He raised his eyebrows, and grinned at me.

'Would I?'

I decided to call his bluff.

'OK then, so tell me what can Time Masters do?'

He scrutinised me intently. The grin faded and he didn't answer.

I waited, frustrated with his silence.

'Oh come on Stanley, you can't go saying things like that and not backing it up. It's such a ridiculous claim to make. If you're a Time Master you must be able to tell me what you can do. Can you tell me?'

He shook his head.

'Why not?'

'Not enough time,' he joked.

I laughed, and the tension between us evaporated as usual, like summer mist.

'Well can you tell me anything?'

He considered me thoughtfully for a moment.

'I could tell you how to master the Art of Dimensional Competence.'

'When you say Art, what do you mean exactly? I get the impression we're not talking painting here.'

'No, we're not talking painting, we're talking of the Magical Art, the Great Art Work of a Wizard.'

'First Time Masters and now Wizards. Really, Stanley, I don't know where you get it from. Anyway, what is the Great Art Work and what could I do with it when I'd mastered it?' I added as an afterthought.

Stanley ignored my facetious tone. 'It would enable you to go backwards or forwards in time and create more time when you needed it. Oh and I could teach you to be invisible, or truly visible,' he threw in carelessly as an afterthought.

I studied him carefully to see whether he was kidding, but his expression was solemn. I stopped being amused.

'Are you saying that you could really teach people to have more time to do things?'

He nodded. 'That's what I said didn't I?'

If he was in earnest, I needed clarification.

'Now wait a minute. I've been on Time Management Courses and they tell you how to organise the time you've got by various methods like prioritising, delegation and cutting out distractions, is that what you mean by being a Time Master?'

His eyes twinkled in merriment.

'That sounds to me more like being a Time Servant than a Time Master. No. I mean you can actually manifest more time for yourself and also speed it up or slow it down at will.'

'Why would you want to do that?' I was puzzled.

'Well, you might want to slow time down to enable you to meet a deadline, or finish a report on time, and you might want to speed it up to find out the results of a test. You could use the Art to manifest more time for yourself so you could be on time for a meeting when you were already late starting out and you could pay it back later when you had more time available,' he grinned. 'It would mean you'd always be in the right place at the right time.'

I stared at him intently. He obviously believed all this. I started to wonder if Stanley was more than just weird. Perhaps he was clinically insane. It was a worrying thought, but on the other hand maybe he wasn't. I had known him for many years and I knew him to be extremely knowledgeable about psychic and spiritual matters.

I was always open to possibilities and I'd had a couple of interesting experiences myself concerning time. Most people I talked to reported incidences of déjà vu. Perhaps he could explain them to me. I decided to humour him and see if I could find out more. It was an interesting subject after all. I tried not to laugh as I asked.

'Could you teach me to be a Time Master?'

He shook his head.

'Why not?' I queried, feeling rather put out.

'You would have to change,' he replied.

Suddenly I wanted to know. A feeling welled up from within me like an underground spring waiting to burst forth from the earth.

'Please Stanley.'

'Do you really want to learn how to be a Time Master?' he asked.

I nodded, in earnest now. If there was such a possibility of being a Time Master outside the realms of fiction, then I wanted to be one.

'Do I get a Time Machine?' I couldn't help joking, possibly to relieve the tension of the moment.

He paused, ignoring the question and continued to stare at me intently, his bony features serious.

A wave of feeling hit me and his question seemed the most important one I had ever been asked. Of course learning was important to me, I was a Training Manager in a local College and my life had been spent enabling others to learn new skills, but apart from this in a sudden flash of insight I recognised within me a deep yearning that wanted this to be real. I wanted there to be more to life than being a nine to five wage slave, caught in domestic routine, with nothing but work, bed and bills.

'Yes, I really want to learn,' I confirmed. 'How long would it take you to teach me?'

'You?' he looked me up and down as if he had never seen me before. His steely blue eyes seemed to stare at me from a great distance.

'If you really made an effort?'

I nodded, waiting for his answer in breathless anticipation. Somehow I knew it was one of the most auspicious moments of my life.

'Are you sure you want to know?' he enquired again, peering at me intently.

'Yes, Stanley, I want to know,' I confirmed.

'You're quite certain?'

'I'm quite certain,' I assured him. As I said the words, I felt the certainty within me. It was a calm, solid feeling that relaxed my body and focussed my mind. I knew that I wanted to do this more than anything else in my life.

'It will be difficult at times, challenging to your beliefs. You would have to trust me.'

'Stanley I trust you. Will you please teach me how to be a Time Master?'

There. I had said the magic formula. I had confirmed that I wanted to know three times and I had asked for him specifically, to be my teacher. I don't know how I knew that this was required, but I did.

His blue eyes took on a luminous quality as they bored into mine to scan my commitment and capability. There was a long pause and I held my breath.

'Alright,' he finally agreed somewhat reluctantly, 'but it will take you, working hard, flat out, about six years.'

'Six years,' I gasped. 'You must be joking. I haven't got six years. You know I'm working full time, and there's my son to consider.'

I had been a single parent for the past few years and my son Laurence was my sole responsibility now my daughter Samantha had left home.

'No, I'm not joking.' He looked thoughtfully at me.

'But Stanley, I haven't got six years. I have to work,' I protested.

'Well, say six months then,' and added, 'just for the basics.'

I considered the situation, my heart sinking. It was ironic but there was no way I could find the time to learn how to master Time. All I had coming up was a weeks holiday entitlement over the Easter period. I decided I would offer to give that up. It was all I could manage, I couldn't take time off without pay or I wouldn't be able to meet my mortgage repayments.

'I can spare a week,' I informed him. I know it didn't sound a lot, but for me it was the only time I had to myself and was a big deal for me.

'A week, is that all?' he said laughingly. 'It's not much of a commitment is it?'

'You don't go to work,' I retorted, 'so it doesn't seem much to you, but it's all the time I have to myself. I'm willing to give up all the time I have and that's all I can do.'

He still looked doubtful, so I pushed it.

'Look, I promise to work all the time. It's a big commitment for me. Come on Stanley, I'm willing to give up my Easter holiday for you.'

He shook his head. 'Not for me.'

'Alright, for Spirit,' I conceded hurriedly.

Again he shook his head. 'Not for Spirit either. This is for you Abby.'

'OK for me,' I agreed. 'Please Stanley, I will work from the moment I wake up to the moment I go to sleep. Is that working hard enough?'

He shrugged. 'I'm not sure.'

I sighed, feeling somewhat disheartened. 'I don't see how I can do any more.'

He looked at me seriously. 'Even your best effort may not be enough for you to grasp the basic principles.'

I was shocked. I didn't doubt what he was saying, but I was after all a psychology and philosophy graduate and had post graduate teaching qualifications and he had nothing whatsoever in the way of formal educational certificates.

He had hardly ever worked since I had known him, at least, not at paid work, his work was not of the paying kind. He gave psychic help, healing and spiritual counsel to others. He made himself available to those who needed him. Many who couldn't see past appearances avoided him, as he was slight and scruffy, with a thin, bony nose. Often dismissed as a nonentity, his rather large ears protruded from his unkempt fair hair which tumbled over the collar of his frayed shirt. The overall impression was of an abandoned elf. He looked out of place in our material culture, which obviously held no attraction for him.

Once I had finished deriding his notions of being a Time Master I began to think that it might explain a lot, and once I believed him I wanted to know for myself.

He studied my disappointed countenance dispassionately and appeared to be listening to something.

'Yes, alright. They're saying you can do it.'

I failed to question him about the 'they' as I felt a burden lift from me. I was as excited as a schoolgirl. Life had been stressful since the break up of my marriage and fun and adventure had been in short supply. Now I felt I was being given the opportunity of leaving the mundane world behind and journeying into magical unknown territory where logical boundaries ceased to operate. What would I find?

'We will need a place where we will not be interrupted for the whole time, and it must be on or near an energy site,' he stated.

'I have a caravan on Gower, we could go there,' I suggested. 'It's still quiet because it's being newly developed and doesn't have many facilities, so we wouldn't be disturbed.'

'But is it near an energy site?' he enquired.

I nodded excitedly. 'Yes, it's the site of the Ritual, you know the one I wrote about?'

He looked thoughtful. 'The one with the excavations of the ancient church?'

'That's right,' I confirmed.

I had bought the caravan as a writing refuge, a space where I could go when I needed peace and freedom from phones and other interruptions.

'It sounds OK, but I must insist on no interruptions of any kind, you cannot bring your son or the dog,' he stipulated.

'There are no phones down there and I'll arrange for Heidi to go into kennels and Laurence can stay with his grandfather in Shropshire for a week,'

Stanley nodded in approval of my plans.

In the event, there was no need for Heidi, my Airedale, to go into kennels, as my friend Cynthia offered to look after her for me.

'Am I invited?' Betty asked when I told her what we were planning.

Betty and I had been friends for many years. Her son Daniel was the same age as Laurence although she was twenty years my senior. She was a striking, well built woman in her late forties who sported square framed glasses. Her short brown hair was permed into soft curls which softened the effect of her rather prominent nose and protruding front teeth. She dressed flamboyantly in vibrant velvets and casual cord trouser suits favouring colours like burnt orange, turquoise and emerald green, accessorised with chiffon scarves and crystal jewellery.

In addition to the jewellery she had a rapidly expanding collection of semi precious stones, including topaz, turquoise, quartz, carnelian and jasper which she kept on the kitchen shelf at the side of the Aga amongst her healing balms, runes and spiritual literature.

Her farmhouse kitchen in the Victorian terrace a few doors down from mine provided a sanctuary from the world where coffee, tea and homemade cakes were always on offer. She was welcoming and wise, enveloping visitors in a strong Druidic energy which cocooned you from the world. Since I had met Stanley at the Spiritualist Church a few years ago and introduced him to Betty, the three of us had formed the core of the regular, almost daily gatherings in her kitchen where we meditated and discussed spiritual issues.

Stanley took her hands in his.

'Of course you're invited Betty,' she smiled at him. 'Thank you. But I wouldn't be able to stay the whole time as I've got Tony and the children to feed.'

Tony was her Catholic husband. Older than her, portly, grey haired and stern, he was strictly old school, and firmly believed a woman's place was in the home, which was unfortunate as Betty was a free spirit and trustee of the local Spiritualist church now known as the old St. John's.

She mostly ignored him, but made sure her house wifely duties were not neglected so as to give him no cause for complaint. Their marriage was a fraught union of opposites concerning their religious beliefs, but held together by their principles, their six children and their commitment to the marriage ideal. As their last child Daniel entered his teens along with my son Laurence, Betty's ties to the home lessened and she now gave herself permission to leave the house for a few hours during the day.

'Well then it appears we have a date. To the Time Workshops,' Stanley held up his mug of tea and drank to us.

'The Time Workshops,' Betty and I toasted in coffee.

A thrill rippled through me as I said the words, although I had no real idea of what I was undertaking.

Chapter 1

Preparations

The next few weeks passed in a flurry of excitement as we made arrangements and preparations. We visited the caravan to check on its suitability as Stanley hadn't been there before. He was quiet on the journey to Gower, taking stock of the landscape while Betty drove across Welsh moor and headed towards Llanrhidian. There were no buses and few cars for the site was still relatively unknown.

The caravan was situated by a hedge, well away from its neighbours and flanked by fields. He mounted the metal step and wandered around, checking the two bedrooms, the living and dining area with its narrow galley kitchen, and then went outside and walked around smoking a cigarette, noting the overhanging trees and the fields at the back and eventually returned nodding his approval.

'Yes, it's quiet, it will be fine. Also, it's on an energy site,' he grinned as if he had a hidden secret.

I glanced at him suspiciously. Just what had I let myself in for?

'What exactly will we be doing?' I enquired as they sat down and I made us some coffee.

'You will be learning the skills of a wizard,' he informed us.

Betty nodded serenely unfazed by this pronouncement.

'Is that the male equivalent of a witch?' I wanted to know.

He looked at me in mock horror. 'Certainly not. It has nothing to do with what sex you are, it's a term for your level of development.'

He was silent then as if that explained everything, but I was not satisfied.

'What are the levels of development?' I wanted to know.

He sighed imperceptibly as if being harassed by an inquisitive child.

'Well, a witch is at the first level of development. They are psychics and seekers, they are just beginners in the Magical Art, though some are really unconscious wizards. The next level up is a Seer. He or she,' he added quickly anticipating my objection to the pronoun, 'is a finder, a trainee wizard, a journeyman, and a Wizard is someone who has mastered the art of dimensional competence. They have completed the Great Art Work, the Pattern, the foundation of the Lore of the Ring of Time.'

I had never heard Stanley say so much before, and I listened, fascinated.

'What do you mean by dimensional competence?' Betty asked, peering at him over the rim of her tortoiseshell glasses.

'Well, they are masters of the elements.'

'By Elements, do you mean Earth, Air, Fire and Water?' I enquired.

He nodded. 'An air wizard for example can control the weather and can transmute anything containing air. A fire wizard can create fire and transmute anything containing fire, such as volcanoes, gemstones, lazers etc. Water wizards are healers and can transmute anything containing water, they can direct flows, including the fluid in people's bodies, and the flow of events. Finally an Earth wizard has the power of the Earth, he – or she,' he smiled at me, correcting himself, 'is more powerful than the other wizards, but there are more laws which bind their power. They can transmute metals. Your alchemist for example would be your typical Earth wizard. Wizards tend to be drawn to the sciences, computing, finances, psychology and the arts, though they don't see themselves as such. Then there are the creative/destructive elements (No Time) and the Spirit element (All Time) Wizards.'

Betty and I listened fascinated.

'So as you know all this stuff I guess you must be a wizard?' I studied him closely to watch for his reaction but he merely bowed his head.

'Indeed I am. I can see behind the scene. I can control my energy and create whatever I want, whenever I want it, and only the power of the one, true living God/Goddess can stop me,' he smiled.

I knew him well enough to believe him. I was suddenly in awe of this man who had transformed from the admittedly mysterious but somewhat insignificant Stanley I knew into this alien being full of authority and power. I suddenly felt nervous about being alone with him.

'So what would I have to do to be a wizard?' Undaunted, Betty was practical as ever.

'You would have to stop seeking and start finding. You would have to learn to create the right relationship between people and things. You would need total commitment and achievement. You would have to have perseverance, courage, endurance and resolve. You would need to set goals and pass them, to learn to perceive yourself in relation to the smallest seed and tallest mountain. You would need to gain knowledge through listening to your intuition, your experiences and your perception, according to the Lore of the Ring of Time.'

I stirred extra sugar into my coffee before taking a gulp. I felt I needed it.

'Oh well, a week should just about cover it then,' I joked, grabbing one of Betty's homemade shortbread biscuits.

They both laughed.

In spite of my joking I felt humbled as I began to realise the enormity of the task in front of me.

As if he knew my thoughts, Stanley placed a comforting hand on my shoulder.

'It'll be OK, trust me.'

'Never trust a man who says trust me,' I intoned automatically, and wished I hadn't when I saw a shadow pass over his face.

The word soon spread out on our grapevine and quite a few friends and associates expressed interest but weren't able to join us. June, a tall, smart, blonde friend of Betty's and as Tony put it, one of Betty's 'coven' requested to attend on an ad hoc basis. Stanley was against it.

'This is a serious commitment,' he insisted. 'She can't just go dipping in and out as she pleases. It would interrupt us.'

I liked June, although she was somewhat older than me and tended to keep her distance. She had other friends and groups that she belonged to and liked to keep everyone compartmentalised, never discussing the activities of one group with another. She kept her private life separate from her spiritual activities and made it clear that her family came first. She attended many spiritual events and workshops, and knew a wide range of people. I protested on her behalf.

'But how can she interrupt us? Surely, if it's in harmony she will come at the right time in order to hear what is right for her. She's very psychic you know.'

'Yes, I know she is, but she won't put what she hears into practice, she's just information gathering.'

'Stanley', I pleaded, 'how can you deny someone who wants to know? Maybe she isn't ready to make a full commitment just yet, but she's obviously ready to make a start.'

Stanley considered my argument reluctantly, held out for a while and then capitulated.

'OK she can come.'

I was delighted. She stipulated that she would only be available for the afternoon sessions. Betty said she would attend two out of the three, but would have to miss out on the early morning ones and be home by 5.30 p.m. in order to accommodate the family's breakfast and evening meals.

No-one else felt they could sacrifice a whole week of their precious time, and Stanley continued to hold out against the merely curious who wished to drop in at their own convenience.

I shopped for enough food for the week and stored it in the kitchen cupboards and fridge at the caravan. I cleaned the place thoroughly and aired the blankets and sheets. Stanley said we should have no contact with the outside world, which is why he was against drop in visitors and made Betty and June promise to leave everything behind when they attended and refrain from gossip or discussing what was going on in the world. There were to be no letters, phones or newspapers and there was no TV in the caravan. Our concentration must be total.

I arranged with Laurence to visit his grandfather in Shropshire and told him I was going on a retreat and could not be contacted. Hugh was fine with that and assured me he could cope. I didn't doubt it. Although now retired, he had travelled the world as a businessman and spoke several languages including fluent German. He was well read and fond of quoting the racy passages of Omar Kyam to me with a hint of suggestion in his voice, which I both acknowledged and ignored. He understood that his silent invitation was not being accepted, even though we were mutually fond of each other and had remained close after his wife had died and his son and I divorced. He and Laurence had a special bond, so I knew they would enjoy each other's company.

To my relief Stanley assured me there were to be no intimacies between us.

'This is a purely professional relationship and I will sleep in the small bedroom during the time of the workshops,' he announced.

I was surprised that he was so forthright, but the clarification put my mind at rest, as I was feeling slightly uneasy about spending the nights alone with him in the caravan.

'We will start promptly at 9 a.m.,' he announced. 'Please be ready as they do not like to be kept waiting. Each session will last for approximately two hours. We will have a break at 11am and re-commence at 11.30 a.m. Betty should be ready to start by 11.30 a.m.'

'I can be there by 10 a.m.,' she said. 'if you don't mind me interrupting.'

He smiled at her. 'You could never interrupt Bett. We will continue until 1.30 p.m. then the afternoon session will begin at 2.30 p.m. until 4.30 p.m., so June can join us after lunch, and you can be home by 5.30 p.m. as you requested.'

He turned to me. 'We will then have an evening walk from 6.30 p.m. until 7.30 p.m. to ground the energies, to be followed by a recap of the day's work, from 7.30 until 9.30 p.m. and then finally we shall meditate from 10.00 to 11.00 p.m. to assist with the integration of the information before retiring. Is this acceptable?'

I agreed that it was. It did not sound like Stanley at all to be so organised or so busy. It was a full programme. He watched while I fetched a pen and notepad.

'What are they for?' he asked suspiciously.

'I need to make notes or I'll never remember it all.'

He went quiet for a moment and raised his eyes upwards as if asking spirit.'

'Alright, they're saying you can make notes, but be sure you pay attention to what is being said.'

'Oh I will,' I assured him, 'it's just that I've got used to taking notes from my student days and I can concentrate better with a pen in my hand.'

He didn't look convinced. He had difficulty writing, mainly I think because he couldn't spell. (Well not in the written sense anyway.) It amused me to think of a wizard who couldn't spell.

We arranged to start on the Saturday morning. I picked Stanley up on Friday evening after putting Laurence on the train to Shropshire. Cynthia assured me Heidi would be fine, as she could play with her dog Bonnie, who was one of Heidi's pups. She said she would take them both for walks together in the parks. All the preparations were in now in place. I had phoned my friends and my parents who were devout Christians, and would have been horrified to learn of my activities. However I merely told them I was going on a retreat and left them to draw their own conclusions. I think my mother decided that I was over stressed.

'You go dear, I'm sure it will do you good to get away from it all,' was her assessment of the situation.

I wasn't convinced I was 'getting away from' anything, and certainly by the time we had unpacked the car and settled in, I was exhausted. My job at the College was demanding and I was looking forward to a break. Stanley pottered around outside having a last cigarette while I made up the beds. I wished him good night and lay in the little double bedroom listening to the unfamiliar sounds around me.

I still had some reservations about giving up my holiday. I didn't know what to expect and wondered if I'd been too gullible in being ready to give up my Easter week to listen to Stanley telling us about being a Time Master. Perhaps I had been wrong to encourage him, it could all be a load of twaddle.

But in spite of my misgivings, I found I was looking forward to the event. It was peaceful in the caravan and if nothing else, I could relax. OK, I could have gone abroad, but maybe this would be more restful. On that first night all was unknown and I slept in blissful ignorance. Fortunately I did not know that this was to be the most strenuous week of my life.

Chapter 2

What is Time?

Day 1
Session 1

I rose dutifully at 8.00 a.m. and headed for the bathroom. Stanley was already dressed and sitting in the living area. I heard him put the kettle on and by the time I emerged he had made coffee for me and a mug of tea for himself.

'Did you sleep well?' he enquired.

'I did,' I confirmed. 'And you?'

He smiled and inclined his head. 'Indeed I did.'

He took his mug of tea outside to the morning air and lit a cigarette. He never ate breakfast he informed me, so I ate my cereal and toast on my own.

By five to nine I had finished and cleared away. I seated myself at the table, ready for our agreed 9 a.m. start. Stanley entered at exactly 9 a.m. He put his hands together and gave me a formal little bow as if he had not seen me before.

'Greetings and welcome to the Time Workshops.' It was not Stanley's voice. I peered more closely at him. There seemed to be an almost Chinese slant to his eyes, which I'm sure I'd never noticed before. I realised with a start, this was someone else.

I smiled back somewhat nervously at this stranger, and returned his greeting.

'The first workshop is called What is Time? Any ideas?'

I wrote the title on my notepad and stared at it hoping for inspiration which didn't come. My mind had gone blank.

What is Time?

I found it hard to interact with him on my own. He just stood there in front of me waiting for an answer and I felt pressurised, especially since he didn't offer any solutions, but expected me to come up with everything on my own. In university the lecturers did just that, they lectured. They gave the information and we, the students, listened and wrote it down if we wished, to absorb and learn later.

I tried my best. 'Well Time provides a framework for our lives. We live by the clock don't we? It tells us when to get up when to go to bed, when to go to work, when to eat.'

He just smiled and nodded and asked for more.

'A framework. Yes, what else?'

I was conscious of him standing over me waiting for an answer. It was a strange situation that made me feel as though I were back again in the French class in school with the teacher speaking only 'en Français' and expecting me to understand.

He moved suddenly and his movement pulled me back to the present moment with a start and I remembered I was supposed to be thinking about time.

Time, what did it mean to me? What was it? Trying to define time was like trying to define mist. It was nebulous somehow and wasn't anything you could get hold of and examine. I tried to think about it. Where did the concept of time begin? Before clocks there were sundials and sand timers, like the old egg timers. People have always felt the need to measure time. I supposed the day and night were the first type of measurement, and the seasons, winter and summer. I guessed it must have been the farmers who first felt the need to measure time. Time and the weather. They had to know when to get the crops in, how long the winter would last to make sure they had enough food. Stanley was waiting. I tried thinking aloud.

'I guess time is tied to survival.'

'In what way?'

'Winter, summer, harvesting the crops, having enough food to last through the cold weather. And then in the hot countries, knowing when the rainy season is coming and how long the drought will last. People would have needed to know these things, and I guess those who got it right survived and those who didn't died and so,' I was on a roll now, 'those who knew about time were more evolved.'

'So time is evolution?' he queried.

That didn't sound right to me somehow.

'No, I don't think so. Oh, I don't know, why can't you tell me what time is? Surely that's the point of the workshop?'

'Is it?' Was all he would say.

I wouldn't let him get away with that.

'Well isn't it? If it isn't what is it about then? We can hardly guess our way to enlightenment can we? It's a ridiculous idea. If that were true then there'd be no need for teachers would there? We'd all sit around and information would come whiz into our heads from nowhere. Wonderful if we could do it, but we can't. We need others to explain things to us. If we have to learn everything by trial and error each person would have to start back in the stone age. We'd never progress, never evolve.'

'So time is not evolution?' he queried.

'Oh!' I growled at him in exasperation.

He refused to tell me anything. He was trying to tease the information out of me and get me to come up with my own answers, but how could I tell him what I didn't know? It was a ridiculous learning method.

I was so pleased when Betty arrived at 10.00 a.m. We heard her car draw up and Stanley opened the door to greet her, smiling in welcome.

'Hi Betty, welcome to the Time Workshops.'

She merely nodded to us both and sat down next to me, keeping to the rule not to exchange pleasantries and disrupt the energies. In this case, I thought it might have been a good idea as I felt quite negative at that moment.

'Have I missed much?' she asked me.

'I wouldn't know,' I replied sulkily, 'if you have, then I've missed it too.'

Stanley giggled as if I had said something really witty and I scowled at him.

Betty glanced from one to the other of us.

'I see I've arrived just in time.'

'Indeed you have, we are attempting to answer the question, What is Time?' Stanley informed her.

'Less of the we,' I muttered.

He laughed. 'Alright then, Abby is attempting to answer the question What is Time? She doesn't appear to be having much luck however. Strange really when you consider that we all use time every day.'

'I wouldn't say use,' I countered, 'more like we are used by it.'

Stanley laughed again. 'Oh dear, you really do need these workshops don't you? So far we have considered that Time is a framework and is necessary for survival, what do you think Betty? What is time to you?'

Betty was quiet for a moment, considering the question and then answered thoughtfully.

'I would say that time is order, without time we would have chaos.'

'Mmmm, order. Very good,' Stanley nodded approvingly.

It was different with Betty there beside me. I felt less pressurised and started to concentrate and get into the swing of it.

I wrote:

Time is order

'Time is measurement,' I contributed. 'A way of measuring seconds, minutes, days, months, years. Centuries ago we had a sundial to measure the passage of the sun.'

I scribbled hastily:

Time is measurement

Stanley looked at me and nodded. 'So time is order and measurement. Anything else?'

'It's a way of meeting people,' Betty said.

I was puzzled. 'What do you mean?'

'Well, without time we wouldn't be able to arrange anything would we? I mean I arranged to be here at 10 a.m., so you knew when to expect me.'

'So time is meetings,' Stanley cut in, 'anything else?'

Betty and I looked at each other searching for inspiration.

'Time is money?' I suggested.

Stanley winced. 'Oooh, that's a bad construct to have.'

'Why?' I was defensive. 'If you worked you might have the same one. We get paid by the hours we put in, so to those of us who do work,' I laboured the point, annoyed at his reaction, 'time *is* money.'

'Nobody pays me for the hours I work,' Betty murmured almost to herself.

'Well perhaps they should,' I suggested. 'The Government was thinking of paying housewives and child carers. Even if you were paid the minimum wage you could claim as a cleaner, cook, laundry maid, child carer, gardener, chauffeur.'

'I'd be rich if I claimed for all that,' Betty looked pleased.

'And then there's shopping, ironing, counselling.'

'Ladies, can we please stay focussed?' Stanley stopped me in mid flow, smiled and paused a moment before continuing.

'Now is that all you have to say about time?'

I felt managed, and as a manager I recognised the technique. It confirmed my suspicions that this was not Stanley speaking. This was an articulate, educated person, totally unlike the inarticulate, semi-literate Stanley.

'I've noticed,' Betty said 'that when you're happy time seems to go really quickly and when you want it to go quickly, like when you're in a dentist's chair or waiting for someone in the rain, it goes really slowly.'

'Yes indeed,' Stanley confirmed. 'But is it time that varies, or our conception of it?'

'Our conception of it,' Betty was quick to agree.

'So time itself stays the same?' Stanley asked.

I was thoughtful. 'That's an interesting idea. I suppose it does, but that means there is what I might call subjective time which is our experience of it and an objective time that stays the same.'

'Oooh, we're getting serious now with all these big words,' Stanley chuckled. 'What do you think Betty?'

'Well I don't understand Abby's subjective and objective, but I think I grasp the principles. It's like everything else isn't it? Something happens and we all respond to it differently.'

'Good,' Stanley nodded to her gravely. 'I'm glad to know you are grasping the principles. Ladies should always hold on to their principles. And Abby, would you agree that subjective time is personal time which we may call the experiencer, and objective time is non personal, the experience itself?'

'Yes,' I nodded as I wrote:

Personal time is the experiencer

Non Personal time is the experience itself

I smiled in contentment. Finally we were getting somewhere and things were starting to make sense. 'Yes I would agree with that. Only last weekend I had some friend's children round and they stayed about two hours. They romped about and played loud music and wrecked the house, while I cooked a meal for them and washed up afterwards. I was exhausted by the time their parents came to collect them. It felt like they had been with me forever, or at least four hours, but they didn't want to go so soon as they said it had only been a few minutes since they arrived. I thought it strange at the time.'

'That's a good illustration,' Stanley turned to Betty, 'And would you agree Betty that we have an experience and an experiencer?'

'Yes, I can understand that. It's clear to me,' Betty smiled.

I was impressed with Stanley's (or whoever it was) ability to define our needs and make the appropriate interpretation.

'Understand that it is important to approach each experience in a new way. If, as the experiencer, we bring old ideas from the past into the present we will have expectations of the experience, either good or bad, which will distort what is actually happening. If Abby offered to have her friend's children again and she remembered the last time they came and was dreading it, she would affect the experience by bringing in the past. We need to live in the present, then we can allow each experience to be fresh and alive, different from any other. To colour it with the past is to live in a stagnant way that prevents us from interacting with the experience. The key phrase to remember here is 'I am the experiencer.'

I wrote it down on my notepad in large letters:

I am the experiencer

and Stanley paused a moment while I did so, before continuing.

'The aim is to become one with the experience, which will enable natural, spontaneous action to take place bringing freedom and understanding. It is the mind and the body which govern the way we interact with non personal time.'

I wrote down:

Non Personal time is affected by the state of our mind and body

Stanley stood in front of me staring down at my writing in a protective fashion, reminding me of my eagle eyed primary school teacher, Mrs. Hudson, making sure I was copying down my letters in the right order.

'No, non personal time is not affected by the state of our mind and body.' He pointed at my pad.

'But you just said it was,' I objected.

'No. I said it governs the way we *interact* with non personal time,' he corrected. 'There is a difference.'

I then wrote:

The state of our mind and body governs the way we interact with non personal time

Satisfied this time with my notes he carried on, pacing the little space between our table and the kitchen and then marching imperceptibly on the spot as if it aided his concentration.

'As our attitude changes towards our experience and we manage to stay focussed in the present without colouring from past associations, so will our experience change. Once this happens, our responses change and so will our understanding of time.'

'Does that mean we will experience time differently?'
I asked.

'What do you think Betty?' he passed the question on to her without her seeming to notice.

She heaved a sigh while she considered. 'Well, I suppose it does. It's interesting isn't it, to think that time depends on our attitude.'

'Does it?' Stanley queried. 'Are you quite sure about that Betty?'

I had a sudden revelation. 'No, it's our *experience* of time that depends on our attitude, isn't it?' I looked at him for confirmation. 'Time itself doesn't change.'

He nodded. 'Very good Abby. I think she's got it. Betty?'

Betty nodded thoughtfully.

'Right then,' Stanley rubbed his hands together, smiling and looking pleased with himself.

Time itself doesn't change.
It's our experience of time that changes depending on our attitude

I was busy scribbling and by the time I had caught up nothing more had been said so I looked up and was just in time to see him give a little bow and bring his hands together in oriental fashion, signalling the close of the workshop.

'Is that it?' I queried looking from him to Betty. Stanley had closed his eyes and Betty nodded. 'Yes, look his guide is leaving.'

'Well that's all folks.' In a moment Stanley was back with his jokey attitude, which was totally different from our workshop mentor.

'You were very good Stanley,' I had to admit I was impressed.

He looked pleased. 'Was I? So glad you liked it. We do aim to please.'

'Was that a guide with you?' Betty wanted to know.

'Ah, our little China man you mean?'

'Oh, that's who he was,' Betty gave a satisfied grin, 'that would make sense of all the bowing. What's his name?'

'His name? Oh his name is Ti Ming.'

'Ti Ming,' I repeated suspiciously scrutinising his face for traces of a smile. 'Are you sure that's his name?'

'Why shouldn't it be?' Betty wanted to know.

'Well, come on, were doing the Time Workshops and they're being held by Ti Ming.'

Betty still hadn't caught on. 'Timing Betty, Ti-Ming,' I spelt it out.

Stanley laughed, 'Oh I see you have discovered our little joke,' he gave a bow, hands together in front of him. 'Ti Ming is very important.'

Joke or no joke, we continued to call him Ti Ming from then on.

I made a last note:

Stay focussed in the present. This changes:

(a) our attitude towards experiences

(b) the experience

(c) our understanding of time

'Can we stop for coffee now?' I pleaded, needing to stretch my legs and take a break.

Stanley consulted his watch in an exaggerated gesture.

'Do you think we have the time?' he asked.

Betty laughed and I felt like throwing something at him.

We were allowed to stop for a break, so I put the aluminium kettle on the gas stove and Stanley went outside to have a cigarette.

'This is proving to be more interesting than I thought,' Betty said. 'I'm glad I came.'

'Me too,' I replied.

Chapter 3

How Long is a Minute?

Day 1
Session 2

'OK, are we all ready? Right, so the next workshop is entitled: How Long is a Minute?'

Stanley picked up his unfinished mug of tea and wandered outside without saying anything more to us.

I duly wrote down the title on my notepad and sipped my coffee.

How Long is a Minute?

We sat and waited for his return.

'Where do you think he's gone?' I asked Betty.

'For a cigarette?' she suggested.

'What another one?'

'Maybe we've stressed him out,' she laughed.

We drank our coffee contentedly and chatted about the previous workshop.

Stanley returned and looked at us expectantly.

'So what have you been doing while I was outside?'

I shrugged. 'Nothing. We were waiting for you to come back.'

'Oh waiting for me to come back,' he repeated thoughtfully, 'and how long did you wait? Any idea?'

'Not long,' Betty contributed.

He pointed to my notepad I looked at the words. It said *How long is a Minute?*

'Oh I see. You were gone for a minute,' I suggested.

He sighed exaggeratedly. 'Well done. I'm glad you're both awake. So this minute, how long did it seem to you both?'

'Not long at all,' Betty ventured, 'in fact, we didn't really miss you, we were chatting.'

'Oh, chatting were you?' he lifted an eyebrow inquiringly. 'So tell me, while you were chatting, what were you aware of?'

'Aware of?' Betty looked startled. 'Oh I didn't know we were supposed to be aware of anything.'

'I didn't know we had started,' I objected.

He paced around the caravan observing us, and I realised that this was not Stanley talking to us. Our mentor, Ti Ming had returned.

'So now we have established that we have in fact, started, could we ask you to cast your mind back to the minute that I was outside – and I can confirm that it was *exactly* a minute,' he smiled, showing us his watch, 'what was it that you noticed? What did you see, what did you hear, what were you thinking?'

'Oh.' Now we realised what he wanted, we considered the question. I answered first. 'I was aware of you going outside.'

'Very perceptive,' he nodded gravely.

I smiled and tried harder. It was difficult to think what I had been aware of, and yet it was only a few moments before.

'I was aware of needing a cigarette and wishing I could join you.' Betty contributed.

'Very good,' he bowed to her inclining his head, 'you were aware of your own needs.'

He waited for us to speak further but neither of us could think of anything to say. He clapped his hands together suddenly making us jump.

'OK. So we will take another minute and can you please retain your awareness this time?' he looked at his watch. 'Beginning now.'

My mind instantly started racing. I wrote:

Retain your awareness

I looked at the words. What was I aware of? What was I supposed to be aware of? Anything in particular? My eyes scanned around the room trying to take in as much as possible. I felt as though I were on a quiz show trying to memorise the prizes as they passed by. I looked around the caravan, noticing the curtains, pink dralon and the nets needing a wash. I was drawn to the view outside, the trees waving in the wind. I could hear a bird singing. I was aware of Betty sitting next to me, her shoulder just touching mine and of Stanley pointedly staring at his watch in front of us. I felt rather silly and self conscious about the exercise and was glad when he called 'Time up.'

He let his watch arm drop and looked at us. 'Before I ask you what you were aware of, can I ask you just to notice whether you were in a positive or negative state while you were observing?'

I cringed and slid back in my seat. He noticed immediately and smiled.

'And Betty, what about you?'

'I think I remained fairly positive,' she announced.

'Trust her,' the little negative voice sneaked in before I could stop it.

'So tell me Bett,' he asked, 'what was it that you were aware of during this minute?'

'I was aware of my foot itching and feeling that I shouldn't move or I would distract Abby. I felt Abby was bored. I heard someone outside call their dog and there was a bird singing. A chaffinch, I think it was.'

'Very good, and you Abby, was Betty right, were you bored?'

'No,' I turned to look at her, 'sorry Betty.'

'There's no need to apologise,' she said graciously.

'The point is,' Stanley interrupted hurriedly, 'in feeling that Abby was bored, you stepped out of what you were actually feeling Betty, and in not moving when you wanted to you were assuming that you would distract Abby, and letting that assumption stop you from taking the action you needed to take for yourself and your comfort.'

'I've been doing that all my life,' Betty confirmed. 'I've been too busy thinking about others to think about myself. I suppose it comes from having six kids and an old man like mine to take care of.'

'Well maybe it's time to stop making assumptions about what other people need and focus on the reality of your own needs.'

I noted:

Stop making assumptions about others.
Focus on your own needs

Without giving her time to comment on this Stanley continued, switching his gaze to me with lazer like precision.

'So Abby, what about you, what were you aware of in this minute?'

I told him what I could remember and added I had felt more self conscious than bored.

'Self conscious? Oh so you were conscious of your self? Very good,' he smiled at me, as I wrote.

Stay conscious of your Self

He had a habit of turning things around. 'So, now let's see how you both do on the next exercise. I'm going to ask each of you to talk for one minute on a subject of my choice.'

'Oh no,' we both groaned in unison.

'I'm sure you'll enjoy it,' Stanley assured us, undeterred.

We were not convinced. However we complied. I struggled to talk for one minute about leaves and fizzled out towards the end. Betty did rather better I thought, talking about the wind, but we both stopped and started, looked at the ceiling, the floor and each other for inspiration. We laughed and complained and stated we couldn't think of anything else to say and was our time up yet, and were glad when Stanley called 'Time.'

'So what were your thoughts when I asked you to speak?' he asked me.

I considered. 'Something like, oh no, I'll never be able to speak for a minute about leaves.'

'Betty?'

'I thought, do I know enough about wind to make the subject interesting.'

'And so ladies, did it seem like a minute to you?'

'Longer,' we both agreed.

'So this time I want you to stand up,' Stanley encouraged us to rise by waving his hand. 'Come on, up you come.'

Reluctantly, we both rose and stood looking at him, waiting for the next instruction.

'Right, now I want you to run around the caravan.'

'What?' we groaned. 'Do we have to?'

'Yes you have to,' he opened the door smiling but determined not to move until we grudgingly complied.

It was not so much of a run as a clomping walk. I was surprised at how heavy I felt. It was as though I were walking through a quagmire and it was dragging me down. I was glad when we finally approached the door, ready to plonk ourselves down. He barred our way.

'Come on, again,' he encouraged, 'faster this time. I said run, not stagger.'

We each took a breath, complained to each other and speeded up. Surprisingly, this time I found it easier and by the third circumnavigation I felt almost weightless. We were out of breath, but laughing as we approached Stanley in the doorway.

'Alright, you can come in now,' he stood aside to let us enter and we gratefully sought the sanctuary of the bench seat.

'Do you know what happened out there?' he asked.

'We ran,' I said laughingly stating the obvious.

'I know you ran, I was watching you, but do you know *why* you ran?'

'Because you told us to?'

'Yes, and why did I tell you to?'

'Because you're a sadist and a control freak?' I ventured.

Betty intervened at this point.

'To clear us of negative energy?'

'Well done Betty,' he ignored my remarks. 'It was indeed to clear you of negative energy, allowing it to Earth as you ran.'

Earth the negative by moving (walking/running)

'And there was me thinking you were a sadist,' I said as I wrote.

'Well you went, so that makes you a masochist,' he retorted good humouredly. 'OK ladies, up you get.'

'I'm not running any more,' I warned him. 'I'm not that much of a masochist.'

'No, no,' he said hurriedly. 'I just want you to stand up and put all your weight on your right foot. Maintain a positive attitude and say to yourself. This is going to be fun.'

This is going to be fun

'What is?' I asked as I wrote it down before I stood up. He ignored me. I looked down at my notes and repeated somewhat dubiously,

'This is going to be fun.'

'And are we staying positive?' his querying little elfin face peered into mine.'

I laughed. I couldn't help it. Stanley always made me feel good humoured (except when he annoyed the hell out me). Just to remind myself before I continued I wrote:

Stay positive

'Alright, now tell us Abby in one minute, everything you know about dust.'

I did so and then he gave the same instruction to Betty to talk for one minute on the topic of shampoo.

'So how did that feel?' he asked us when we had both finished.

'Wow!' I exclaimed. 'I'd never have believed it would have made that much difference, and that I knew so much about dust.'

Betty agreed. 'Yes, it was a completely different experience being positive, it was really fun and the time went so quickly.'

'And did it seem like a minute?' Stanley wanted to know.

'No much shorter,' Betty replied.

'Yes shorter,' I agreed.

'Now isn't that curious?' Stanley asked in a mock question. He inclined his head to us in a little nod. 'We are pleased to have been able to demonstrate this point to you. It is necessary to understand that when you adopt a negative attitude towards a task, you are sabotaging yourself.'

I nodded thoughtfully. 'Yes, I can see that and I know I do it a lot at work in meetings and presentations and so on. No wonder I have such a hard time of it. Thank you Ti Ming that was very helpful.'

Another little bow acknowledged my thanks. I wrote in my book:

Adopting a positive attitude towards a task makes it easier.

We stopped at this point for a lunch break. Betty had brought sandwiches, so I made some for Stanley and myself. June arrived in her blue Citroen just after two. Her eyes were sparkling and her cheeks flushed. She looked like one of Enid Blyton's Famous Five, out on an adventure.

'This is fun,' she announced. 'What have I missed?'

'Running around the caravan,' I replied somewhat morosely. Stan and Betty laughed but she looked horrified.

'I'm glad I missed that.'

'Don't worry, you'll get your turn,' Stanley assured her.

I watched her face drop and, like a new convert, was tempted to ask if she was staying positive with it, but managed to restrain myself. She would find out soon enough.

Chapter 4

Does Time Affect Reality?

Day 1
Session 3

Stanley gave his usual little bow to indicate the commencement of the workshop and that Ti Ming was present.

'This workshop is entitled Does Time Affect Reality?' he announced. 'What do you think?'

I dutifully wrote it down to give me something to do while I thought about the question.

Does Time Affect Reality?

Well, we had two choices.

'Yes,' I said.

Betty went for 'No.'

'I'm not sure what you mean,' June looked confused. (Obviously there had been three choices.)

Stanley marched on the spot while he considered us.

'Alright. I will tell you a little story,' I relaxed back into my seat and put the pen down. The pressure was off for the moment.

'Suppose you were out walking. It is a beautiful day and you are on a narrow pathway going over some mountains. As you round the corner there is a dog standing on the path and barking at you, refusing to let you pass. What would you do?'

'How big was the dog?' I wanted to know.

He smiled. 'It was quite a large dog.'

'Then I think I'd turn back,' I replied. 'I'm not keen on ferocious dogs, I got bitten as a child by an Alsatian.'

'Who said it was ferocious?' Betty wanted to know.

'Who said it was an Alsatian?' June said. 'Some large dogs are quite friendly. Well you should know Abby, you've got Heidi and she's quite big isn't she?'

I turned to Stanley. 'Was it a ferocious Alsatian?'

Infuriatingly, he just smiled and didn't answer.

'I'd talk to it. I'm good with dogs.' June lowered her voice to a conspiratorial whisper. 'You know, I don't tell everyone this but I'm something of a dog whisperer.'

'I'd approach it and offer it a biscuit,' Betty decided.

'Hang on,' I protested, 'where did you get the biscuit?'

'From my bag.'

'No biscuits allowed,' I maintained, 'that's cheating.'

'No it isn't.'

June laughed, she was enjoying herself I could tell.

'Stanley, are you going to let her get away with cheating?' I demanded.

He looked around at our animated faces and took control of the situation in a masterful tone that was quite foreign to him. Usually he stayed out of discussions when they got heated.

'OK. Can we forget about biscuits please? I know it might still be on your mind because we've just had our coffee, but what you need to be thinking is, whose right of way is it?'

'Ours of course,' I thought it was an obvious question.

Betty was not so sure. The fact that he'd asked the question meant that here was something to consider. I wrote hastily:

Whose right of way is it?

'The dogs?' she answered hesitantly, making it a question.

'The dogs?' June repeated and laughed. 'How can the dog have a right of way?'

'Well let's suppose that he thinks he has, whose right of way is it from whose point of view?' I admired the way Stanley (or Ti Ming) had got us back on track.

I put my hand up as if I were in school and Stanley nodded for me to answer.

'I guess from our point of view it was our right of way, and from the dog's point of view it was his right of way. He was defending his path.'

39

Stanley smiled, looking pleased.

'Correct. From your point of view the dog was in the way of the path and from the dog's point of view the path was in the way of the dog.'

It sounded confusing, so I wrote it down in order to look at the written words. Things always looked clearer when I could see them. June looked over my shoulder as I wrote:

From our point of view:
The dog was in the way of the path

From the dog's point of view:
The path was in the way of the dog

Stanley waited until I'd finished and then continued.

'Then we need to consider the path itself, which didn't have a point of view at all.'

'What?' I looked up from my writing in amazement. 'The path?'

Stanley nodded.

'I don't understand what you mean, could you please explain?' June looked thoroughly confused now.

'Well,' he began patiently as if talking to children, 'there are three elements here. You, the dog and the path. As we have just ascertained from the previous workshops, we have personal subjective time and non personal objctive time. Now who do you suppose was operating in personal time?'

'Us,' I replied.

'The dog,' answered Betty.

'Correct,' Stanley grinned at us looking from one to the other and waiting for our reaction as if it were a wonderful game and he was enjoying every moment.

'Well, which?' I asked. 'We can't both be correct.'

'Oh but you are.' He looked delightedly at my confused expression as if I had confirmed his predictions.

Poor June looked thoroughly out of her depth. This was not proving to be the jolly she had at first thought.

'Can you explain please?' I asked, sighing resignedly, realising that I had fallen into his trap.

'Certainly,' He bowed formally.

'The dog, thinking that the path was in his way was operating in Personal Time. You as pedestrians, were thinking that the dog was in the way of the path you were on, were you not?'

'Yes,' Betty spoke for us as we nodded.

'So, you were operating in Personal Time also.' He waited while I wrote it down:

We were operating in Personal Time

The Dog was operating in Personal Time

He then continued, 'The path however, not thinking at all was operating in Non Personal Time. The Path was the experience and you and the dog were the experiencers.'

The path was operating in
Non Personal Time
The Path was the experience

'Remember what we said in the first workshop?'

'No,' said June unnecessarily.

'Ah, can either of you tell June please?'

He paused and waited for us to remember. I'm ashamed to say I had to turn back the pages of my notepad to show her.

'The state of our mind and body
affects the way
we interact with non personal time'

41

So what were you thinking when you encountered the dog?' he asked.

'I was negative, because I thought the dog was going to bite me,' I suggested.

'I was positive because I thought he would be fine if I gave him a biscuit,' Betty decided.

'And what about you June?' Stanley enquired. 'How would you feel if you encountered a large dog on your path.'

'As I said, I'd be quite happy, I'd just talk to it.'

'So would you continue on the path or turn back?' he asked her.

'Continue,' she replied.

He looked at me.

'Turn back,' I said very definitely.

'Continue,' Betty answered.

'So you Abby allowed the dog to dictate to you and impose his reality on you, that it was his right to be walking where he was, and you and the path were an inconvenience that was in his way. Betty and June on the other hand decided that it was their right of way and the dog was inconveniencing them, so they dictated to him, via the biscuit and the whispering, so they imposed their reality on him.'

He waited to allow what he had said to digest and then asked.

'So which one of you was operating in personal time?'

'Abby was,' replied Betty.

'Abby, what do you think?' he asked before replying.

'I think Betty and June were,' I decided.

'Ah!' He smiled at us. 'We have divided opinions. The truth is, you all were.'

'Oh,' we looked at each other, surprised.

'And just for you to know,' he added, 'so was the dog.'

He surveyed our blank faces with amusement.

'All of you including the dog, had your own point of view. With me so far?'

We nodded.

'And all viewing points must necessarily be personal. It is only the path with no point of view that was in non personal time. OK, so do you agree that personal time can vary depending upon our viewpoint?'

We all nodded, so he continued.

'And our viewpoint will vary depending on whether we are positive or negative?

Again we nodded.

'Non-personal time however remains constant.'
We nodded once more. I picked up my pen and I wrote on my pad:

All viewing points must necessarily be personal.
Personal time can vary depending upon our
state, but Non Personal time remains constant

'Personal time is created by us, and what we create depends on whether we are operating positively or negatively.'
I summarised:

Personal reality is created by us.
What we create depends upon whether
we are positive or negative

He waited until I had finished before continuing.
'The Path, being in non personal time stays constant and operates in All Time. All time operates within the Time framework and creates the experience.'
There was no way I had understood what he had just said, but I dutifully wrote it down for future reference:

All time operates within the Time framework
and creates the experience

'When we are in a balanced state between positive and negative we are in Natural Time. But that is the subject of another workshop,' he added hurriedly as he saw our faces and realised we were near overload.
'Right, now let us consider positive Time. Positive Time is the result

of positive self talk and we can use it to balance out our accumulations of negative Time. Once we have done this we will be able to create our own reality. Some people are content to stay in this state, thinking that they have arrived, however they are still operating in duality.'

He paused and considered us.

'OK. Question. You set off from the house with 1.5 miles to walk and you have only got five minutes to do it in, otherwise you will miss your appointment. You make it with one minute to spare, how do you do it?'

I shrugged and stared at him wide eyed.

'I've no idea. It wouldn't occur to me to try and walk one and a half miles in five minutes anyway, because I know it's impossible.'

'Oh you do, do you? June, is it impossible for you?'

'Yes,' she agreed without hesitation.

'Betty?'

She regarded him thoughtfully over her glasses.

'It obviously isn't, or you wouldn't be asking us the question.'

He grinned impishly. 'Very good. So how would you do it?'

'Well, it must be by using positive Time,' she decided.

'Not quite correct.' He was gleeful, enjoying himself immensely, pleased that Betty had at least partially understood.

'In fact you would be travelling in positive No-Time. To travel in No-Time we need to be able to balance our energies. Time, like energy cannot be destroyed, but it can be changed and used to our advantage. The energy that made up the original reality was negative.'

'Why was it?' I interrupted.

'Well, you would have been thinking, it's late, I'll never make it on time, etc, with other emotions like panic, fear of being late, anger possibly at whatever, or whoever had made you late. You get the idea?'

I nodded my agreement. I could relate to that.

'So, this negative energy has to be changed by throwing it into Negative No-Time. Positive energy from Positive No-Time will then replace it, as Positive No-Time can create reality. So you would really have walked the whole way, but would have only taken four minutes to do it.'

'Could you do it instantaneously?' Betty wanted to know.

'Yes, you could,' he agreed. 'You would appear to have tele-ported, but in fact you would still have merely walked the distance as usual, only taken No-Time to do it. There, is that clear?' he aimed his question at me.

'As mud,' I replied gloomily.

This brought shrieks of laughter from him.

'Don't laugh at her,' June defended me, 'I don't understand it either.'

'I feel a run around the caravan coming on,' he threatened. 'Don't worry about it. If you can't understand, you will in Time,' he laughed at his own joke. 'In time,' he emphasised, willing us to join him in the fun, but our faces remained blank and he looked disappointed.

'Hmmm. So to conclude this workshop, Does Time affect reality, the Universe must always be in balance, therefore if negative energy is generated, then removed, positive energy must come in to replace it. So a change has been created within our Time Reference Frame.'

'What kind of change?' Betty wanted to know.

'All kinds of inexplicable and synchronistic events can occur, including psychic phenomena. If a sufficient amount of energy is moved, we might call it a miracle. So I think the answer is Yes, Time does affect Reality,' he gave a little bow. 'This is the end of the workshop. I thank you.' There was a few moments silence until Stanley rejoined us.

'Now off round the caravan with you.'

'Just a minute,' I protested, and noticed that he pointedly looked at his watch while I wrote down:

Yes, Time does affect Reality

'Right. Your minute is up. No excuses now, up with you.'

'But I have to go,' June protested, 'and I'm too tired to run.'

'You can't go before you've grounded the energy, then you can rest all you want.'

'Rest,' she retorted, 'I have to drive home and then get Eddie's tea.'

'Well your brain can have a rest. Now off you go, the sooner you start the sooner you'll finish.'

Betty and I knew better than to argue and once June realised we were going, she joined in.

'I didn't realise it was going to be this hard,' she panted, running to catch us up.

'I know,' I agreed, 'and it's only the first day.'

'I've really enjoyed it,' Betty was breathing hard, but obviously determined. 'I think I'll join you at nine tomorrow, if that's alright by you and Stanley?'

'It's fine by me,' I puffed, 'in fact, I'll be glad of the company, it's hard trying to answer everything all by myself.'

When we had finished our circuit she put the question to Stanley.

'Of course you can come my Angel, the more the merrier. June, what about you?'

June shook her head and tried to catch her breath.

'One session a day is more than enough for me to cope with thank you.'

Stanley sighed dramatically. 'No stamina the young these days.'

I had to smile as June was obviously his senior by quite a few years.

After they had departed I cooked us a vegetarian meal. We had our recap session on the days workshops before our evening meditation at 10.00 p.m.

Although I was tired, I hardly slept that night because, my brain was processing all the new information. I realised this kind of mental intensity was far more tiring than any physical labour. I had to admit I was impressed with Stanley's (or Ti Ming's) delivery and content of the workshops so far. I hadn't known quite what to expect and half thought that I could be wasting my time on a wild goose chase, but so far, so good.

This was a side of Stanley that I hadn't seen before and I was excited as I realised that I had learned so much already and this was only day one. There were still six days left to go.

Chapter 5

Practical Time

Day 2
Session 4

The birds were singing their morning chorus when I awoke to hear someone moving around the house. It took me a few moments to remember I was in the caravan and that it was Stanley I could hear in the kitchen next door, running the water and lighting the gas.

I groaned as I staggered to the bathroom to shower and dress. It was just past seven.

'Good morning Abby,' his voice was unusually bright and cheerful as I appeared yawning in the doorway. He was obviously taking his duties very seriously. I smiled a silent greeting as I sat down and yawned again. He presented me with a steaming mug of sweet, black coffee which I gulped gratefully.

He wandered outside with his mug of tea and packet of cigarettes.

The sun was streaming through the little window and the bird song engulfed me. I stretched my feet out under the table in the little dining area and sighed contentedly. It was a beautiful place to be, better than working. I savoured the moment, closed my eyes and extended my awareness as I had been taught to do yesterday. Stanley returned quietly and seated himself on the bench opposite.

'Fancy a walk?' he enquired when I opened my eyes.

I nodded my agreement and stood up. 'It will be nice to stretch my legs before we start.'

He smiled. 'It's going to be a busy day today.'

'No different to yesterday then,' I grinned.

Betty was sitting in her grey Vauxhall Astra when we returned from our walk at quarter to nine.

'Hi both, lovely morning.'

'Yes, isn't it?' I agreed.

'Glad you could join us Bett.'

47

'Well, I didn't want to miss anything after yesterday,' Betty laughed. 'I think poor June was out of her depth.'

'June was out of her depth! She wasn't the only one, so was I and I had no excuse, I was present the whole time.'

'Were you really? I'm pleased to hear that,' Stanley couldn't resist the jibe at me.

'Well you're on form Stanley so early in the morning,' Betty approved.

'Indeed I am.'

We all laughed and hugged each other before making our way into the caravan.

Betty and I settled ourselves into the bench seats and Stanley stood in front of us as usual. At precisely nine o'clock he began.

'Greetings.'

He gave the little bow we had come to expect from Ti Ming.

'Greetings friend,' Betty replied.

I merely bowed in return.

'The subject of this session is entitled Practical Time. It is called Practical time because it is time that can be used. It has a positive application.'

I duly wrote it all down on my notepad, pleased that he had actually given us a definition without trying to tease it out of us bit by bit. Perhaps he was starting to grasp the principles of teaching, or was it because Betty was there?

Practical Time

Practical Time can be Used. It has a positive application.

'What do you mean it can be used?' I wanted to know.

'Good question Abby. Betty have you got any ideas?'

'Use it to get things done, to be ahead of yourself?' Betty replied.

'I like that,' Stanley smiled encouragingly. 'Tell me, how can you be ahead of yourself exactly?'

'Well, if you've allowed two hours to do something, say cleaning the house, you finish in one and a half hours. You've got half an hour to spare.'

'And what would you do with that half an hour Betty?'

She shrugged. 'I don't know. Take a break, have a coffee perhaps?'

Stanley laughed. 'If that was a hint Betty, I'm sorry, but you'll have to wait until after this session. You may have some water though,' he indicated the water jug and glasses I had placed on the draining board.

She shook her head. 'No, I'm fine, but coffee would have been nice,' she admitted.

'Apart from drinking coffee, what else could you do with the half hour you'd saved?' Stanley looked round at me. 'Abby?'

'Well, anything you liked,' I answered puzzled that he was making a big thing of it.'

'Betty?' he looked hopeful.

'You could save it,' she replied thoughtfully.

'Save it. Yes. Well done Bett.'

'I don't understand,' I objected, 'we've already said we could save it.'

'Save as in bank it,' Betty explained.

'You mean, to use in the future?' I asked, somewhat incredulous, as I wrote down:

You could save it

'How would that work exactly?'

'Well, it draws on the workshop which we did yesterday, Does Time Affect Reality? Remember Negative No Time and Positive No Time? You can get ahead of yourself, as Betty puts it, and then keep that time in Positive No Time to use for a purpose of your own in the future, say to balance out an appointment where you would have been half an hour late, or to cancel out a debit.'

'What do you mean, cancel out a debit?' I wanted to know.

'Well, supposing you had generated some negative energy. As we know, normally if you act while you are negative you will create a negative outcome, arguments, illness, debt, the sort of days when you wished you'd stayed in bed. A bad hair day. But if you know about the Time Workshops, if you really couldn't manage to stay positive, you could at least put that negative energy on hold.'

Put it on hold

'What would that do?' Betty asked.

'Well, it would stop things getting chaotic and allow you to achieve a positive result.'

'But isn't that cheating?' I objected.

He laughed. 'There's only competent energy management and incompetent energy management. It's like money management, would you say it's cheating to borrow money and buy something that you can't afford now, but will pay for later?'

'Well, no,' I had to admit, 'I mean, even if you don't agree with borrowing, most people have a car or house loan these days, or a student loan.'

'Exactly my point,' Stanley beamed at me and waited while I wrote:

There's only competent energy management and incompetent energy management

'It's the same with energy, you would have to pay it back at some point, and so you could use the positive energy you have already banked.'

I was amazed. 'You mean you can actually move time around as if it were a commodity?'

'It *is* a commodity,' he reminded me gently, 'for those who are capable.'

Time is a commodity

'So you could take half an hour saved from last week, or pay back half an hour taken in advance?' Betty clarified.

He smiled at our enthusiasm. 'Yes, it's possible, but it's better not to have to pay it back. If you have accumulated enough practical time you wouldn't need to. It's like having savings in the Bank so you don't have to go into debit.'

It was an interesting concept to me. I had heard of saving time, but it never occurred to me to bank it.

You could Bank it

'What do we have to do to accumulate practical time – Betty?'
Betty visibly jumped.

'Oh, what did you say Stan? Sorry, I was miles away. I was just thinking that I've been wasting my extra time by drinking coffee.'

'No time is ever wasted Betty. Now can you tell me how to get ahead of yourself?'

No time is ever wasted

Stanley rephrased the question in the hope that she might answer this time.

'Oh, you would need to stay positive and focussed,' she replied easily.

'Yes, thank you Betty, we would need to stay positive. So now we need to consider how to stay positive. Any ideas?'

'Focus on the positive viewpoint,' I suggested.

'Meditate regularly, and ask God for help,' was Betty's contribution. I decided to write it down:

(a) Focus on the positive viewpoint
(b) Meditate regularly
(c) Ask God for help

'Well done,' Stanley congratulated us, looking at my list, 'they're all very good. What else could we do?'

The ball was back in our court and no-one spoke. We had made our contributions and couldn't think of anything else to say.

'Do you think conscious will affirmations might help?' he enquired with mock enquiry.

'Of course, I was just about to suggest it.' I joined in with his jokey attitude, as I wrote:

Make conscious will affirmations

'Oh, were you now? Well, in that case Abby, you could give us an example of a conscious will affirmation couldn't you?' he enjoyed watching me squirm as Betty stared expectantly at me. I laughed, it was a fair cop. I tried to think of something wonderful to say but all that came out was Mmmm.

'Interesting affirmation that, Mmmm. How about we try I am conscious of ummm?' Stanley scanned us both and must have realised that he was conscious of us needing to be told.

'Alright, in order to break negative thinking habits, you need to use conscious will affirmations. You start by thinking "I am conscious of," in order to bring the state into your awareness. You can also use, "I am being, I am worthy of, I am capable of, or I am independent." Make sure that you always use a positive statement to follow a conscious will affirmation. For instance, I am capable of doing this, or I am being focussed. Make sure you avoid following a conscious will affirmation with a negative, such as I am being a nuisance, or I am conscious of feeling embarrassed.'

I duly wrote:

Conscious will affirmations.
Use to eliminate negative thoughts.
Be careful to follow with only positives.

I am conscious of

I am being

I am worthy of

I am capable of

I am independent

He waited until I had finished.

'Good,' he approved.

'So ladies, what else can we do that will change the pattern of our activity and keep us positive?'

'Laughter?' Betty enquired.

'Yes indeed. A sense of humour is always very useful in helping to keep us positive, especially if we remember to laugh at ourselves as well as others,' he raised his eyebrows and made a silly face to accentuate the point and had us giggling.

Remember to laugh at ourselves as well as others

'If we are one of those more enlightened people who are more positive than negative, then we will find that we can cope with the circumstances of our life quite easily. Our situation will be relatively happy, we will be financially secure and able to turn our attention to being creative, or helping others who are not as developed. We will you might say, have become part of the solution instead of part of the problem.'

'So are there any other ways to stay positive?' I asked. I might have known I wouldn't get a straight answer.

'It's a good question. Anyone got any ideas?'

Back to us again. I was still hoping he would teach us, but maybe he didn't have enough positive energy to do it,' I thought and then realised that it was a negative thought. I glanced quickly at him in case he had read my mind, but if he had he showed no indication. He was too busy trying to inspire us.

'Well,' Betty began, 'I suppose the first step is to recognise that we are being negative.'

I cringed. Maybe it was Betty that had read my mind. I wasn't sure if I felt bad about thinking negatively, or good because I had recognised it.

'Good,' Stanley looked pleased. 'Yes, indeed, bring it into consciousness. You can't do anything unless you are aware of what it is that you are doing.'

He suddenly broke into song.

'You need to accentuate the positive and eliminate the negative and they won't mess with Mr. In between.'

He was tone deaf and his voice was flat. I cringed at the awful noise he was making, it was painful to me. But presumably oblivious to the caterwauling, he finished with a little bow, very pleased with his rendering.

'That ladies, concludes the Practical Time workshop,' he put his hands together in the usual Ti Ming bow.

I wrote down:

Accentuate the positive and eliminate the negative

Betty stood up. 'Thank you Stanley, I am conscious of needing to use the bathroom.'

I took my cue from Betty and stood up as well.

'I think I'll go for a walk, in case he sings any more.'

'I am conscious of having a wonderful voice,' Stanley informed us unrepentant.

'A wonderful voice for clearing the pubs at closing time,' I retorted.

He laughed good naturedly and joined me for a walk around the caravan site to stretch his legs and indulge his habit.

When we returned Betty had made coffee and put out the home-made biscuits she had brought.

Chapter 6

Non-Practical Time

At eleven thirty we began again.

Stanley waited until we had settled ourselves.

'We are now going to consider the meaning of Non Practical Time.'

There was silence for a few moments until his guide, Ti Ming stepped in with a little bow of acknowledgement.

'Greetings both and welcome to the Non-Practical Time Workshop.'

I wrote the heading in my book:

Non-Practical Time

'So what do you think we mean by Non-Practical Time?'

'Well,' Betty began, settling herself back on the cushions, 'earlier we agreed that Practical Time is time that can be used, so maybe Non-Practical Time can't be used?'

'It's a good answer and is partly right. Abby, do you have anything to add to Betty's definition?'

'Can it only be used to create negative situations?' I suggested.

'That certainly seems to be the way most people use it,' he agreed nodding vigorously.

'So you mean then that non-practical time is negative?' Betty asked.

'Not exactly,' his demeanour changed to become more thoughtful. He was obviously trying to find a definition for us and failing.

The thought crossed my mind that he might have trouble in translating from Chinese, or was it from a higher level of awareness?

'But you may call it negative time I suppose if that is your under-standing.'

'So, are you saying then that if we think negatively we generate a kind of negative time that cannot be put to any creative use?'

He listened while I spoke with his head cocked to one side, as if analysing what I was saying.

'In a way, although that is not quite right. There is a way of being creatively destructive or destructively creative.

Betty and I exchanged puzzled glances.

'If we have generated non-practical time for ourselves we need to burn up this negative energy in a harmless way. Any ideas?'

There was silence so he tried again.

'If we try to be creative when we haven't got enough positive energy to work with, what do you think would happen?'

'We'd get it wrong?' Betty suggested.

'Create more problems?' I added.

He nodded. 'When you are negative, all you can create is chaos. You'd end up making more of a mess and having one of those days when everything just goes wrong, no matter how hard you try. You would be being destructively creative, creating destruction,' he paused and we all smiled. We knew just what he meant. Satisfied, he continued.

'If we are generating more negative than positive in our thinking then we are generating more and more non-practical time in our lives, which will manifest in negative consequences for us. Can you think of anything else that might happen?'

'Arguments?' I suggested.

'Yes indeed,' he confirmed.

'Illness?' Betty contributed somewhat hesitantly.

'Correct. Arguments and illness. Yes. Anything else?' he waited for a moment and then moved us along with another question.

'What else would happen in our lives if we were negative most of the time?'

'Things would go wrong?' I offered.

He nodded. 'Things would go wrong indeed, and what would we say had happened?'

I was confused, but Betty answered in a flash of insight.

'We would say we'd had an accident.'

'Ah, yes. That's what I wanted to hear. An accident. Now that's inter-esting isn't it? To consider an accident to be the result of our own think-ing, rather than a chance occurrence? What does this mean?'

56

'That there are no accidents,' I said, picking up my pen and scribbling furiously. I had been so involved that I had forgotten to keep up with writing it down. Now I wrote in large letters:

Negative thinking creates non-practical time.

*Non-practical time is negative time
and creates chaos,
i.e. arguments, accidents, illness.*

There is no such thing as an accident.

Stanley marched up and down on the spot, watching as I wrote it down. Betty looked worried.

'Do we have to take notes?'

'No, it's just that Abby wants to,' Stanley explained, 'but I don't mind if you want to as well.'

'And do you?' I enquired looking amused, as I knew that Betty shared his views on writing.

She hurriedly shook her head. 'No thanks. I'm fine just listening.'

'OK then. There is a way we can be creative and use up our negative energy. Can anyone think how we might do that?'

We didn't speak. He waited for a moment, looking from one to the other in an encouraging kind of way, but eventually realised that no answer would be forthcoming.

'Well, think about tasks you could do that might require you to be destructive.'

'Throwing out rubbish?' Betty suggested.

'Well done Betty, that's a very good example of being creatively destructive. Any more, – Abby?'

Betty looked pleased with herself.

'Clearing out cupboards?' she offered once more.

'Yes, very good Betty. Abby do you have an example for us?'

'DIY,' I blurted out.

'DIY?' It was Stanley's turn to look confused. Yes! I felt triumphant.

'You know,' I explained, 'tearing down walls and ripping out fire-places. That's best done when you're angry.'

Stanley nodded in agreement. 'Yes, this would be an example of being creatively destructive. However we would have to be careful of accidents wouldn't we?'

I wrote down:

Examples of being Creatively Destructive

(a) Throwing out rubbish

(b) Clearing out cupboards

(c) DIY demolition work

'So what else could we do to use up accumulated negative energy?'

'Sleep,' I suggested.

'What makes you say that?' he enquired.

'Well, it's just that if I'm feeling stressed out I feel tired all the time.'

'You're quite right. Sleeping is an example of being passive and passivity uses up negative energy. Can you give me any other examples of being passive?'

'Daydreaming,' Betty said. 'I know I often used to get told off for daydreaming as a child. The Devil makes work for idle hands, they used to tell me.'

'My mother told me that too,' I agreed.

'Again correct. Daydreaming is an example of a passive use of negative energy,' Stanley confirmed. 'Anything else?'

'Would meditation count?' Betty asked rather timidly.

'It would indeed.'

'But I thought meditation was a positive thing to do,' I objected.

Stanley laughed. 'Well, so it is. It's using up negative energy and enabling the meditator to remain positive.'

'Ah, that's why they do it,' Betty was thoughtful. 'Does that mean then that the more they meditate, the more negative they are?'

'An interesting observation Betty. Not necessarily, but possibly. In any event, meditation is always a recommended practice,' Stanley bowed to us in Ti Ming fashion.

'Other ways that negative energy can be harmlessly dissipated is by going to the cinema, watching television, attending the theatre, reading fiction, drifting off into trances, spectator sports.'

'Spectator sports?' I questioned. 'How is that using up negative energy?'

'Because all of these activities we have spoken of are passive and do not engage your conscious will.'

'What about playing a sport?' Betty asked.

'What about it?' Stanley retorted.

'Would that count as passive action?'

'Well, is the player being passive?' Stanley asked.

'Depends on who we're talking about,' Betty chortled at her own humour.

'We are not discussing the proficiency of the player,' Stanley rebuked gently, 'we are trying to decide if playing a sport is a passive example of how to dissipate negative energy.'

'Yes, I know,' Betty sighed. 'I suppose it isn't then?'

'You are correct Bett, it isn't. All actions such as dancing, singing, playing sport or music, the arts and crafts, are all examples of creative action. But what happens when we try to follow these pursuits when we are negative?"

'Things go wrong,' I suggested.

'Indeed they do,' he confirmed. 'And I'm sure we could all provide examples of when things have gone wrong. We say we're having a bad day or we blame somebody else. If we try to carry on when we are negative we are just going from bad to worse.'

'Hey do you think my employer would agree to me having the day off on the grounds I'm having a bad day?' I laughed.

'Probably not, but it would be a good idea if they did because they would be saving themselves a lot of errors and bad workmanship and possible accidents. Work done on 'bad' days as you call it may take many future days of work to rectify. It would be far better to take the day off and remain passive, as they do in the East I believe.'

'Unless it was an enlightened firm who allowed you to be creatively destructive,' Betty suggested thoughtfully.

'I can't see that happening can you?' I said.

'Well they could allow you to destroy all the out of date paperwork or redecorate the office.'

'Depends on how many 'bad' days you get doesn't it?' I said. 'And what about everybody else? The office would be redecorated every day I should imagine.'

'Of course they could have outings for bad days and take everyone to the cinema,' Betty suggested

'Yes,' I agreed, 'they could put it down as staff training and call it motivation or team building skills. It's got to be better than some of the courses they are running at the moment. The last course I was on they got us building a bridge with elastic bands and sheets of paper.'

'What kind of films would you see?' Betty was still considering her idea.

'You'd only be drawn to the negative and that would hardly be motivational.'

'Ah,' Stanley had been watching the interaction between us and now he interrupted. 'Good point. Passive input from films, TV, books or the theatre should always be positive. You can't change your negative state by inputting negative.'

'OK then, how about the classics like the The Wizard of Oz?' I suggested.

He nodded with approval, 'That would be a good film to watch if you were attempting to passively dissipate negativity, and it's about a Wizard.'

I wrote down:

Strategies for dissipating negative energy

(a) Creatively Destructive

(b) Passive

(c) Destructively Creative

'So,' Stanley noted that I had caught up, 'what would happen if we were equally balanced in our negative and positive thinking?'

We both stared at him in silence, we hadn't thought of that. He waited, raised his eyebrows encouragingly and looked to each of us in turn.

'Ladies, anybody? No? Oh well?' he heaved an exaggerated sigh and continued.

'Well, it means that negative things will still happen, but we will have the positive energy to deal with them.'

'Well that's good isn't it?' Remarked Betty.

Stanley stared at her in consternation. 'I wouldn't say good exactly, it means we will be moving from one crisis to the next and we will have no surplus energy to maintain us, so we will be feeling tired and stressed and always fearful about what is going to happen next. The future we are generating is unknown and scary and it feels as if nasty things are just around the corner waiting to jump out at us. They are, because we are continuing to create them.'

He paused, looking at our shocked faces in amusement. 'BOO!' he suddenly shouted, making us jump.

'If it goes Boo, it's the Negative You.'

He watched me write:

If it goes Boo, it's the Negative You.'

As soon as I put my pen down he picked it up from the table and threw it at me.

'Catch,' he shouted.

I was surprised, but caught it deftly and was pleased with myself.

'Good catch,' Betty clapped her hands.

'Now how do you feel?' Stanley asked me, as I put the pen down.

'What do you mean?' I was confused.

'Check please,' he instructed and waited while I thought about it. Moments before I had been negative, ashamed of myself, now I felt pleased that I had caught the pen. How had that changed so quickly?

'You feel better yes?' Stanley enquired.

I nodded. 'Yes, but I don't understand why.'

'Was it something to do with the pen?' Betty asked. He nodded, saying nothing, and continued to look at Betty.

'In throwing the pen, you changed the energy,' she concluded.

61

'Yes,' he threw his hands wide in an exaggerated gesture as if showing us the situation.

I picked up the pen and stared at it. There was nothing special about it, just an ordinary ball point, a blue Bic with a fine tip.

'Are you saying this pen changed my mood?'

'Not exactly.'

'What then?'

'Any ideas?' he looked hopefully at Betty.

'When you threw the pen at her, did you throw energy with it?'

He shook his head, looking disappointed.

'Look at the pen,' he instructed me. 'Now throw it from hand to hand.'

I did as he asked, staring at it as I did so. Betty also watched me intently, all eyes were focussed on the Bic.

'Why am I doing this?' I asked after a few moments.

'Now that's a good question,' he looked round hopefully to see if Betty would provide the answer.

'Ah,' Betty had the insight. 'It's the movement. You are changing your state as you do it.'

Stanley clapped. 'Very good. Now you understand. It doesn't have to be a pen, anything can be a regulator. You don't even have to have an object. You could just drum your fingers on the table, tap your feet on the floor or fiddle with something,' he smiled conspiratorially. 'You could clap your hands. All movement will do the same thing, regulate the state of energy that is around you.'

'Is that why you tap your feet a lot?' I suddenly realised why he had persisted with that irritating habit in spite of my objections.

His eyes flashed with merriment. 'Oh I'm giving away all my secrets now aren't I?'

'So,' I clarified, 'you're changing negative energy when you do that?'

He nodded. 'I am indeed.'

It explained a lot. I started to realise why he was always so quiet in our meetings. There was obviously a lot more going on than I had realised.

'You can use anything to break state, you could throw a crystal from hand to hand, or get up and move around,' he continued.

'Is that why you made us run around the caravan?' I asked light suddenly dawning.

'Yes, exactly. It works doesn't it?'

Betty and I nodded. I was silent as I let the new information filter into my brain. I picked up my pen, looking at it with some awe and wrote:

Use a regulator to change negative energy

'So you all now realise that when you are being negative you need to use a regulator to change your energy?'
We both nodded.
'Good,' he approved. 'You should also thank the person who brings chaos into your life.'
Stanley looked at me and at my pen and I hurriedly wrote:

Thank the person who brings chaos into your life

'Why would we do that?' I questioned him.
It sounded suspiciously religious to me, akin to turning the other cheek, and I was surprised that Stanley, being a Wizard should subscribe to such a Christian sentiment.
I just couldn't see why we would want to thank people who brought negative experiences into our life, surely that would just encourage them even more?
He was silent for a while.
'You should thank them because a great service has been done for you,' he eventually replied.
'A great service?' I repeated, puzzled. 'What was it and who did it?'
He didn't answer and I looked at Betty to see if she could provide any insight as I was totally confused.
'The service is the learning experience they are offering us,' she said.
I had to admit, Betty was good. I wrote it down:

A great service is being done for us by negative people
They are offering us a learning experience

'You are right Bett, it is indeed the learning experience,' Stanley agreed.

'And who do you think decided that we needed the learning experience?'

'They did,' I answered.

He laughed. 'I agree that they might think you needed it, but who really decided?'

There was silence while we thought about it.

'The Universe?' Betty suggested.

Stanley ignored this and looked at me.

I had to say something, so I made a wild guess.

'I did?'

'Well done Abby,' he congratulated me with exaggerated euphoria.

'Of course it was you, it's always you.' ·

'But why would we want to bring chaos into our life?' Betty spoke for both of us.

'For fun.' He looked as though he meant it.

I couldn't let him get away with that. 'Fun? Chaos isn't fun.'

'Isn't it? I find it quite hilarious.'

I was beginning to feel exasperated with him. I think I was getting hungry, it was near lunch time and I was flagging.

Betty came to my rescue.

'I think he means that learning about ourselves is fun and that we should thank the people who give us the opportunity to learn about ourselves.'

He beamed at Betty but remained silent while I wrote:

Learning about ourselves is fun

'Up you come. Run round the caravan. Yes both of you, and remember, it's fun.'

'Fun is it?' I mumbled, but I complied.

As I ran I considered the suggestion of fun carefully, but the logic niggled at me.

I challenged Stanley when we returned.

'How can it be fun if someone does something to hurt us, surely we're not supposed to thank them are we? I mean, what about criminals, murderers and child molesters? We can't just say, oh thank you for killing or raping my child and forget about it can we? We can't just not punish people because they are bringing us a learning experience. It doesn't make any sense.'

Stanley waited to see if Betty would answer me, but when she didn't he explained.

'Just because it's right doesn't mean that it's not wrong.'

'What?' I was totally confused.

'An action is always both right and wrong, – unless it's in Natural Time, but we will come to that. It's right for us because we can learn and integrate the energy they bring back to us, enabling us to complete a learning experience, but that doesn't mean that the bringer of the experience shouldn't be punished for what they have done if punishment is required. No-one gets away with anything, on any level. The Law is absolutely just.'

'I take it you mean Spiritual Law?' Betty clarified.

No-one gets away with anything on any level
Spiritual Law is absolutely just

'Exactly so,' he agreed. 'If someone appears to be getting away with something it's for a reason, and there will be lessons to be learned from that, but it's not for us to figure out someone else's learning experiences, we have enough to do figuring out our own, wouldn't you say? Now are you both clear on the point that negative thinking generates non-practical time?'

We were silent, taking in the implications of what he had just said. I wrote down:

Negative thinking generates non-practical time

'Any questions? No, well I have one for you. What can we do supposing that we have been thinking negatively. Heaven forbid,' he raised his hands in mock horror, 'and we have generated Non-Practical Time for ourselves?'

Again we were silent.

'What nobody? How extraordinary. I would have thought you were all Non-Practical Time experts by now.'

'How can we be?' Betty protested, 'we're only just doing the workshop about it.'

Stanley smiled. 'But Bett my dear, you've been living it all your life.'

I was angry at his chauvinistic tone and rushed to her rescue.

'That's not very nice, implying that Betty is negative.'

My nose turned up even more than was natural for me as I sniffed haughtily, 'We didn't come here for you to be insulting to us.'

'Whoa,' Stanley laughed and clapped his hands together above his head.

'Well done. I'm impressed that you've created a practical demonstration of this point. Hands up those of you who are feeling negative at this precise moment.'

I raised my hand. Betty looked at me in obvious surprise. She didn't rise to the bait quite so easily.

'Are you thanking him for the learning experience?' she enquired.

I met her eyes and we both giggled.

'Stanley, stop playing games,' I demanded.

'Oh, but I told you it was fun.'

'Well it's not my idea of fun,' I remonstrated.

Stanley stood up. 'Time for a run round the caravan.'

'Oh no, not again,' we groaned, Betty stood up, but I remained seated.

'I'm not going again this time, we've only just been.'

Stanley said nothing.

Betty looked at him and pleaded with me.

'Won't you come with me?'

'No,' I was adamant.

'Are you being negative?' Betty enquired, raising an eyebrow.

At that I stood up, suddenly defensive.

'No, of course not. I'm never negative.'

We smiled at each other. Stanley held the door open.

The fresh air was welcoming. It gave me a chance to switch my mind off and invigorated me. By the time we had done a couple of rounds I was feeling quite refreshed.

'That seemed to be easier, I must be getting used to all this running,' said Betty dryly as she plonked herself back down to catch her breath. 'By the end of this week we shall both be a lot fitter.'

'I think I shall be more frustrated.'

'So shall I add frustration to the list of negatives?' Stanley enquired brightly.

I threw a cushion at him and he dodged it easily.

'Just using a regulator,' I smiled innocently. He picked up the cushion and looked at it thoughtfully.

'Abby could you stand up please?'

I thought he was going to throw it back at me, so I stayed put. He looked up and realised my reluctance.

'I just want to demonstrate something,' he explained.

I stood up warily, expecting a sudden throw, but he merely held it aloft.

'Right, could you please observe this cushion.'

We both duly stared at it. It was a green corduroy cushion of medium size with a zip down one side for easy cleaning. I wondered if he was going to ask us to talk about it, so I was ready with my observations.

'Now Abby, catch,' he threw it at me, but I wasn't ready and it dropped to the floor behind me.

'Can you pick it up please?' he waited while I did so.

'OK now we'll try again. Throw me the cushion please.'

I complied, wondering where this was going.

'Right, now this cushion is my problem.'

We both looked at the cushion with renewed interest. Why was it his problem, what was wrong with it?

'Now I'm going to throw it to you again Abby.'

This time I caught it.

'Right, now can anyone tell me what has just happened?'

'Abby caught the cushion you threw at her,' Betty replied.

'Yes, anything else?'

I looked down at the cushion in my arms as if it would provide the answer.

Betty knew. 'You have just passed your problem to Abby.'

He beamed. 'Well spotted Betty. Do you both see that? I am demonstrating how negative energy can be passed from one person to another. I had a problem and by giving it to Abby I am problem free, but now she has it. What can she do about it?'

I promptly threw the cushion back and he laughingly caught it.

'Yes, that's one way. Hand the problem straight back. Any other ways we could deal with it?'

He paused for a moment to give us time to think, but as no answers were forthcoming he held up the cushion in front of us again.

'OK. Abby, this cushion is my problem and I'm going to pass it to you. Catch,' he threw it at me and I stepped back, letting the cushion fall to the floor. I wasn't going to be had a second time.

'Very good. Did you see what happened that time?'

'She dropped the cushion,' Betty observed. 'She didn't take the problem on board.' She was on a roll.

'Exactly,' Stanley agreed. 'So, to recap, if someone has a problem, and you sympathise with them and take their problem on board, you've caught the cushion. You've taken their problem off them, but now you have the worry of it and will spend your energy helping to sort it out.

It will cost you time and/or money to do that, and it will certainly drain your energy and leave you feeling exhausted. Another way of dealing with other people's problems as Abby so kindly demonstrated, is to just stay detached and not take them on board. You leave the cushion coming at you to fall on the floor and do not pick it up, which means that you accept that others are responsible for dealing with their own problems and let them do that without interfering.'

'That doesn't sound very nice,' I objected.

'It's not about being nice,' he countered, 'it's about being aware. Other people's learning experiences are nothing to do with you. They cannot learn if you constantly interfere and deal with their problems for them, so you could say that it's not very nice of you to help them. What happens if you insist on helping everyone?'

'You could end up by being taken advantage of,' I suggested.

'And are you?' he enquired.

'Yes,' I admitted.

'It's diverting you from dealing with your own problems,' Betty delivered the blow.

'I don't have time for my problems, I'm too busy with everyone else's.'

'Exactly. So if you would pick up the cushion again please Abby.'

Stanley was anxious to move on and let me think about it in my own time.

Was being caring and compassionate really an excuse for not taking responsibility for myself?

'I shall now demonstrate another technique for dealing with negative energy that others attempt to off load.'

68

'Throw me the cushion please Abby.'

I did as he asked and he caught it and quickly threw it up into the air. 'What did I just do?' he asked.

'You threw the cushion into the air,' I replied, stating the obvious.

'You handed the problem up,' was Betty's contribution.

'Well done Betty, that's exactly what I did.'

I looked confused. 'But you caught the cushion first.'

'Yes, the best way to deal with negative energy coming at you is to acknowledge that it is your energy returning, but not necessarily from that person. Then you ask for the energy to be transmuted.'

'Ask who?' I wanted to know.

'The One,' Stanley replied.

'What One?'

'The One you call God or the Goddess.'

'Oh.' I was silent while I considered this.

'So you're saying that we should ask God to deal with other people's problems?'

'Not quite, although that is an option, but we would have to decide whether that was appropriate.'

'Why wouldn't it be?' Betty asked.

'They might not want us to,' he replied simply.

'It is for them to ask for themselves. I'm saying that we should allow other people to deal with their own problems, unless directed otherwise by the Higher Self, as that is the way they will learn and grow, but that we should ask the One to transmute our own negative energy that is returning to us from those around us.'

'I don't quite understand the difference,' I frowned in concentration.

'The difference is that some people are unwilling to deal with their own problems and try to dump them on us, and some people are wanting to give back problems to us that we have dumped on others in the past. By handing up all problems to God/Goddess, or the One as I like to say, we are freeing ourselves from carrying their cushions and freeing others from carrying ours. Now are we all clear on cushion management?'

We laughed and I nodded, busy writing down what had been said in my notepad.

Stanley watched as I wrote down:

Cushion Management

1. Catching cushion = being sympathetic
   allowing others to dump on us

2. Dropping cushion = being detached
   not allowing others to dump on us

3. Catching cushion and throwing it up
   = being aware
   handing their/our problem
   up (to the Higher Consciousness,
   God/Goddess, or the One)

When he spoke, it was in a tone too formal to be his own.
'Thank you ladies, this concludes the Non-Practical Time workshop.'
Ti Ming gave his usual little bow.

Chapter 7

Time Strategies

Day 2
Session 6

I was so glad it was lunch time, I needed the break for thinking and besides, I was starving. I lit the gas to prepare beans on toast and Betty opened her pack of sandwiches.

'I've brought some for you Stanley. While I'm making some for me I may as well make some for you. Abby is providing all the other food for you, so consider lunch my contribution.'

As if she didn't have enough to do, but I didn't argue as I knew they would contain meat and it must be hard for Stanley to exist solely on my vegetarian fayre.

She handed one to him which he gratefully accepted.

'Thanks Bett.'

We decided to wait for June to arrive before we began our run round the caravan. Stanley said it would help to integrate her energies into the group.

She rounded the corner in her little Citroen waving cheerfully at us.

'Hi everyone, lovely to see you. How's it going?'

She managed to keep her smile even after we told her about the run. Stanley stood watching us thoughtfully while he puffed at his cigarette.

'Why don't you join us?' I invited as we completed our first circuit. He just smiled and waved us on. We returned with five minutes to spare and seated ourselves in preparation. At exactly 2.30 p.m. Stanley was ready to begin. He stood up and waited a few moments in silence. I assumed he was tuning in to spirit.

He gave a little bow, with his hands together. I felt the energy change, Ti Ming was here.

'This afternoon we will start with Time Strategies,' he announced in an authoritative tone. I duly wrote:

Time Strategies

'So tell me Abby, what kind of time strategies do you use?' he enquired of me.

I shrugged and reeled off a list. 'Prioritising, organising, delegating, is that the kind of thing you mean?'

'Not quite. I mean what state of consciousness do you use in order to obtain the outcomes you require?'

This definitely didn't sound like Stanley. 'I don't think I'm aware of using a state of consciousness to obtain outcomes,' I confessed. 'I didn't know you could.'

He laughed, amused. 'Oh but you do, we all do, and the outcome we get will depend on the type of state or strategy we have used, so it's a good idea to bring our strategies into consciousness, wouldn't you agree?'

I nodded twirling a lock of hair around my finger distractedly.

'But how would you do that?' Betty asked.

'Well, suppose Abby was under pressure at work to produce a certain document, how would she react do you think?'

'I don't know, how would you react Abby?' Betty looked at me.

It was an easy question for once, it happened to me all the time.

'Well, I get stressed out, work through my lunch break, and stay late until it's done.'

'OK,' Stanley started his marching on the spot, shifting his weight from one foot to the other.

Regulating the energy, I remembered. Now I understood that his little habit had a purpose, I stopped being annoyed by it.

'So would you say you were driven by time?' Stanley enquired.

'Definitely,' I agreed.

'So that is your time strategy,' he informed me. 'Can you give me another example of ways in which you are driven by time?'

It was another easy question. 'Oh loads of ways. Getting to work on time, taking Laurence to school through the rush hour traffic on Mumbles Road, trying to meet deadlines, quarterly reviews. I constantly feel driven, there just never seems to be enough time to get everything done.'

'Indeed,' Stanley nodded gravely. 'This is the outcome of the Driven by Time Strategy.

'You mean there are other ways we could do things that would get us more time and different outcomes?' Betty asked.

June laughed. 'It sounds wonderful to me. I mean we could all use more time couldn't we?'

He nodded gravely. 'Indeed we could June.'

I was amazed. It had never occurred to me that there was any other way of doing things, or that if there was, it would result in changing the amount of time I had available.

'What are the other time strategies?' I was desperate to know and leaned forward, eager to hear more. I wrote down:

Negative Strategies

(a) Driven by Time

'Well now that you know there are others, what do you think Abby?'

I sighed, leaning back against the wall of the caravan. I might have known. Stanley was never one to give a straight answer. I wished the others would say something to help me out.

'What other kinds of things do you do under pressure?' he enquired.

'Ask for help?'

'Yes, asking for help is always a useful thing to do, but in this instance I am asking what *you* actually do.'

I considered. 'Sometimes I just keep on regardless. If there's no-one else to help and I've got to get something done I carry on until I finish, even if it's getting late.'

I looked at him hopefully, wondering if I had said the right thing inadvertently. It felt like being back in French lessons, I was struggling to understand a foreign language and make sense of what was being said. In a way that was correct, I was struggling to understand my own unconscious mind, which speaks in a language that is foreign to the concious mind.

'So you might say you are ignoring what time it is, in order to concentrate on the task?'

'Yes, I suppose I am,' I agreed.

He beamed at me delightedly.

'There you are, your next strategy, Ignoring Time.'

'Is that one?' June asked dubiously.

'It certainly is,' he confirmed. 'Unfortunately, to be driven by time and to ignore time are both negative time strategies. To be driven by time is to respond unconsciously to past conditioning and experiences and to ignore time is to refuse to acknowledge that time is passing. Tell me what are you thinking when you are ignoring time?'

It was such an odd question. I had no idea. 'Well I don't think I'm thinking about time at all, I'm concentrating on what I'm doing.'

'So you're not aware that time is passing?'

'Well yes I am, I mean, I suppose I do look at the clock, but then just kind of blank it out and quickly focus on something else.'

He listened attentively to my description, like an eager puppy waiting for you to throw the ball for him. He was almost quivering with excitement.

'So you are quite literally ignoring time?'

He pounced on the ball and laid it at my feet, tail wagging, pleased with himself.

I felt like a naughty schoolgirl who had been caught talking in class. For some inexplicable reason I felt guilty. It seemed rude to be ignoring time.

(b) Ignoring Time

'And when you feel driven by time, what are you thinking then?'
He was relentless.

'Well, when I'm in panic mode it's something like 'Oh no, it can't be that time already, I'll never get it done in time.'

Stanley nodded, still on the trail.

'And would you say that this self talk is positive or negative?'

I pulled a face at him and grinned. 'Negative.'

'So do you think it would be better to be more positive about time?'

'Yes of course,' I agreed.

'So how could you do that?'

I was silent.

'Anyone?' he opened it out, speaking as if there was an audience of hundreds.

It suddenly occurred to me that perhaps there were in the spirit world, perhaps they had all gathered to attend the Time Workshops and learn from Ti Ming.

'Say I've got all the time in the world?' Betty suggested.

He laughed. 'No that would be lying to yourself. I don't think lying counts as being positive.'

'Anyone else? June?'

She shrugged without answering.

'Abby?' he was back to me again.

I was stumped. 'I don't know. I mean obviously, if I knew I would be doing it, wouldn't I?'

He was silent for a moment considering us and marching on the spot. He must have realised we were not going to get it, so he decided to give us the answer.

'Alright then. You could consciously manifest time.'

'Consciously manifest time?' I gasped. 'Can it be done? Are you serious?'

'What does that mean?' June enquired, looking puzzled.

'Well, he means make more time, at least, I think that's what he means. Is it?' I asked him.

He nodded.

'How would I do that?' Betty wanted to know, practical as ever.

He held up his hand. 'Could we have one question at a time please ladies? Yes, it can be done, we are serious. It is possible to consciously manifest time. You would use conscious will affirmations.'

I wrote:

Consciously manifest time

'Like we did earlier?'

'Yes indeed,' he confirmed.

'So,' I consulted my notes, 'I would start off with I am?'

He nodded encouragingly.

'I am what?' June wanted to know. (She had missed that workshop.)

'Whatever you want,' he replied.

'I am confused.' Somehow it sounded like a true statement of her condition.

'Ah, be careful. You must only follow the I am statements with positives.'

'But I'm telling the truth. You told Betty that lying to herself was a negative. We can't win.'

Stanley winced. 'Is that a positive statement June?'

'No,' she admitted, smiling ruefully, 'but I don't know what else to say.'

'You could say, I am capable of understanding this.'

'I am capable of understanding this,' she repeated dutifully, and then added, 'do I have to believe what I'm saying?'

He chuckled. 'Well it does help.'

'So I could say I am capable of finishing the work on time, or I am conscious of my own efficiency,' I suggested to take the heat off June who was looking somewhat perplexed.

'You could indeed. They would be excellent examples to use to consciously manifest time.'

'And does this stuff work?' June demanded somewhat ungraciously.

Stanley (or Ti Ming) took no offence.

'Ah now this is something for you to find out. You have after all found out what does not work have you not?'

June nodded, she had to agree it was true.

'You can also use positive affirmations as a time strategy. You mentioned one earlier Betty, but unfortunately it was not quite realistic.'

'I've got all the time in the world do you mean?'

He laughed. 'That's the one. What you could say to make it more practical is; I have all the time I need, or I have plenty of time. Other positive affirmations include, Time is on my side. It's always the right time. Help will arrive when needed, or what's past is past. There's also, today is a new day.'

I held up my hand. I had forgotten to write anything on my notepad. I quickly caught up.

Consciously manifest time by using

Conscious will affirmations, e.g.

(a) *I have all the time I need*

(b) *I have plenty of time*

Positive affirmations, e.g.

(c) Time is on my side
(d) It's always the right time
(e) Help will arrive when needed
(f) What's past is passed
(g) Today is a new day

Avoid negative strategies, e.g.

(a) Driven by time
(b) Ignoring time

He waited patiently. 'Have you got all that?'

'Just about,' I put my pen down and heaved a sigh of relief.

'I meant all of you. Do you understand what has been said and will you use it to manifest more time for yourselves?'

'Oh,' I looked up, somewhat startled. 'I don't know about that.'

Stanley smiled with glee. He had caught me out again.

'It's not just about making notes you know, or reading about it at a later date. This is about you living your life in a new way. Tell me what positive action will you take NOW that will enable you to live your life in a new way?'

He made me jump by shouting the word now at me, as if he knew I was sneaking a look at the clock and wondering how long it would be before we finished. Then I looked down at my notes and thought about the answer to the question. Positive action. Hmmm. Get up and put the kettle on?

'I could ask for help,' Betty suggested, breaking in on my thoughts.

'Good. What else?'

There was silence once more. I considered the question more sensibly this time. What positive things could I do to make more time for myself?

'Delegate?' I answered.

If Stanley knew I had cheated by looking at my notes, he gave no indication.

He nodded. 'Yes, similar to asking for help, only when you delegate, you must realise that you are giving the task over to someone, so you need to let them do it in their own way. You must let go of trying to control the outcome. What else? Anyone, June?'

She shrugged. 'I don't know. Be prepared to change?'

Stanley looked delighted. 'Excellent. An essential point in all these workshops. What is the point of acquiring new information if we are not prepared to change?'

I wrote:

Be prepared to Change

I saw Stanley's glance lower to my notepad and felt he was making the point to me. Maybe I was just feeling paranoid, but I knew he didn't approve of my writing everything down because he thought I might miss something. His next words made me realise that I had merely been assuming what he was thinking.

'Now I'm going to give you all an exercise to do. I am going to make some statements that I want you Abby to write down and you can all decide whether you say them out loud or think them to yourself, and Abby can tick the ones that apply and cross the ones that do not. Are you ready?'

We nodded eagerly.

I held my pen in readiness.

'It will reveal itself in time,' he said.

1. It will reveal itself in time.

I wrote down dutifully.

'Yes I say that, put a tick for me,' Betty said.

'Me too,' I agreed.

'And a tick for me,' June added.

Stanley observed us and when we were ready gave us the next one. 'Time heals,' was the second one he gave.

2. Time Heals.

I wrote it on my pad.
We all agreed to that one.
I wrote the third one down that he gave us.

3. Hold on, or wait a minute.

'I don't think I say that,' said Betty thoughtfully, looking at my pad.
'I do,' I admitted.
'So do I,' said June, so I put two ticks and one cross against the statement.
The next one was:

4. I'm having the time of my life.

None of us ticked that one. Interesting, I thought that none of us said that, and maybe we were at that precise moment.
'The next one is, I didn't know it was that time.'
I wrote it down.

5. I didn't know it was that time.

Betty and I agreed we said that.
'I'm always saying it,' Betty admitted. 'I lose track of time.'
'I don't wear a watch,' I said, 'they never seem to work on me, so I never know what the time is.'
'Next.' Stanley interrupted.

6. It will all come right in time.

'Yes, I think I say that,' Betty nodded.
'Me too,' I agreed.
'Similar to the first one wasn't it?' June asked.
I consulted my notes. 'That was, it will reveal itself in time.'
Stanley coughed to keep us on course, and gave me the next statement.

7. Time is money.

'No, I don't say that, put a cross for me,' Betty watched while I did so.
'Nor me. I never worry about money,' June announced.
'I do,' I put a tick against my name.
'Well you're working aren't you? It makes a difference when someone is paying you by the hour.'

I thought it was nice of June to acknowledge I was the only one of the party who had to earn my own living. Both she and Betty had husbands who provided for them.

Stanley moved us on, obviously thinking there was not enough time to discuss it, I thought wickedly. As if to confirm, the next one was:

8. There's not enough time to do it.

We all agreed to that one, so I ticked accordingly.
'OK,' said Stanley, peering at my notes, 'what number are we up to?'
'Number nine,' I informed him.
'Right then number nine.'

9. Take your time.

'I think I get a cross for that one,' I laughed. 'I never say that, I'm always too impatient.'
'I get a cross for that one too,' Betty agreed.
'Oh I think you can put a tick for me on that,' said June, 'I'm never in a hurry.'
'OK last one.'

10. I want to be free.

'Oh yes, I say that all the time,' I said, 'should I put two ticks?'
'Just one will be fine,' Stanley smiled. 'What about you Bett?'
'Well I don't usually say it out loud, but I often think it, does that count?'
'It does indeed. A tick for Betty then please Abby. And June, what about you?'
'No I don't say that. I am free.'
'Right then ladies, let's see what you have been manifesting for yourselves.'

I was puzzled. 'What do you mean?'

'Well, read out the first one.

'It will reveal itself in time.'

We all had it.

'Right, now that statement is positive, so that will give you a positive outcome. Next.'

'Time heals.'

'Good. Also positive, next.'

'Hold on, or wait a minute.'

'Ah,' Stanley paused. 'Now this one is negative. Who has it?'

'Me,' I confessed.

'And me,' June admitted.

'So, Abby and June, do you have any idea why this should be negative?'

I shrugged somewhat petulantly. 'Because I'm asking someone to wait?'

Stanley nodded. 'Yes, indeed. You are actually programming their subconscious and preventing them from using their time in a positive way. This will come back to you. Do you find you are kept waiting by others, or that you can't always do the things that you want to do, even though you've got the time available?'

'Yes,' I agreed,

June said, 'It always annoys me when I'm kept waiting, I make sure that I'm always on time.'

'Maybe you are June, but if you delay others by telling them to hold on or wait a minute, you have placed a time lock on them which is going to come back on you. That time has to be repaid somewhere, even if it's not the same people you put on hold, someone at sometime or another will keep you waiting.'

I was horrified. 'You mean that just because I make a casual remark to someone it's going to have an affect?'

Stanley was grave, the smile for once absent. 'Everything we do has an affect, what we say, even what we don't say, it's just that we don't always notice what we are doing.'

'I feel terrible,' June looked miserable for once.

'So I have been putting other people on hold?'

Stanley nodded. I couldn't help noticing that Betty looked rather self righteous that she didn't do such an awful thing. Then I suddenly wondered if it was negative of me to notice.

'What usually happens when you say it?' Stanley enquired, pulling me back to the moment.

'What do you mean?'

'Well, do people ignore you, or do they wait?'

I considered. 'I suppose they wait.'

'Yes, they wait. They have no choice but to wait because you have used the power of the spoken word. What would be a better way to handle the situation?'

'Be on time?' Betty offered.

'Yes, but if that's clearly not going to be the case?'

June and I looked at each other, searching for answers.

'Tell them not to hold on?' I suggested.

June volunteered, 'Tell them I'm going to be late?'

'That would be a considerate thing to do, but how would you tell them without putting a time lock on them and making them wait for you?'

Stanley scanned our blank faces, and realising that we didn't have a clue, continued.

'You estimate how long you are likely to be and give them that information.'

'But I don't see how that's different to what I'm doing already,' I objected.

'If you say, it's likely to be another five minutes before I'm ready, that gives the other person the option of finding something else to do in those five minutes. You have not given a subconscious command to hold on or wait. When you do this you have taken control of someone else's time and this will have to be paid back at some point.'

'Oh I see, but what if I was going to be an hour late?'

'The same rule applies. An hour, a day, a week, a minute, a lifetime, whatever.'

'But surely people can't put others on hold all that time?' Betty sounded alarmed.

'You'd be surprised,' Stanley's voice was grim. 'They can put people on hold indefinitely.'

'But how?' I was intrigued. 'I'm sure people wouldn't buy "wait a week for me".'

'What about "don't start till I get there", or "just wait for me"?'

'Wait for me could be years if it was lovers parting from each other,' I mused.

Stanley nodded. 'You see what a time lock can do? It could even be lifetimes.'

'And you say it all has to be paid back?' June enquired.

'Indeed. Eventually everything we send out has to return to us, just like a homing pigeon,' Stanley flapped his hands at us in a bird like manner, obviously happy with his analogy, but for once I was not amused by his antics, I was too busy considering the implications.

'So, next statement,' he moved us swiftly on.

'I'm having the time of my life,' Betty read it out, looking across at my notepad.

Stanley smiled. 'Positive, next.'

'I didn't know it was that time.'

'Ah. Who has it?'

Betty and I admitted to it.

'I don't do that. I always know what time it is. I have a watch,' June proudly displayed an obviously expensive gold watch.

We were about to comment on how lovely her watch was when Stanley thwarted the distraction.

'This statement you will be pleased to know does not affect anyone else, but it does affect the speaker. It will throw your subconscious into a state of panic because it thinks it has lost track of time and you will find yourself clock watching in a neurotic manner.'

'Oh, that's why I do it,' Betty looked pleased to have an explanation.

'So what should we say instead?' I wanted to know.

'Good question,' Stanley approved, but as usual gave no direct answer.

'Should have been a politician,' I thought to myself.

'What would be a better choice of language?'

He waited, but we were not forthcoming.

I was flagging. It felt like it had been a long session at the end of a long day and I wanted a coffee break. Still, I rallied myself, if he could do without nicotine, then I could do without caffeine.

'How about, it would be that time?' he suggested.

'What do you mean?' I asked, forgetting about coffee for the moment.

'Well, when you look at the clock and get a shock because it's later than you thought, you need to stop and consider what you have been doing because you have used the time in some way, even if it's to pay back, and by affirming 'it would be that time,' the mind will provide you with details of what you've been doing.'

He gave us a moment to digest the information before moving on to 'It will all come right in time.'

We all agreed that we said this.

'Good. That's a positive statement that is fine to use. What about Time is Money?'

'I say it,' I admitted. 'It's a negative isn't it? I know you've mentioned it before.'

He nodded. 'Any idea why it's negative?'

'Because you shouldn't think of everything in terms of money,' Betty provided.

'And why shouldn't you?' Stanley enquired, probing to see where Betty was coming from.

'Well, you'd be being materialistic wouldn't you?' Betty avoided meeting my eyes while she was saying this.

'No. It's not about being materialistic.' Stanley was brisk, he knew Betty's views on materialism and realised the discussion was in danger of veering off track once more.

'It's about equating one thing with another, thus making the subconscious unable to distinguish between them. What would be the consequence of this?'

We looked at him blankly.

'If the subconscious thinks they are the same, it can give you one or the other, but not both. You can therefore have money without time, or time without money.'

I loved to read. I thought of the time when I had no job, so I had plenty of time to read books, but couldn't buy the ones I wanted because I had no money, and now I had a good job, I had the money to buy them and bought loads of wonderful books that had been on my wish list, but I had no time to read them. It was so frustrating. I regarded Stanley with awe.

'Thank you, that explains so much.'

He bowed. 'Glad to be of service. Now the next one.' He looked at my pad. 'There's not enough time to do it. Ah I see you all have that one.'

'Another negative?' Betty asked.

'You have guessed correctly. Any idea why?'

'Well, we're telling ourselves that we don't have enough time.'

'Well done Betty. And just to make sure that you don't have enough time, your obliging little subconscious will provide you with interruptions and complications.'

'Why would the subconscious do that?' I wanted to know.

'Well you see, your subconscious is like an on board computer and it has to obey the commands given to it. If your programme says I will not have enough time to complete this task, it has to make sure that you won't, because logic tells it that this is the situation you want.'

'I'm starting to realise why it's so important to be careful what you think,' June said.

'Me too,' I agreed.

Stanley looked as if he were enjoying himself. 'I do love it when the penny drops,' his impish grin peeped out at us from under the thatch of untidy fair hair.

'I don't know about the penny dropping, it feels more like a brick to me,' I said.

'So what about "Take your Time"?' He moved us swiftly onward.

Betty and I shook our heads.

'What, neither of you?' he asked in mock surprise. 'Oh what a pity, it's a positive too. You might try it in the future.'

'I say that,' June looked smug.

'Well done June,' he congratulated.

'So, the last one, I want to be free. Any takers?'

He winced as Betty and I raised our hands.

'Oh, this is not good. This last one is a negative time binder. You have programmed yourselves into making sure that you will never be free of the negative time zone you have created. You are caught in a vicious circle and you will need help to break out of this.'

'Can you help us?' I asked anxiously, not liking the sound of it at all.

'I can indeed,' he confirmed and waited. There was a few moments silence when no-one spoke.

'Well, will you then?' I asked exasperated.

He waited expectantly, looking at Betty.

'Can you help me too,' Betty asked hastily.

He smiled. 'I thought you'd never ask.'

'Basically, you have to hand up to your Higher Self and ask for Divine intervention. If you are caught up in a subconscious loop you have to reach outside the loop and call in help from outside. Your Higher Self can then step in and release you.'

'How do I contact my Higher Self?' I wanted to know.

'Close your eyes,' he instructed, waiting while I did so. 'Now, reach up with your inner sense.'

I tried to do as he said, but it was difficult with them watching.

'I'll try again when I'm alone,' I said, opening my eyes.

'Me too,' said Betty, but how will we know if we've succeeded?'

Stanley smiled, 'You'll know. It's like dialling a number on the phone, you know when someone has picked up. So, to recap, the Time Strategies workshop,' he caught June's eye and repeated, mostly for her benefit, 'we have decided that negative strategies like ignoring time or being driven by time can be replaced by consciously manifesting time. And we can do that by?' he looked at me.

I hurriedly looked down at my notes.

'Conscious will affirmations, positive affirmations and positive actions,' I looked up at him defiantly. It had been a lot to take in and I couldn't be expected to remember it all at once.

He sighed in mock exaggeration.

'Thank you Abby for listening so attentively. Perhaps when you have typed everything up you could give copies to Betty and June and maybe in the repetition you will begin to understand what has been said. How can you put it into practice if you can't even remember it?'

'It's been a lot to remember,' I protested.

'You're right,' he agreed. 'It has, and now it's time for a break I think. That ladies,' he gave a little bow, 'concludes the Time Strategies workshop.'

June and Betty said they had to get home so we went out to wave them goodbye. When they had driven out of sight I went back inside to light the gas under the kettle.

'Walk?' Suggested Stanley appearing in the doorway.

'In a minute,' was my first reaction and then I met his eyes with a horrified stare as I realised what I had just said.

'Sorry,' I apologised cringing inwardly, 'I mean, I am just going to have a cup of coffee before I go for a walk, but if you want to start now I can catch you up later.'

'Well spotted,' Stanley approved. 'You were just about to use a time lock on me. I'll tell you what, I'll nip outside for a cigarette while you have a coffee and then we'll go for a walk together alright?'

'Alright,' I agreed.

'Do you see how that respects the rights of both parties and allows us to be co-operative rather than controlling?'

'I didn't realise I was being controlling,' I said feeling ashamed as I wrote:

Be co-operative rather than controlling.

'Of course you didn't,' he agreed, 'it was unconscious controlling. But that's what the workshops are all about, bringing our unconscious behaviour into consciousness, and learning the consequences of our actions, so that we are then in a position to choose what we do and accept responsibility for the outcomes.'

He smiled at me. 'The kettle's boiling.'

Chapter 8

Is Time a Major Factor to Life?

Day 3
Session 7

It was Monday morning and I was not at work. What a delicious feeling, to be on holiday, albeit a working holiday, and one that was proving more arduous than my teaching at the College. I lay in the tiny caravan bedroom and listened to the wind in the trees outside. It was still early, I had slept well and without dreams, as if I had gone too deep for dreaming, probably processing all the new information I had acquired.

I extended my awareness as I had been taught. I was aware of the leaves brushing the roof, of the birds singing, of a spider weaving a web outside the window. I brought my awareness inside. I was aware of my body, still warm and drowsy from sleep, reluctant to move just yet, of my mind, crisp and alert and a sense of excitement and a realisation that for the first time in many years I was happy.

I explored the feeling of happiness within me, and with my attention upon it, the sensation expanded and swelled like the waves on the ocean. I let the feeling roll over me and felt a tingling ripple through me from top to toe. I heaved a deep, involuntary sigh and closed my eyes to experience the bliss more fully.

It was another twenty minutes before I felt ready to move and greet the day. I stumbled into the bathroom still in a daze and showered myself awake.

Stanley was nowhere to be seen. The door to his room stood open, so I presumed he had gone for a walk. He returned after about ten minutes and joined me for a cup of tea, although, as usual, he declined breakfast.

Betty arrived just before nine, bright and breezy in a turquoise blue velvet leisure suit. She looked smart and cheerful as if she had chosen something special to wear for the occasion.

'Morning both, how are you?' she enquired, looking from one to the other.

'I'm fine thanks,' I answered, as I went forward to embrace her.

'All the better for seeing you Betty my angel,' Stanley gushed, putting his arms around her. 'Come on in Bett, we are just about to start.'

'Yesterday was very interesting and gave me a lot to think about.'

'Well hopefully you'll do more than just think,' Stanley raised his eyebrows in a joking way, although he left no doubt from his tone that he was serious.

'Yes of course,' Betty sat down, somewhat flustered and I handed her a mug of coffee.

Without giving us time to converse his manner changed and he began with his usual bow.

'Welcome ladies, today our workshop is entitled, Is Time a Major Factor to Life?'

I opened my note pad and wrote down the title:

Is Time a Major Factor to Life?

I finished and looked up expectantly to find Stanley's piercing blue eyes staring expectantly back at me.

'So ladies, do we think, it is?'

'Well yes, of course it is,' to me it seemed obvious.

Betty was more cautious, she had come to realise that not everything was straightforward with Stanley, or Ti Ming.

His gaze shifted to Betty. 'Well Betty, you haven't given me your answer yet, what do you think?'

'I'm not sure,' she was not going to be drawn.

'OK,' he said lightly. 'Well supposing we accept Abby's answer and explore why we might say that yes, Time is a Major Factor to Life.'

I wrote down:

Reasons why Time is a Major Factor to Life

We both waited.

He waited as well. After a few moment's silence he gave up expecting us to come out with the answer.

'Now come on ladies, I know it's still early but will someone please give me a reason to start us off. Abby, you said yes, so can you tell me why you think time is a major factor to life?'

'Well,' I began, 'I suppose that time is a major factor to life because we need to interact in society. I have to start work at nine o'clock every day, – I couldn't just turn up whenever I fancied. We started these workshops today at nine. Everyone knows where they are if we agree a time. Betty knew when to arrive and June knows the afternoon sessions start at two thirty.'

'OK,' Stanley nodded.

Betty looked thoughtful. 'We've already done this haven't we in the first session, What is Time? Can you look it up Abby?'

I obediently flipped the pages of my notepad.

'Hmm,' Stanley looked on disapprovingly.

Betty looked defiant. 'Well, what's the point in reinventing the wheel?'

'Oh, yes, here it is,' I found the place.

'I said it was a framework, a way of measuring the seasons. It was survival and evolution. You said Betty that it brought order and was a way of meeting people – which we've already said.'

'Oh yes,' Betty peered over my shoulder, 'there was the bit about personal and non personal time wasn't there?'

'Yes,' I agreed, 'personal time is "I am the experiencer", and non personal time is the experience.'

'Well thank you so much for your input ladies. Well remembered both of you.'

We smiled back sweetly, unrepentant.

'You're welcome,' Betty murmured.

'And would you therefore say that all those reasons are indications that Time is a Major Factor to Life?'

'Yes,' we both concurred.

'Right, so can you now please tell me what are the consequences of having Time as a Major Factor in your Life?'

'Well, it's stressful,' I remarked, 'there never seems to be enough time to do all the things you want to do.'

'Or need to do,' added Betty.

'So it causes stress?' Stanley repeated, and indicated with a wave of his hand towards my notepad. I duly wrote:

The effects of saying
Yes, Time is a Major Factor to Life

(a) Stress

'You also said there was not enough time.'
I nodded agreement.
'So you could add that another effect is to limit your actions, as you don't get everything done that you want or need to do. Would that be right?'
We both nodded and I wrote:

(b) Limits actions

'And if it stops you from doing the things you want to do, you might say what?'
I shrugged, my mind had gone blank all of a sudden.
He looked at Betty hopefully, but she was looking at my notes.
'That it inhibits your self expression maybe?' he offered.
Betty nodded 'Yes, I would say that.'
Stanley waved at me. I hurriedly added:

(c) Inhibits self expression

'I would say it inhibits bodily expression as well,' Betty remarked, watching what I was writing.
'Why would you say that?' enquired Stanley.
'Well, often you don't have enough time to allow the body to have all its needs, digestion for instance, or exercise. People rush around gulping food down as quickly as possible, or worse still, eat while they're working, and give themselves little or no time for rest and relaxation or exercising.'

'It's a good point Betty,' Stanley waved at my pad once more and I added:

(d) Inhibits bodily expression

'So do you think ladies that saying Yes, Time is a Major Factor to Life is a good thing?'

'Well perhaps not good, but necessary,' Betty answered.

'What's the point of asking us that anyway?' I asked, somewhat petulantly, 'I mean, what choice do we have?'

'Well you have the choice to say No,' Stanley suggested.

'How can we do that?' I demanded.

'Well let's investigate it shall we and find out?' he invited.

'Tell me what would be the consequences of saying No, Time is not a Major Factor to Life?'

'Well, if Time was not a Major Factor then we'd be able to slow down,' Betty looked thoughtful.

'And if we slowed down, what would happen?' Stanley probed further.

'Well, you could be yourself.'

'Betty, you could be yourself, and Abby, what about you?'

'Mmmm,' I wrote down what he had said and considered it before answering.

Consequences of saying No, Time is not a Major Factor to Life

'Well, if Time was not a Major Factor in my life and I had all the time I needed, I suppose I would be more organised.'

'And if you were more organised what would you do?'

'I'd complete all the projects I've got on the go, so I suppose I'd feel happy, successful and fulfilled.'

'Wow, that's a lot, is there more?'

'Well for me, I would be a more interesting person,' Betty decided, 'I could do more than just housework, I could live life to the full.'

'And what would happen if you lived life to the full?' Stanley enquired.

'I'd be a more loving and generous person. I'd be peaceful within myself.'

'Would you like to write all this down?' Stanley suggested and I jumped in surprise, I had been too busy thinking to write. Now I wrote:

(a) *Could be yourself*

(b) *Be organised*

(c) *Happy*

(d) *Fulfilled*

(e) *Loving*

(f) *Generous*

(g) *Peaceful*

'So,' Stanley asked with a smile, 'Which do think is the better thing to do, make Time a Major Factor in your life or not?'

'Not,' said Betty firmly.

'But it's not that easy, you can't just make a decision to do away with time,' I objected.

'We are not suggesting that you do away with time,' Ti Ming reproved gently, (I could tell it was Ti Ming by the altered pronoun) 'we are merely pointing out that when you make it a Major Factor in your life then this creates negative consequences for yourself, by your own admission, look at your lists.'

'So what do you suggest we do?' Betty asked, ever practical.

'The key, as always is in the question, Is Time a Major Factor to Life? It is the making of time a major factor that causes the problems.

'But what else could we do?' I asked puzzled.

'We would suggest that you make the moment or the task the major factor, because as explained in a previous workshop (Does Time Affect Reality?), it is only the experience that exists in non personal time, and therefore is real. The experiencer, that's you the ego,' he pointed to me, 'can only exist in personal time, which is illusory and therefore can bring the negative consequences that you have identified.'

My head spun for a moment, trying to grasp what was being said.

Make the moment or the task the major factor

'What about if we stay positive?' I asked.

He laughed softly, 'That is always preferential to staying negative.'

'But didn't you say we can be either positive or negative? I thought that negative no-time was still and positive no-time was moving?' I was confused.

'You are correct, I did indeed,' he confirmed.

'So what's wrong with Time being a Major Factor if it's positive?' I wanted to know.

'Ah, you're getting technical now, I'm glad to see that you are grasping the subject.'

'I can't say that I am,' Betty intervened, looking worried.

'Betty my dear, I'm sure that you are conscious of being able to grasp the subject. Aren't you?' he enquired seemingly amused by her confusion.

'Oh, yes of course,' she agreed hurriedly.

'In answer to your question Abby, you are quite right, you need to say yes, to positive time and no to negative time, but it still does not need to be a Major Factor to your life.'

I considered what he was saying and thought I understood, but just to make sure I checked back with him.'

'So you're saying that Time is not a major factor to life, we should focus on the experience which is non-personal, and make that the major factor.'

He nodded encouragingly. 'That's right, go on.'

'So it's our interpretation of the experience that is personal and can be either negative or positive.'

'Yes, that's correct,' he agreed. 'And what happens if we become negative with the experience?'

'We can't do anything with it?'

'Very good Abby.' He looked impressed.

'Stay positive with the experience or task.'

I was quite impressed with myself. Betty still looked worried.

'And as we know, being negative creates negative consequences but we don't exactly create negative consequences, we just stop creating positive consequences.'

'I don't understand,' Betty bleated helplessly. 'You've lost me Stanley.'

'I think you've lost yourself,' he commented, and then beamed at her, 'but I'm sure you're capable of finding yourself aren't you?' he nodded encouragingly at her.

She didn't look convinced.

'I thought negative thinking created negative consequences, now you're saying that isn't the case. Make up your mind please Stanley, it's confusing enough as it is.'

Stanley marched on the spot regarding her. I realised it was the way he did his thinking. Finally after what seemed like a lengthy pause he said,

'OK. 'Imagine yourself in your car driving along and then you stop. While you are driving you are engaged in activity aren't you, changing gears, looking in the mirror, turning the wheel, yes?' he kept his eyes fixed on Betty.

She nodded. 'So far so good, but where is this going?'

'Well, where would you like to go?' he gave her a conspiratorial wink. He was obviously having fun, but it felt as though it was at our expense. His tone changed to a serious note when there was no response from her, maybe Ti Ming had arrived to take over.

'We are engaged in attempting to answer your question and thus eliminate your confusion so that you may find yourself,' he gave a formal little bow.

'Now, back to your car. Consider please, when the car has stopped, what activities are you engaged in?'

Betty shrugged. 'Well, it depends. If I'm getting ready to get out I would be grabbing my coat and handbag on the back seat, collecting my shopping from the boot, but if I was waiting for someone I suppose I might listen to the radio, select a CD, look through my handbag or the glove compartment.'

'Ah, but what activity regarding the moving of the vehicle?'

'Well none, because it's not going anywhere. You just sit there and wait to get going again.'

'Thank you Betty. I trust that makes it clear?'

'Makes what clear?' she looked at him suspiciously.

'Well, negative time is analogous to the car that is stationary. We might say that we make the car move, but we don't need to make it stay still, it does that on its own.'

'But we bring it to a stop,' I interrupted.

'Exactly my point,' Stanley looked thrilled.

'What?' I stared at him in confusion, my mind suddenly turned to cotton wool. 'I think I've just joined Betty.'

'Welcome friend,' she laughed, and I observed that at least my bewilderment had lifted her spirits.

'Look it's simple enough . . .' Stanley or Ti Ming tried again.

'In negative time nothing is moving, it's not that we have created the stillness, that implies that something has been created, whereas negative no time is just an absence of something moving.'

'Ah, I think I see,' said Betty doubtfully.

'Yes I do,' I cut in excitedly. 'It's like darkness isn't it? There's no such thing as 'the dark,' because there is no quality of darkness, there's just an absence of light.'

'Correct,' Ti Ming beamed, and for a moment when I glanced at him, Stanley looked decidedly Chinese.

'So negative time is merely an absence of positive time,' Betty was not to be outdone.

'Wonderful, I think you've got it. So can you tell me Abby what happens if our approach to the experience is positive?'

'We create positive time for ourselves that we can use.'

'Right again. Well done. So can you see the difference between time that can be used and time that uses you?'

I nodded. 'So that's the difference between practical and non-practical as well isn't it?'

'That's right,' Stanley agreed, looking more relaxed now that we had grasped the point.

'Thank you for that Abby, it makes it much clearer,' Betty smiled at me. 'I remember now, positive time is the thing about banking time and using it to pay off our negative.'

Stanley nodded.

'All we need to do now is put it into practice,' Betty remarked.

I laughed. 'That's the difficult bit.'

'I'm sure you are conscious of being able to put it into practice aren't you?' Stanley immediately picked me up.

'Yes, of course I am,' I answered quickly.

Betty joined in with 'I am conscious that I will be able to understand these workshops and put them into practice.'

'I'm pleased to hear that Betty. And that ladies is the end of the Is Time a Major Factor to Life workshop,' Stanley gave a bow in conclusion.

We both inclined our heads in recognition.

'Thank you Ti Ming that was very helpful,' Betty nodded appreciatively and he nodded back, there was a instant's pause, the energy shifted once more and Stanley was with us again.

Chapter 9

Does Past relate to Present Time?

Day 3
Session 8

We had our coffee break and then continued. Stanley consulted his watch so that he could begin at precisely 11.30 a.m. Then he gave a bow and Ti Ming arrived.

'Greetings ladies. The next workshop is entitled, Does Past relate to Present Time, so what do you think, does it?

'Yes,' I answered without hesitation.

'No,' Betty was equally as assured.

'Here we go again,' I laughed, and wrote down the title and stared at it for inspiration, willing it to give up its secrets.

Does Past relate to Present Time?

'I'm not sure,' I frowned and shrugged, 'maybe.'

'So,' Ti Ming bowed to us, his hands together in front of his chest, 'we have a yes, a no and a maybe. That about covers it I should think. And so ladies, which do we think is right? Abby, you said yes, maybe, so tell us please why you think it does.'

'Well, because we learn from our experiences. If the past didn't relate to the present then we'd have no way of knowing whether something works, or doesn't work for us.'

'It is a good point, but Betty, you said no, so perhaps you could explain to Abby why you think the past does not relate to the present time. What would happen to our learning experiences?'

'You integrate them as you go. You don't carry stuff forward, because otherwise you are living in resentment or stuck in the past. You can't live your life based on what has happened before, because each situation is different.'

'Yes but,' I interrupted, 'what about situations that keep repeating themselves until you learn the lesson?'

'Each situation is different,' she insisted.

I didn't agree. 'What about Groundhog Day?'

'That's just a film,' Betty objected.

'Yes I know, but it demonstrates the principle. It shows the same situation repeating over and over again.'

'But his reactions weren't the same were they? Each time the day repeated, he learned a new way of reacting.'

'But that's just the point,' I argued, 'if he hadn't remembered that it had happened before, which was the past as far as he was concerned, he wouldn't have been able to do something different would he? If we don't take past experiences into account we might just keep making the same mistakes over and over.'

'Situations do come round again, but they are similar, not the same, remember the saying, you can't step on the same piece of river twice.'

'But what about déjà vu?' I insisted. 'That's an experience that repeats itself.'

'Déjà vu is not the same thing,' Betty contradicted.

'Thank you ladies,' Ti Ming interrupted, walking forward and gently banging the table in front of us with his hand. We looked up at him in surprise. We had almost forgotten he was there, we were so involved in our discussion.

He stood back and took up his usual position in front of us.

'Now let me summarise. So you Abby think that by studying the past we can solve the problems of the present?'

'Yes.' I gave an emphatic nod. 'If mankind had to learn by trial and error each time humanity would never progress, we'd keep reinventing the wheel and having to start from scratch every time in science, mathematics and technology – we'd still be living in the Dark Ages.'

'Ah but do we progress?' Betty was on my case again. 'Surely that's just the point? Progress can only be made in the present moment. This day is a new day, it's not a repeat of yesterday. If we think that it is we will just keep making the same mistakes as yesterday. If mankind had to learn by past mistakes humanity would never progress.'

'Ah very interesting,' Stanley smiled happily. 'You both make opposite points but arrive at the same conclusions.'

'So tell us,' I demanded in exasperation, 'what is the right answer?'

'Oh, the *right* answer. Well let us consider. Would you all agree that everything in life has been created by us as a learning experience?' he checked our faces which nodded our agreement.

'OK Good. So let us continue then. Do you also agree that if we are not open to see and understand what the situation has to teach us then similar events will keep repeating in our lives?'

(The same point is made today by the self development gurus who tell us, 'if you always do what you've always done, then you'll always get what you've always had).

We nodded once more our silent agreement, waiting to hear what he would say and reluctant to interrupt him.

'So we need therefore to remain alert in each moment in order to recognise the learning experience that we have created for ourselves. If we merely consider life to be a repeat of the past we will bind ourselves in beliefs that are out of date and no longer serve us, but merely serve to date us.'

We groaned as he laughed, amused by his own joke.

I wrote:

> *If we consider life to be a repeat*
> *of the past we will bind ourselves*
> *in beliefs that are out of date*

He continued, serious once more.

'Although it is reasonable to learn from our mistakes and events that occurred in the past, it is essential to understand that whilst we may recognise the similarities in the present, we remain open to the differences also, otherwise we will be making the mistake that history repeats itself. What we believed in the past may have been relevant at that time, but we should allow the relevance of the present to present itself to us afresh in each situation.'

I was busily writing down his remarks as he spoke. He waited for me to catch up.

'So you're saying that the past does not relate to present time?' I clarified.

Past does not relate to present time

'I am saying that to consider the past as relating to present time will involve you in certain consequences. Can either of you tell me what these might be?'

'We might miss the learning experience,' Betty contributed.

He nodded. 'That is correct. Why might we?'

Betty considered a moment before she answered.

'Because the way we used to look at things won't be relevant for what's happening now.'

'So you're saying it's no longer relevant?'

'Yes,' she agreed.

Stanley indicated for me to write, and watched while I wrote:

(a) No longer relevant

'The past can certainly influence us in the present, either unconsciously or consciously, but a relationship implies a two way flow, and the present cannot change what is already past, so if we allow the past to change the present, then we have lost the art of being here and now. What else?' he asked. 'Why is it no longer relevant?'

'Because we've moved on,' Betty replied.

'Yes, it represents outmoded beliefs, they are like junk in the attic, we need to take a good look at what we have taken on board in our life and get rid of beliefs that no longer serve us.'

I wrote:

(b) Represents outmoded beliefs

'What else?'

'We might respond from past conditioning,' I replied.

'That is correct, we might. And what would happen if we did respond from past conditioning?'

'It might be inappropriate, we might be basing our responses on what we think is happening, rather than what actually is.'

'So, point number three, it represents a conditioned outlook. We may end up behaving like our parents or teachers or other significant people in our lives who have had authority over us, or who we have admired and want to emulate. Make no mistake, we are not them and we cannot live our life in the same way that others live theirs. It is a useful exercise to take some time to identify where we have given over our power. We will be covering this in a future workshop,' he added.

'If we fix ourselves in a rigid pattern, we are not flowing, there is no new growth, no new life force and at this point we will stagnate, our energy will remain static and we will deteriorate and grow old, whatever our chronological age.'

He paused, marching up and down on the spot while he waited for me to catch up.

I wrote:

(c) It represents a conditioned outlook

'So it's as I said in the beginning,' Betty recapped triumphantly, 'each day is a new day.'

'Yes it is a new day, but it is also important to recognise the seed from which the day sprang, for the seeds of today were planted in the garden of yesterday.'

'Are you talking about karma?' I asked.

'Indeed I am,' he confirmed, so I wrote:

(d) Involves us in karmic consequences

He waited until I had finished before continuing.

'It's in reviewing the past that we are led into making judgments. If we are constantly thinking about past injustices that other people have done to us we are in danger of setting up negative consequences for ourselves in the future.'

'What goes around comes around,' commented Betty.

'Yes, thank you Betty,' he acknowledged.

'Not understanding where others are coming from or why they do what they do causes people to make judgments and creates a Karmic wheel which will bring more learning situations to them. Unless they are very alert and aware of what is happening, it is difficult to stop once it is set in motion. It is better to deal with circumstances as they arise in the present and then let them go, otherwise we can become weighed down by the weight of the past.'

'So not only do we stay young, but we lose weight,' I joked.

'What more could you ask for?' he bowed.

'So although it is reasonable to learn from our mistakes and from events that have occurred in the past, it is important to remember that if similar circumstances keep recurring in our lives, we may be caught in a Karmic Wheel and need to ask the Higher Self for help to give us new insights to enable us to respond differently.

If we make the mistake of just seeing the similarities and missing the differences then we will fall into the error of thinking that history repeats itself. If we find ourselves blaming someone or something in the past, that is a sure indication that we are trapping ourselves in Karmic consequences.'

'So how do we avoid that?' Betty wanted to know.

'By avoiding blame,' he laughed as if it were obvious.

'That's all very well,' I leapt to Betty's defence, 'but if someone has done something to hurt us or someone we love, then it's very difficult not to blame them.'

Betty shook her head. 'No, it's easy, we just, turn the other cheek, that's the Christian way.'

'Is that what you are advocating?' I demanded.

'I am certainly not advocating following a doctrine of any kind, for how can following a doctrine lead to freedom?'

'But are you saying we should not have any religious beliefs?' Betty was a devout Christian Spiritualist.

'Yes, believe in the One of which you are a part,' he suggested, 'because any other form of belief is rooted in past conditioning.'

'So, if we don't turn the other cheek, how can we not blame?' I still wanted to know.

'By seeing differently,' was his answer. Anticipating our objections he carried on, not giving us time to interrupt.

'Always, in any situation there are many ways of seeing. We will be covering more of this in other workshops, and giving you the opportunity of practising seeing differently.

For now I just wish to reiterate the consequences of bringing the past forward into the present. When we do this, negative time occurs where there is no outcome or growth. If we believe the past does affect the way we experience, then we are binding ourselves into past conditioning and inappropriate responses based on past experiences which are no longer relevant. If we do this it will involve us in karmic consequences that will keep repeating in our lives.'

I wished I had persevered with my shorthand as I struggled to keep up with him.

Bringing the past forward into the present creates negative time

'So you're saying we would bind ourselves in negative time by bringing the past into the present?' I asked.

He nodded. 'That is correct. So it is important to realise that the past does not relate to present time. I wrote it out so that I would remember.

The past does not relate to present time

Betty looked at my pad thoughtfully.

'So you're saying that by living in the present, we will stay young?'

'Certainly,' Ti Ming bowed.

'For how long?' Betty wanted to know eagerly.

'Well our attitude will stay young and therefore we will appear youthful to those around us.'

'So you're not really saying we will look younger?' Betty seemed disappointed.

'Surely it is how we act and how we enjoy the allotted lifespan that is the important thing,' Ti Ming enquired gently, 'not our physical appearance or how many years we survive? What would be the point in living forever if we never aged but were miserable and doomed to constantly relive the past?'

Betty nodded her agreement, but still looked disappointed, as if she had hoped that living in the present moment might provide the key to eternal life, and keep her looking physically young each day.

Each day is a new day

I stared at the words I had written.

'That's easy enough to remember,' I commented.

'I do indeed hope so,' Stanley bowed his head gravely, 'and that ladies concludes the workshop, does Past relate to Present time.'

Chapter 10

Does Future relate to Present Time?

Day 3
Session 9

We had a break for lunch. Betty had brought the sandwiches and I scrambled some eggs for myself. We cleared away the pens and notepad from the dining table and sat and ate, gulping mugs of steaming coffee and tea. Afterwards there was time for a quick stroll in the afternoon sunshine. June arrived and waved happily at us as she passed and drove on to the caravan to park beside Betty's Astra. We headed back to greet her and Stanley lingered behind to smoke before joining us for the next session.

As soon as we sat down the energy changed. Somehow the little caravan became a formal meeting place for the Time Workshops. We could feel the spirit presence and Stanley confirmed it by giving us the Chinese type bow. Ti Ming was back.

'Good afternoon ladies. The title of this workshop is Does Future Time Relate to Present Time?'

I dutifully wrote it down and waited for the answer, which as usual wasn't forthcoming.

Does Future Time Relate to Present Time?

I sighed and put down my pen.

I considered the question. Did the future affect the present? How could it, it hadn't happened yet, so the answer must be no, mustn't it? On the other hand that would be a short workshop and knowing Stanley, or Ti Ming there was a lot more to the question than I could understand.

'Well does it? What do we all think?'

He waited for me to make my considerations, smiling at me as if he could follow the train of my thought.

I had to answer something, as no-one else was contributing.

'No, I don't think the future relates to the present time,' I stated boldly confident.

Now I had made a start the others joined in.

'I don't think it does either,' June smiled at me conspiratorially, she was on my side.

Betty, as usual decided to play Devil's advocate.

'I think it does,' she announced, equally confident.

'Why?' Stanley asked her curiously.

'I've no idea,' she said honestly, and laughed. 'I just thought I'd be different.'

'Have you ever had a premonition?' he enquired still smiling. 'Or a déjà vu experience?'

'Well, yes, I suppose so,' she replied.

'You suppose you have. What about fortune telling, have you ever been to a psychic and have they ever been correct?'

'Yes, I have to admit, I have.'

'So do these things mean the future relates to the present?'

'Well yes.'

'Yes, because all of these things I have mentioned are examples of the flow from the future to the present. Have any of you ever had an experience of living backwards?'

'Yes, I have,' I was excited now. 'People have always said I was mad whenever I mentioned it.'

It was something that had troubled me for a long time. I did things that seemed inexplicable at the time, only to be resolved at some point in the future, almost as if I knew what was going to happen and was acting in advance of my knowledge. Time flowing from the future to the present would explain my experiences. I preferred it to the explanation that I was mad.

'I had a dog Angus that bit me every time I pulled his beard.'

'So why did you do it?' June asked.

I don't know, it seemed to be a habit. I was surprised every time he bit me because I expected him to like it.'

'I think I'd have stopped after the first time – if it ever occurred to me to do it at all,' June looked at me rather disapprovingly.

'I know, I don't know why I did. I never understood it until we had Heidi, and she loves having her beard pulled. It's almost as though I formed the habit with her before I ever met her, and mistook Angus for Heidi.'

'I've met people who I've mistaken for someone I haven't met yet, which I suppose is the same kind of thing,' June said thoughtfully.

'I treat them as if they are the other person I haven't met yet, which causes a great deal of confusion in both of us. I could never understand why I didn't get the responses I was expecting.'

'That's happened to me too,' I interrupted excitedly.

'It's only when you meet the right person in the future and get the right responses that you realise your mistake and everything falls into place,' June continued, with me nodding in agreement.

'That kind of thing has happened to me with animals and places,' Betty remarked.

' So that explains it,' June looked quite excited.

'You see,' Stanley explained, 'future time does relate to present time because . . .' he paused and looked pointedly at my pen and notebook lying on the table, 'are you going to write this down?'

'Oh yes,' I hurriedly picked up the pen.

He continued, 'It's conceived out of the present, it's determined by the present, it's constantly arriving in the present. Unmanifest time flows into manifest time and manifest time flows into unmanifest time.

Future time does relate to present time because:

(a) It's conceived out of the present

(b) It's determined by the present

(c) It's constantly arriving in the present

'Is this the Lore of the Ring of Time you mentioned?' I asked.

June looked confused, as she had not heard it mentioned before.

'Yes,' he confirmed, looking pleased that I had remembered.

'What's that? Can you tell us about it?' June asked.

'Yes, but only when the time is right,' he laughed at her disappointed face. 'I will teach you all about the Lore of the Ring of Time in a separate workshop,' he assured her. 'At the moment we are focussing on whether the future relates to present time are we not?' and hastily continued, without waiting for confirmation.

'If we say no, the future does not relate to present time, then we are denying personal responsibility. We are denying that the consequences of our actions are caused by us.

Everything that we think has a consequence. Just because we cannot see it doesn't mean that it doesn't have an effect. Thinking is an energy and energy manifests. The way we think affects the way we feel and the way we feel determines what we do. Our actions are a direct result of our thinking and feeling.'

I decided to make a note of what not to do to remind myself in the future.

If we say that the future does not relate to present time, then we are:

(a) Denying personal responsibility

(b) Denying consequences of our actions are caused by us

'So what determines our thinking?' I asked him. I regarded his slight frame, quivering with energy and power, yet quiet and controlled, standing over me. It was a unique experience, pressurising but exciting. I felt more alive than I ever had before in my life. (Now I realise that to be in the presence of higher beings speeds up our vibrationary rate, and it is this 'quickening' that is experienced as a flutter of excitement.)

'It is your level of understanding that determines the way you think,' he answered me.

'So how can we raise our level of understanding?' Betty wanted to know.

'Through experience,' he answered.

We were silent for a moment while we considered his answer, then a thought occurred to me.

'Is there anything we can change in the present which can bring the future experiences to us faster so that we can speed up our rate of understanding?' I asked him.

He nodded. 'Yes, you can use a regulator. You remember the pen I threw at you? Anything that will remind you to stay centred and help break up negative energy is called a regulator, because it regulates your energy. Lighting a candle is also a good way of changing the emotional energy, it acts as an ioniser.

You can also meditate regularly, take up yoga practice or Tai Chi. These practices will help you to stay centred and keep a clear focus.'

I nodded writing it all down as he spoke.

To speed up rate of understanding:

(a) *Use a regulator*

(b) *Light a candle*

(c) *Meditate regularly*

(d) *Practice yoga or Tai Chi*

He observed me and when I had caught up, stood for a moment with his eyes looking upwards as if checking his memory.

'Oh and of course you could throw something away.'

June looked at him surprised. 'Throw what away?'

'Anything that you don't use. Hoarding things that you don't need or have finished with accumulates dead energy, it will slow you down. Use it or lose it is a good motto to have.'

'Right, there's plenty of things I need to lose,' Betty instantly resolved to have a spring clean.

(e) *Throw something away*

(Use it or lose it)

'If throwing things away will speed me up, I'm going to get rid of everything,' I resolved.

'Are you saying that we shouldn't be materialistic?' June enquired.

'That depends upon your definition of materialistic,' he replied. 'Remember what I said earlier about materialism.'

June shook her head, she hadn't been present.

Betty enlightened her. 'Well, you know, rich people can't get into the Kingdom of Heaven and all that. It's only the poor who can become enlightened, because they don't have so many things to slow them down. That's right isn't it Stanley?'

Stanley, or Ti Ming sighed almost imperceptibly and smiled at her lack of understanding.

'It is not things that slow us down but our management of things, and our attitude towards them. If we can own things and not be owned by them, or we get a positive charge from them whenever we look at them, then it is safe to be rich. But bearing in mind that everything is energy and energy needs to be moving or it will stagnate. It is the stagnant energy that will slow you down, not the things, so you either need to be giving your positive No-Time to your things, or the things will send you into negative No-Time. That is why having material possessions can be a drawback, they will take your time one way or the other even if it's only cleaning them and make it hard for you to reach beyond the positive or negative into natural time.'

Another thought occurred to me.

'If, as you have said, the future is constantly arriving in the present, does that mean that if we have created negative time in the future, it will arrive in the present and create problems?'

Stanley nodded. 'That is correct.'

'What!' June was horrified. 'You mean that something that I'm going to do in the future can affect me now?'

Stanley looked amused at her distress.

'Well yes June, because whatever it is, is created now.'

'So what can we do to stop it?' she wanted to know.

Stanley did some marching on the spot.

'June wants to know how she can eliminate negative time that she has set up for herself in the future. Anyone?'

There was silence while we gazed at him, hoping that he knew the answer and would give it to us.

After a few moments he continued, looking from one to another of us and realising that we were not about to elucidate with words of wisdom.'

'Well, there are various things that you can do and we shall be covering them in future workshops.'

I sighed. 'You always say that Stanley.'

'Because it's true,' he laughed.

'Alright then,' Betty decided to be clever, 'tell us how we can create positive time for ourselves in the future.'

'Well Betty you have already had some answers for this question in the Time Strategies workshop that we did yesterday. Anybody remember?'

I was about to start flipping through my notes when he shook his head. 'Shall we try to remember first?'

I dropped my hand, duly chastened.

'Time Strategies, that was about ignoring time or being driven by it, wasn't it?' It was all coming back to me.

He acknowledged my answer with his usual little bow.

'Very good.'

I smiled. 'Yes, but I still don't see how those strategies can create positive time for us in the future.'

'Don't you?' he sounded disappointed, as if by remembering what he had said I had automatically absorbed and understood all the consequences.

'Can anyone?'

There was silence.

He gave another imperceptible sigh.

'OK. June, if you were to draw me a picture of time, what would it look like.'

She gave a start, not expecting to be put on the spot, and glanced swiftly at Betty and myself as if we had the answer for her.

'Well, it's a line isn't it? A time line?' she asked hopefully.

'That's right. I have an NLP book called Time Lines,' I agreed.

'No,' Betty's eyes lit up with inspiration, 'not a line, a wheel.'

Stanley looked pleased. 'Well done Bett. It is indeed a wheel. Now all of you picture a wheel with spokes radiating out from a central point. Where on this wheel is the present?'

'On the rim,' I suggested.

'The spokes,' was June's contribution.

Stanley laughed. 'That leaves you with the centre Bett.'

Betty frowned at him, picturing it in her head and still thinking.
'Can you draw it for me please Abby,' she asked.
I obliged.

Time Wheel

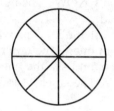

Betty stared at it.

'Yes, I think the present is the centre and the outside rim is the future and it's a two way flow.'

'You're quite right,' he confirmed. 'The centre point is the time core, and the present spreads out from the time core down the spokes and into the rim. If the time core is negative, then that influence will spread out from the core in much the same way as ripples spread out when a pebble is thrown into a pond. It can also flow from the future to the present. As you said, it's a two way flow.'

She looked very satisfied with herself. I guess it was nice to be more right than wrong and realised that it would be an expression of her having more positive energy than negative. In which case the opposite was also true, if I was wrong more often than right, it must be an expression of my negativity. Whoops. I veered sharply away from that thought and instead stared fixedly at my drawing of the Time Wheel. I still didn't get it, even though I wanted to.

'If the future affects the present, then we've had it,' I remarked.

'In what way?' Stanley enquired, looking faintly amused.

'Well I can understand that if we think negatively in the present then that can create negative situations for us in the future, but if the future creates the present then I don't see how we can change the future.'

'You don't?' Was all he would say.

'No I don't.'

'Can anyone?'

June shrugged, looking totally confused.

'I can,' Betty remarked, almost casually.

'Well how then?' I was getting somewhat exasperated.

'Well, all time is NOW,' was her reply, making June and I jump with her emphasis on the now.

'That's about as clear as mud Betty,' I was glad June had said it not me.

'Don't you see, there's only NOW?' she insisted.

'No.' June shook her head.

I was watching Stanley watching us. He was observing the exchange between us by looking from one to the other as if he were following a tennis match. I realised he could see the energy interactions that were taking place. I wished I could see them. I looked down at my pad and wrote:

All time is NOW

'Abby, do you understand what she means?' Stanley spotted me taking an observer's role and attempted to draw me back in with his question.

I considered it. 'Well I understand that all time is now, that we don't have power in the past, but I would also have said we don't have power in the future either, and that's why I can't see how it can affect us in the present, because the moment of power is in the now.'

Stanley marched on the spot for a moment before answering me.

'Time flows from the manifest to the unmanifest and from the unmanifest to the manifest, it is a two way flow.

'OK I can understand that, but surely the future hasn't manifested yet?' I protested.

He smiled his enigmatic smile and I fancied I saw a tinge of pity in his eyes.

'You are right, it hasn't.'

'But it will,' Betty attempted to explain, 'that's the point, if we are negative then our unmanifest negative energy will create a negative future for us.'

'Yes, but he's saying that the negative future is what causes us to be negative in the present. As I said, you can't win.'

Stanley winced.

'I'm sure it's possible for you to win, if by winning, you mean under-standing.'

'He's cancelling out your negative,' Betty supplied helpfully, while she watched me writing, but the knowledge still didn't assist me to be positive.

Time flows from the manifest to the unmanifest and from the unmanifest to the manifest. It is a two way flow.

'Well I can see what Abby is saying, but I don't think I quite get the point that Stanley is making,' June remarked.

I liked June, she was always supportive.

'I think the point Stanley is making is that it's vital to remain positive in the present moment, or we will be caught in a negative cycle that will spiral downwards and result in even more negativity.'

Negative Spiral

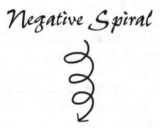

Stanley nodded watching me draw the negative spiral.

'Well put Betty, and of course the opposite is also true,' he laughed as I hastily drew another diagram.

Positive Spiral

I think at this point, in order to demonstrate how to change our energy it is time for a run round the caravan.'

'Oh no,' we groaned.

'Oh yes,' he smiled.

'And this concludes the workshop Does Future Time Relate to Present Time.'

He gave his little bow before walking over and opening the door.

'But I have to go,' June protested.

'Not before you have grounded your energy. Would you want to go home taking negative energy with you?' he enquired.

'No, of course not,' June replied, getting up in a hurry.

'Me too?' Enquired Betty.

'You too,' he confirmed laughing.

'You have been very positive so far Bett, you're not having negative thoughts now are you?'

'Certainly not,' Betty replied briskly and rose to her feet rather more energetically than usual.

I was amused at their reactions and felt myself feeling more positive by the minute.

After we had run three revolutions, we decided to reconvene for coffee before we separated for the evening. There was a reluctance in us to split up, as if we had forged bonds in doing these workshops that held us together even stronger than family ties. These were spiritual bonds that bound us in the friendship, love and the understanding of a spiritual family. I realised that it is our understanding that creates bonds between people. If our understanding is different, then we live in separate worlds however close our familial ties.

Chapter 11

What is Natural Time?

The sound of rain on the caravan roof woke me the next morning. It was the first cloudy day since our arrival. I lay in bed and listened to the dripping rain in the trees above. The birds still sang their dawn chorus to the world, sounding cheerful even though the sun wasn't shining.

I wondered what today would bring. The workshops were going well and Stanley surprised me constantly with his knowledge and delivery skills. I felt ashamed when I recalled my arrogant attitude at the beginning. I had never realised he could be so articulate and professional in his expression. In fact it went further than that. I had attended many workshops in my management career and I had not encountered the humour and caring intelligence that was present in Stanley's workshops. Also the content was vital and relevant, which was another deviation from usual management courses.

I thought that people should have access to this information, it should be taught in schools, so that children could learn the basic fundamentals prerequisite for living a successful life. Without this knowledge we are as blind people feeling our way cautiously in the darkness and never realising there are obstacles in our path until we trip over them. We can (and frequently do) get ourselves entangled in negative consequences that can then take years of our life in trying to extricate ourselves, if we manage to at all. Many people merely become their own casualties in life and never really gain the fulfilment of their hopes and dreams.

I roused myself and went for a shower in the little cubicle next door to the bedroom. Stanley was not in sight, so I breakfasted as usual. He returned from his walk as I was tidying away the dishes. At 9 a.m. precisely we were ready to begin, the table cleared ready for action, my notebook and pen at the ready. There was no sign of Betty, which surprised me as she was usually so punctual. I wondered if we should wait for her, but Stanley bowed formally to me, and announced the title of the next workshop. Obviously, Ti Ming did not expect to be delayed.

'This morning we will consider the question, What is Natural Time?'

I wrote the title in my notebook.

What is Natural Time?

I waited for the explanation, but of course none came, for as usual, Stanley was expecting me to answer the question.

I put my pen down and stared at the title hoping for inspiration and thankfully heard Betty's car drawing up.

Stanley opened the door, bowing to her as she entered.

She took her cue from him and bowed silently in return, albeit somewhat breathlessly.

'Sorry I'm late,' she puffed to me, as she sat down, 'I got stuck behind a tractor up on Welsh moor.'

Stanley smiled and deliberately ignored her explanation. 'I'm glad you could join us in time to assist Abby to answer the question, What is Natural Time?'

'Ah,' she settled herself beside me. 'That would be Nature time then?'

Stanley cocked his head to one side as if listening. 'Well, there is such a thing as Nature time, but it is slightly different to Natural time, we will be coming to that in another workshop.'

I found it very teasing when he hinted at other workshops in that way, but he obviously couldn't do everything at once.

I considered his question. 'Well, we've had practical time which is positive, and non-practical which is negative, so I suppose natural time must be neutral.'

'Excellent, Abby, it is indeed neutral, although not in a way that would imply that it is static. It is balanced time.'

'Like a see-saw, with the balance being in the middle?' I suggested.

Stanley frowned. 'No, not really, it's the whole see-saw.'

'So it's not a balance between positive and negative then?' Betty asked.

'No, it's not,' he confirmed 'It's both ends and the middle.'

'So, you must be talking about a balanced spiritual state,' Betty muttered to herself.

'Yes, that's right, balanced time means we are in a balanced spiritual state, and have balanced, conscious awareness and take balanced, intuitive action.'

'So would that be non-personal or personal?' I wanted to know.

'It would be both, because we need to be able to see the wood from the trees in order to maintain an objective viewpoint regardless of the play unfolding before our eyes, or the actions of the individual player.'

'But isn't that just Practical time?' I objected.

'No, it is a step beyond Practical time. Practical time can cancel out Non-Practical time. Practical time is time that we can use to bring us positive consequences. Natural time can only be accessed through practical time. You can't get to Natural time through Non-practical time.'

'So negative people can't reach it?' Betty wanted clarification.

'Correct,' he confirmed.

'I still don't understand the difference,' I objected.

'Well, in Practical time we are interested in achieving practical outcomes. More money, a better job, reaching targets and goals, etc. Natural time enables us to progress in our understanding. Instead of doing we are Being, learning to let go and relax. We are aware that each situation has something to show us about ourselves and we are alert to ask the question, 'What is this showing me about me?' When we ask this question we may learn and grow in consciousness.'

'You mentioned intuition,' Betty reminded him.

'Yes, that's right, what is it you wanted to know?' he enquired, still not willing to tell us anything without a direct question.

'Well are we supposed to act on our intuition to get to Natural time?' Betty asked him.

He smiled at her delightedly. 'You see, you knew all the time.'

She drew a sharp intake of breath. 'So when we act on our intuition we are living in Natural time?'

'Exactly. Well put.'

I wrote down:

Natural Time is accessed through our intuition.

'But what if we're not intuitive?' I asked.

He roared with laughter at that one.

I didn't see what was so funny.

'Everyone is intuitive,' Betty explained.

'But not everyone is aware that they are,' I objected.

'You are correct,' Stanley had stopped laughing by this time.

'When people are existing in Non-Practical time they will not be aware of their intuition. As they become more positive however and start to live more in Practical Time they will become more and more aware of their intuition. It is at this time that they will need to start trusting themselves and taking spontaneous action without thinking about it, so that they can progress into Natural Time.'

'But negative people can be spontaneous,' I objected.

'Indeed they can,' he agreed, 'but spontaneously negative people are merely spontaneously aggressive. Positive people can be spontaneously positive, arising from a desire to please someone, or do good for them, but neither are being intuitive.'

'Now I'm confused,' Betty admitted.

'Natural time does not have an I want content,' Stanley explained to us patiently. 'There is no personal motive when the action takes place. There is no negative or positive thought behind what is being done. It is a state beyond ego. Have you ever done anything and not known why you've done it?' he looked at Betty.

'Yes, I think so,' she replied doubtfully, 'but I can't think of an example right now.'

'What about when I arrive hungry and you've already cooked more food than you needed, but you didn't know why?' I suggested.

She brightened. 'Yes of course, come to think of it, I often do things and don't know why I'm doing them, and when people ask me I just shrug it off and say, I'm doing what I'm doing.'

Stanley nodded in satisfaction.

'Exactly, Bett, that's a wonderful example of a Natural Time affirmation.'

I wrote down:

Natural Time Affirmation
'I'm doing what I'm doing.'

'So the difference between the positive state and the natural one is that when you're in the positive you know what you're doing, but when you're in the natural you don't?' I queried.

They both laughed, but I didn't see what was funny.

'Well you could say that,' Stanley agreed, 'but in Natural Time you have a greater understanding.'

'So why is the Natural state better?' I wanted to know.

'Well, I wouldn't say it's better exactly, but it's higher.'

'Why is it?'

'Well, if we take the example you gave us, that you call round to Betty's when you're hungry. If she knew you would be calling after College without having eaten and so invited you for a meal, then that would be positive.'

I nodded. I could follow that.

'Of course if she planned it as a surprise and thought that you would be hungry so she cooked a meal without telling you, that would also be positive.'

I nodded again and he continued. 'But if you didn't want to put Betty out by arriving hungry and knowing that she would most likely put herself out to feed you, you might take responsibility for your own stomach and eat before you went to see her. In which case she would be very disappointed that her surprise had backfired and that she couldn't please you and end up annoyed that she had wasted her time and her food and dropped into a negative state.'

'That actually happened once,' I confided.

'When?' Betty asked curiously, 'I don't remember that.'

'Well, I didn't tell you,' I said.

'What do you mean?'

'Well, once I had just eaten a huge dinner, and when I got to you, you had prepared a lovely meal specially for me, and I just didn't have the heart to tell you I had just had my dinner, so I ate yours as well.'

'Oh no,' Betty was horrified. 'Why didn't you say anything?'

'I didn't want to spoil your surprise,' I said simply.

Tears came to her eyes. 'Oh Abby, you must have felt so bloated, having to eat two dinners and you didn't say anything just to make me feel good. I feel terrible now.'

'No need,' Stanley intervened briskly. 'It is merely a demonstration of how positive time can sometimes be inappropriate, whereas natural time is always appropriate. Do you both now understand the difference?'

We both nodded, half laughing, half crying, appreciating our friendship and realising how much we valued each other's feelings. Stanley paused for a moment observing us, marching on the spot, (to settle the energies I now realised), reached into his pocket and handed us each a tissue before continuing.

'When you operate in Natural Time you have no preconceived ideas of what you or other people want. You allow events to unfold moment by moment.'

'But does that mean we should never plan?' I asked.

'You can plan,' Stanley agreed, 'but be prepared to change your plans or for others to foil your plans. It is best to hand your plans 'upstairs' to spirit and then wait and see what you do. Follow your feet.'

I wanted to make a note of that and resolved to put it into practice.

Hand plans upstairs
Follow your feet

I could see it was a more effective way of acting. You were not bound by ordinary consciousness, which is how Betty managed to cook the meal without knowing I would need it.

'To be in Natural Time is to be part of the Time Core, or the One.' Stanley informed us.

I was quiet while I digested this information.

'Natural Time does also have a practical application,' Stanley continued, 'we can use Natural Time to actually alter time by changing our focus of attention. When we focus outwardly we find that we can slow time down so that we can accomplish much in a short space of time, and when we focus inwardly on contemplative thought or esoteric conversation, then we will find that time has speeded up.'

'Yes, I've experienced that,' Betty agreed.

'Both?' I asked.

'Yes,' she nodded.

'I've experienced that time can speed up,' I said, 'but I haven't managed to slow it down yet.'

'It's very useful when you need to get things done.'

'I'm sure it is. I could do with some of that.'

'We can also regulate the time of others when we exist in Natural time,' Stanley continued.

'What do you mean by that?' I wanted to know.

'He means that when he is around he can give us more time, isn't that so Stanley.'

He smiled silently at us, neither confirming or denying.

I was incredulous.

'Now that I think about it, I do manage to get more done when he's around, although he never appears to do anything to help.'

'I'm getting offended now,' Stanley interrupted, 'never help. I always do everything to help.'

'Well, perhaps he's doing more than you thought,' Betty suggested quickly.

'Come to think of it he has said that he does more when he's not doing anything, but I always thought it was an excuse. Thank you Stanley, I'm sorry I was rude to you.'

He inclined his head to me, pleased to be vindicated.

'Isn't it manipulative though?' I asked. 'I mean, even though it's useful, it means that you have power over others.'

'The idea is to use a balanced mental state.'

'Balanced mental state?' I repeated. 'What's that?'

'It's a good question,' he replied as usual. Fortunately Betty answered me.

"Well, it's not us being positive or negative, it's the real us, as we really are,' she informed me.

He nodded. 'Good. As we are. Yes, that is balanced awareness, a balanced mental state.'

As we are
Balanced awareness
Balanced mental state

'And how can we achieve this balanced mental state?' he enquired.

'Through watching the Natural Mirror,' Betty answered.

'Yes. Very good Bett,' he looked pleased. 'Though we haven't reached that workshop yet.'

Balanced Mental State achieved through watching the Natural Mirror

'What about following your feet? What is that?'

'Action,' she suggested.

'Yes. Balanced action. And balanced action is – Abby?' he asked to get me to look up from my writing. I did so reluctantly.

'Acting without planning,' I answered.

'Yes,' he confirmed. 'And balanced action comes from a balanced emotional state.'

'And how do we achieve a balanced emotional state?' Betty asked.

'It's a good question Bett.'

'And it deserves a good answer,' I muttered defiantly.

He just laughed good naturedly.

'It does indeed and who's going to give it?' he looked at us hopefully, and waited a few moments before continuing.

'OK then, to achieve balanced actions through a balanced emotion, attune to Spirit through intuitive, spontaneous action.'

'Can you say that again,' I pleaded, 'I need to write that down,' he complied.

To achieve balanced actions through a balanced emotion, attune to Spirit through intuitive, spontaneous action

'Got that?'

I nodded.

'Right, so how do we achieve balanced Time?'

I was surprised at the question. 'Isn't that what we've just done?'

He shook his head. 'No, we've just done, as you put it, balanced action through balanced emotion.'

'No, before that.'

'Before that we considered how to achieve a balanced mental state.'

'Oh, so are we now considering how to achieve a balanced spiritual state?' Betty enquired.

'Congratulations Bett. Balanced Time means a balanced spiritual state, and can you tell us please how to achieve a balanced spiritual state?'

'Through surrendering to the One,' she answered immediately.

I was impressed.

'Surrendering what to the One exactly?' Stanley enquired cautiously, he was obviously not that easily impressed.

'Well, everything,' Betty answered surprised. 'Your mind and emotion.'

'Yes. Thank you Bett. So to recap, Natural Emotion comes from spontaneous action, Natural Mind comes from learning from the Natural Mirror and the Natural Spirit comes from surrendering the Mind and Emotion to the One.

Natural Emotion comes from spontaneous action

Natural Mind comes from learning from the Natural Mirror

Natural Spirit comes from surrendering the Mind and Emotion to the One.

Stanley marched while he watched me write it down, when I had finished he continued.

'Right then Abby will you please draw me a straight line.'

———————

I did so. Betty and I looked at it curiously.

'Now this is the concept of Negative Time,' he announced.

'Why is it?' I immediately wanted to know, staring at the line. He couldn't just go making these pronouncements without explaining them.

'Because it is the concept of birth, life and death as a straight line. There is no concept of an afterlife. When you're dead you're dead. I'm sure you've both met people like that.'

We nodded.

'Exactly. Now Abby, please draw a circle.'

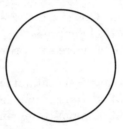

We both duly considered the circle.

'This is the concept of Positive Time,' he announced and hurried on before I could interrupt him again.

'This is the concept of re-incarnation, of life incarnating again and again until you "get it right". This also represents the belief in rising from the dead on Judgement Day to see whether you "got it right". Can you now draw me an infinity symbol?'

I found that more difficult, but I did my best.

'Right, now this represents Natural Time. Life as a cycle. Seasons, Nature. It is made up of both Positive and Negative, and incorporates both belief systems, that one lifetime is made up of many lifetimes and the understanding that you are both your own cause and effect. There is an awareness of personal responsibility and spiritual growth.'

I stared at the infinity symbol in awe.

'Right, now can either of you tell me how we can use Natural Time?'

That stumped us. I continued staring at the symbol, hoping it would inspire me.

'Would you say we can use it to regulate our growth?' he enquired after a pause.

We both nodded vigorously.

'If we are giving out, our focus is outward, we speed our own internal time up and everything else slows down. If we are taking in from the One, then our focus is inward, we slow our own internal time down and everything else speeds up. Can you give me examples of this?'

'When you come out of a meditative state sometimes it feels as though only five minutes has passed whereas we may find that 30 minutes has gone, which would confirm what you said Stanley,' Betty agreed.

'But,' I added, 'the opposite can also be true. Sometimes when I meditate I feel sure I've been doing it at least half an hour but only five minutes has gone.'

'Interesting,' Stanley commented, 'your focus must have been outward with stray thoughts interrupting you.'

'Yes, you're right,' I confirmed grudgingly.

'So, what happens if we meditate in a group?' Betty asked.

'Well, whenever two or more people are together, you will be speeded up or slowed down by the strongest vibrationary rate.'

'Do you mean that the strongest person has power over the others?' I asked feeling worried.

'Haven't you ever noticed that other people can either uplift or drain you?'

'Yes, I often get a migraine when some people call, and other people give me healing energy,' Betty admitted.

'That's right,' Stanley nodded at her.

'What happens if both people are the same vibrationary rate?' I asked.

'In that case there will be conflict until one or the other gains the upper hand or retreats, unless they are two naturals.'

I nodded, I had experienced that at home. It explained a lot.

He continued. 'Two people who consider themselves to be positive will believe their truth is the only truth and each will argue for their own point of view.'

'As in two people of different religious beliefs?' I inquired.

He nodded. 'Exactly.'

'What happens when two negative people come together?' Betty wanted to know.

'Two negatives together will try and outdo each other in recounting their tales of woe and misery, each trying to gain the sympathy of the other by wallowing in self pity.'

'That happened to me once,' I said, 'when I had someone who only ever phoned me to tell me their troubles. They used to go on for hours, until one day I had troubles of my own and got in first.'

'How did they react?' Betty asked.

'Well, funnily enough I've never heard from them again. I heard on the grapevine later that they thought I was too negative.'

Betty and I laughed. Stanley coughed and continued.

'And two naturals together will merge and become one.'

'That sounds like the best option,' I observed.

'I suppose it's the only way two people can exist in harmony,' Betty observed. 'It explains a lot.'

'It's a good reason for living in Natural Time,' Stanley agreed.

'Another spin off from existing in Natural Time is the ability to become invisible to those living in Practical or Non-practical Time.'

'How? Betty asked.

'By changing our vibrationary rate. Operating in Natural Time gives us the ability to change our vibrationary rate at will, and so if we wish, we can become invisible to those around us.'

'How does that work exactly?' I asked him.

'Well, you've seen me do it,' he laughed.

I had. He had often startled me by seeming to appear out of nowhere when I had been walking along. I had just thought it was because he was insignificant in appearance and didn't say much, but now I realised what he had been doing, operating in Natural Time.'

There was definitely more to Stanley than I had thought.

'You see,' he explained, 'apart from our senses, we also pick up the energies of the life forms around us in the form of vibration, the people, the plants, the animals, even the places, because rocks and trees have a vibrationary rate as well, which is why we say there are 'bad' places that make us feel creepy or uneasy. It's a two way communication, animals sense our vibrationary rate, as do plants and places. It is mostly the humans who are unaware of these energies consciously. In this way the animals, plants and the planet itself is more evolved than we are, as they are already operating in Natural Time, but once we start to operate in Natural Time, we can join them.'

'Does that mean animals can make themselves invisible?' I asked.

'We shall never know until we operate in Natural Time will we, because they will be invisible.'

Stanley raised his eyebrows at me and grinned cheekily.

'Come to think of it,' I said, 'they can, at least, my cat can make me forget he's in the room so that he can get up on the sofa as soon as I leave.'

'Yes,' Betty agreed, 'and children try it on when they go very quiet as soon as it's bedtime, hoping you'll forget that they are there.'

'If they're natural beings, it works,' Stanley smiled, 'I got away with it all the time when I was little.'

I was shocked. 'You bad man.'

'Ah, but I was only a child then and I didn't realise what I was doing.'

'You still do it,' I accused him. 'You appear from nowhere at times and frighten me to death.'

'That's an interesting observation, I appear from nowhere, how right you are.'

'What do you mean by that?' Betty asked suspiciously.

'Well, when your mind is still and your emotions are still, you could be said to be existing nowhere.'

'But your body is still existing somewhere,' I objected.

'Indeed, and how is it then that you do not see me when I am right in front of you?'

I was silent. It was something that had puzzled me for years.

He laughed.

'We see with our senses, our sight is a compilation of sensory input from the vibrations around us. Blind people develop an awareness of vibrationary rate because they need to rely on it. In some cases they can interpret the data visually and will say they can 'see' inside their head.'

We nodded, we had heard about that.

'When you still your vibrationary rate and your thoughts and do not move, you will find that other people's busy minds will decide that there is nothing there and so you will not be seen, but as soon as you move of course, you can be seen by them and it's as if you have emerged from nowhere.'

'Wow. That's amazing.' I was impressed. I couldn't wait to try it.

Stanley as usual read my thoughts.

'Of course it's more impressive to be able to heal others than jump out at them from nowhere.'

'How does that work?' Betty was already a healer but wanted to know the mechanics of it.

'Well, you simply lift off the excess positive or negative energy from the person to allow them to experience the balanced state and then the body can heal itself.

'What do you do with the excess?' I asked.

'Well it's stored until they can deal with it later at a more convenient time.'

Stanley observed us for a moment, marched up and down and then announced, 'and that ladies, concludes the What is Natural Time workshop.' He gave a bow.

I jumped, I had been so engrossed that I had forgotten to make my notes and hurriedly wrote:

To Become Invisible

(a) Still mind

(b) Still emotions

(c) Still body

'Whew I think I need a walk after that,' I told Betty.

'Don't you mean a run?' Stanley asked.

Betty agreed. 'Yes Abby, I'll join you – in *a walk*,' she emphasised laughing, 'and perhaps we can have coffee when we get back?'

'I'm going for a cigarette,' Stanley announced, and we all donned our coats before exiting the caravan into the rain.

Chapter 12

Time Manifestation

Day 4
Session 11

We returned from our brief walk dripping, but refreshed and ready for coffee and biscuits. It was not a coffee break as such, but more of a coffee continuation. We did not chat or discuss what had happened previously, but went straight into the next workshop, which Ti Ming informed us was called Time Manifestation.

'Any ideas what a time manifestation might be?' Stanley enquired of us looking exaggeratedly hopeful.

I hoped Betty might say something as I didn't have a clue.

She merely sipped her coffee thoughtfully, her eyes down.

I wrote on my notepad:

Time Manifestation

When I had finished I looked up and Stanley smiled at me encouragingly.

I sighed, feeling pressurised to answer something. Anything. This was worse than being in school.

'Let's take the words one at a time,' he suggested. 'Give me an example of a manifestation.'

'An event, something that happens?' I asked hopefully.

'An experience,' Betty contributed.

We were getting into the flow now.

'A disaster.'

'A blessing,' Betty countered.

'A thought.'

'A word.'

'A deed.'

'Thank you,' Stanley interrupted us. 'I think you have the idea. So now consider the word 'Time'. What is time?'

'We've done this,' I said. 'It helps us to learn.'

'To grow,' Betty put in.

'So what is a time manifestation?' Stanley asked again.

'Time that we have manifested?' I enquired not knowing at all what I meant by that answer.

'Very good,' I was relieved to hear him say. 'It is indeed time that we have manifested, or created. It's nice when the title gives you a clue isn't it?' he grinned impishly at me, knowing full well that I had guessed.

'So you're saying that we create our own time?' Betty wanted clarification.

'Yes, our own time and our own reality.'

'But I'm not conscious of doing that,' she objected, while I wrote:

We create our own time and our own reality

'Ah, now there's the problem,' his smiled faded and his eyes became serious for a moment. 'If we are not conscious of creating our own reality then it is being created for us.'

'Who by?' I asked incredulously.

'Our own unconscious?' Betty enquired.

'Yes, our unconscious will can create our time and our reality, but it is also possible that other factors are involved. Any ideas what they might be?'

Our unconscious will can create our time and our reality

'Someone else's unconscious will?' I asked, hoping that wasn't the case, but to my horror he nodded.

'Yes, someone else's conscious or unconscious will.'

'So we can be manipulated without even knowing it?' I was aghast.

Someone else's conscious or unconscious will can create our time and our reality

'It is even worse than that.'

'I don't see how it can be,' I argued.

He was silent, having delivered his blow, and his small, slight hands reached out for his mug of tea.

Betty was the first to see it. 'We can manipulate others either consciously or unconsciously.'

He nodded.

We can create others time and reality either consciously or unconsciously

I sipped at my coffee while I thought about the implications and wrote:

We can have our time and our reality created by:

(a) Our conscious will

(b) Our unconscious will

(c) Others conscious will

(d) Others unconscious will

If Stanley was right, then we weren't the free beings that I had always thought we were. For the first time the workshops had given me information that made me feel negative and depressed.

Life, it seemed was more complicated than I had imagined. I had known of course that things didn't always go as planned and that situations threw up many obstacles for us to deal with, but it hadn't occurred to me that either we or someone else had created that situation deliberately and put the obstacles there. The problem was, as I saw it, if we were unconsciously doing things, how could we bring it into consciousness?

'How can we know what it is we are doing?' I asked him.

'We have to remain aware,' Betty answered me.

'If we make sure we are not manipulating others then it will not come back to us.'

'Of course others may be demonstrating to us how we manipulate ourselves,' Stanley pointed out. 'The first thing to realise is that as we manipulate, so we will be manipulated. We can start to become conscious of how the process works and to halt the effect of others upon us by the use of affirmations.'

'What affirmations?' I wanted to know.

'Well, if someone is trying to dump their negative onto you, you can just say, Stop,' Stanley held up his hand like a traffic policeman. 'You could also say, Go,' he pointed at the door.

'Other statements you could use are I hear you, I understand, thank you. never mind and what do you think?'

'Why would you thank someone for dumping their negative on you?' I wanted to know, feeling puzzled.

'Because if someone is giving you negative, then it's only your negative returning to you. Remember the cushion exercise in the Non Practical Time Workshop?'

As if I could ever forget that green corduroy cushion.

'But what if I haven't been negative to them?' I protested.

'You could have been negative to someone in the past,' Betty pointed out, 'or even a past life.'

'So you're saying that every negative I've ever given out to anyone will come back to me?'

Stanley smiled at me delightedly. 'Of course. Fun isn't it?'

I ignored him and wrote:

Affirmations to stop others using you:

(a) *Stop! Go!*

(b) *I hear you I understand*

(c) *Thank you Never Mind*

(d) *What do you think?*

Stanley observed my dismay, and clutching his mug, marched on the spot.

'You know manipulation isn't always negative, it is the art of re-organisation. It can organise order out of chaos. The choice is ours. When we create order, the Creator is working through us.'

'So who is working through us when we create chaos?' I asked, not really wanting the answer to that question.

None was given.

'Abby, can you give Betty some paper and a pen? I want you both to write down what you have manifested so far in your lives.'

I handed Betty the pen and paper as requested and she stared at it in horror.

'I wouldn't know where to begin.'

'Put down the headings, relationships and possessions.'

He watched while we did so and waited for us to think of things to write.

Relationships   *Possessions*

'Write down all the people you have in your life and all the things. Every person and every thing has been created by you.'

'Or someone else,' I muttered to myself.

'We didn't choose our relatives,' Betty commented.

'Didn't you?' he countered. 'On one level you did. Every person in your life is there for a reason. Every one has something to teach you and something they can learn from you.'

I wrote a list of the people in my life, family, friends, work colleagues, and my possessions, my car, house, caravan, pc, tv, stereo, furniture, plants, books, appliances, ornaments and clothes.

'You need to do an inventory of the things in your life, remember anything that is not in use can be creating negative in your life. Everything you have is there because of an act of conscious will on your part.'

'What if someone gave it to me?' I queried, not deliberately trying to be awkward.

'Then you consciously accepted it into your space,' Stanley countered.

'It's difficult to say no to a gift,' I objected.

Consciously accept gifts into your space

'Which may be the very reason that someone would present you with a gift,' he suggested gently.

'So Abby is vulnerable because she is polite?' Betty asked.

He nodded grave for once.

'But how could you refuse?' I wanted to know.

'You could say, I am grateful for the thought, but I do not require further things in my life at this time, I am on a diet.'

'A diet, what's that got to do with it?' I queried, looking puzzled.

'Attempting to lighten up.'

Betty and I laughed, and he relaxed and laughed with us.

Consciously refuse gifts into your space

'But it might be a gift we need,' Betty suggested, 'What do we do then?'

'Well you are always free to accept a gift, providing that it is free.'

Stanley smiled.

'How will we know the difference?' I wanted to know.

'A gift from the One will always be exactly what is needed, or will create genuine delight in the recipient. One that is a Trojan horse and comes with hidden intent, will be felt as a burden and received with reluctance. It will be something that is not required and will cause resentment rather than joy in the recipient.'

A thought occurred to me.

'I've just remembered, I sometimes have accidents with those kinds of gifts.'

'What do you mean?' Betty enquired looking at me suspiciously, and no doubt thinking of all the gifts she had given me in the past and wondering about their fate.

'Well I do have a family member who insists on dumping us with awful gifts, especially at Christmas. I remember one year my daughter received a very ugly figurine and she complained that she would be stuck with it for ever. I asked to see it and threw it to the floor deliberately smashing it. She was horrified and asked me why I had done such an awful thing with her present.

'But you didn't want to be stuck with it for ever,' I told her.

'Yes but I could have given it to someone else,' she countered.

'What, and have them stuck with it for ever? Shame on you.'

She saw the point, and laughed and ever since then we have what we call in the family 'accidents' with things we don't like.'

Betty looked quite shocked.

'I hope you don't do that with things I give you?'

'No of course not Bett, you always give me wonderful presents.'

She didn't look convinced and I wished I hadn't shared that with her. She'd probably never give me anything again.

'Of course Abby was merely trying to earth the negative charge attached to the object,' Stanley attempted to vindicate me.

'It is a way of dealing with it, but perhaps you would be better using your will to decline the gift in the first place as then you wouldn't be left with it. You need to bring your will into consciousness. If your will is conscious then it cannot be dominated.'

'So if it's not conscious then it can be dominated?' Betty asked nodding to herself and answered before Stanley had a chance. 'That explains a lot.'

'Yes,' he confirmed, 'you can be dominated by your own subconscious or other people's subconscious or conscious will. So now look at your list and see who and what you do not want in your life. Try to decide which things you have manifested and which things you think others have manifested on your behalf.'

I scrolled down my list underlining the things that I thought were not of my own making. Betty did the same, circling hers.

'Ok. Now I want you to look at the ways in which you think you have influenced others in their lives.'

'That's a hard one,' Betty protested. 'If it was unconscious, then I wouldn't know, would I?'

'That is correct,' Stanley conceded, smiling. 'However, consider only the ways you have influenced them consciously, and I don't just mean negatively.'

'You've helped loads of people Abby,' Betty observed. 'Especially in your role as therapist.'

'Well so have you,' I answered.

'Not in that way,' she contradicted.

'Well, maybe not, but you've got six children remember,' I reminded her, 'and anyway, I help people mentally, and you help them spiritually, and practically,' I added, 'my stomach is still grateful for all the meals you've given me.'

'So are you beginning to see,' Stanley cut in hurriedly, 'that all these influencing factors are what we call a time manifestation?'

We both brought our focus back to the moment and agreed with him that we did.

'Good,' he nodded. 'Remember then to be more conscious of what you are manifesting in your life and in the lives of others, for whatever you send out will return.

'So those meals that Betty cooked for me are in repayment of meals that I have cooked for others?'

'Well not just meals, although you have just agreed that you feed others on different levels.'

'So a spiritual feast may be repaid by a physical one?' Betty clarified.

'Yes,' Stanley agreed, 'and vice versa, a physical feast may be repaid by a spiritual one,'

'I like the sound of that,' Betty smiled to herself.

'I suppose we could say that these workshops are a spiritual feast,' I suggested.

Stanley smiled. 'You could indeed, well spotted Abby.'

'That's a lot of cooking we've been doing,' Betty remarked.

'Certainly a lot of cooking in one way or another,' Stanley agreed.

'You should be due a lot of meals then Stanley,' I remarked.

He ignored me.

'So you see it's important to be aware of what you give others and what you receive from them.'

'And what we give ourselves,' Betty reminded him.

'Quite so,' he agreed, and watched while I wrote:

Be conscious of what we are manifesting in our gift giving to ourself and others

'That then ladies, concludes the Time Manifestation workshop,' he gave his little Chinese type bow and put his hands together in farewell.

We reciprocated and then continued to discuss the implications of the workshop and how we might have influenced others, or been influenced by them, over the meal break.

Chapter 13

Timely Intervention
or Accidental Process?

Day 4
Session 12

June arrived just before the next session. We greeted her without inquiring about her day, as instructed. She merely said Hi and sat down at the little caravan table. Her short blonde hair was neat and she was immaculate as always in a pale green silk shirt and grey slacks. Betty always looked groomed with her casual velvets, corduroys and cottons.

I had not bothered much with my appearance that day and felt a little dishevelled beside them. I had merely pulled on a pair of jeans and a sweater and brushed my hair, catching it with a scrunchie into a pony tail to stop it falling across my face when I bent over the page to write my notes.

Once we were settled, Ti Ming arrived and Stanley began the workshop with his usual little bow.

'Good afternoon. The title of this workshop is Timely Intervention or Accidental Process. What would you say is a Timely Intervention?'

I opened my notebook and wrote the title.

Timely Intervention or Accidental Process?

June was on the ball and answered him before we could say anything.

'Something that happens to stop me putting my foot in it.' Betty agreed with her.

'Yes, it's something that saves my bacon. It's as though an outside force has taken a hand in what is happening and stops me from making a mistake.'

Stanley looked at me, waiting for my contribution.

'It's an example of the Natural Mirror in operation,' I said.

'Well, yes,' he agreed. 'You're all right, but we haven't come to that workshop yet Abby.'

'I'm in future time,' I countered quickly.

He laughed.

'OK. So tell me now, what is your understanding of an accident?'

'There's no such thing?' June decided.

'It's a misperceived example of the Natural Mirror,' I said, feeling rather superior and on a roll for once.

'It's a timely intervention,' Betty decided.

'Betty is correct,' Stanley declared. 'It's a timely intervention that has not been recognised.

'I don't understand,' June protested.

'Well, to demonstrate this I will provide you with some examples. I would ask you all to consider the following. You are in a china shop and have browsed around for some time selecting a beautiful object for your newly decorated room. You have just decided to buy something when a young child runs past, swinging his arms and smashes it. There is no chance of replacing the object as it was unique. What do you do? June?'

'Wring his neck,' she laughed. 'No, I suppose I would just feel disappointed and angry at being thwarted. It's strange you should say that because it happened to me only last week.

Stanley nodded. 'And Abby, what would you do?'

'Accept that I wasn't meant to have it.'

'Well, that's what I did in the end,' June agreed.

'OK, and Betty?'

'I would wonder why it happened and look to see what it had to teach me.'

'So you would all have different reactions to the same situation. You understand from your own point of view, and depending upon your understanding, your reality is created. Let me ask you another. Abby, you answer first this time please.' I wrote hurriedly:

Your reality is created from your Understanding

I knew he asked me to interrupt me writing and draw me back into the flow of the workshop.

'You are decorating a room.' (He knew that I was.)

'You are on top of the step ladder painting the ceiling when the phone rings. What do you do?'

'Rush to answer it I suppose, and knowing my luck it would stop just as I got there.'

'OK, June, what would you do?'

'Let it ring. There's no way I would risk breaking my neck to answer it in time. And anyway, they must be negative beings to ring at such an inharmonious time,' she smiled triumphantly, pleased with her assessment of the situation.

He made no comment. 'And Betty?'

'I think I would try to answer it and wonder what the interruption was showing me.'

'OK, very good so far. Please observe again that you all responded differently. Alright. I will give you another scenario. This time Betty, you answer first. It's a lovely day and the sun is shining. You are driving your car when you run out of petrol. You remember that you passed a garage a quarter of a mile back. What is your first thought?'

'I'm being taught a lesson here. At least the sun is shining and it's only a quarter of a mile to walk. Perhaps I'm being told I need to get more exercise.'

June and I laughed.

'Don't laugh,' she admonished, 'it happened to me only three days ago and the garage was more than half a mile away and it was raining at the time.'

'And you really thought that?' June asked. 'I don't think I'd be thinking, at least it's only a half a mile. More like, damn and blast, I'm out of fuel, I'm going to be late, and have I got my can with me?'

'I'd be thinking, "what an idiot I am", and make sure I checked my gauge next time,' I said.

'So, what is it that we observe in these scenario's?' Stanley asked. 'Can you tell me June what is your initial response to unexpected situations?'

'Annoyance and frustration at things not going as smoothly as expected.'

'And would you say this was a positive or a negative response?'

'Well, I suppose negative, although the one about the decorating I think was positive because I didn't let it interrupt what I was doing.'

142

'But suppose it was an emergency?' I asked her. 'Somebody could have had an accident and wanted you to go to the hospital.'

'Which brings us nicely to the point Abby, are you still saying that there any such thing as an accident?'

'Well, yes of course there is,' June declared, interrupting, and I nodded my agreement.

Betty frowned at us and murmured, 'No, there isn't. I mean if everything is showing us something, whatever happens is already planned.'

'But it wasn't planned, that's just the point, that's what the word accident means,' June sounded frustrated with her lack of understanding.

'Not planned by us,' Betty emphasised the *us*, 'that's the point.'

'Well by who then?' June asked surprised.

'Spirit of course.'

'Betty, I don't think spirit can use the phone,' I quipped, 'and even if they could, why would they try and make us break our necks by phoning when we were up a ladder? It's bad timing.'

'They ought to do these workshops then,' June suggested and we all laughed.

'Who says they aren't?' Betty joined in with the joviality.

'Well, Ti Ming is anyway,' I cast an amused look at Stanley, but he only observed us quietly without saying anything and for some reason this made us all the more amused. He liked to laugh at our expense, so why shouldn't the joke be on him for once?

'Let's try another scenario,' was all he said. We sighed in unison. He obviously couldn't take a joke. Or Ti Ming couldn't, perhaps it wasn't funny in Chinese.

'Go on then,' I agreed for us all.

'Right, you have just bought a new coffee table for your living room.'

'Isn't that weird,' Betty interrupted. 'I have too.'

Stanley ignored her. 'You go out for the afternoon and when you return you find that the leg has been damaged. Your partner admits to kicking it accidentally. What do you do?'

'Kick him,' I laughed. 'No, I suppose I would just moan at him and say he should have watched what he was doing.'

'I'd want another one,' June insisted. 'I wouldn't want to live with a damaged table, and I'd make him pay for it as he did it.'

I was surprised by this. 'Do you know,' I said, 'It would never occur to me to demand a new table. I would just live with the damaged one.'

'Ah, victim thinking,' June announced. 'You don't love yourself

143

enough to demand perfection. I never put up with second best. Would you Betty?'

'Well as I said, this actually happened and Tony did damage it but I kept the original one, as I decided it was my fault for putting it in a place that might trip people up.'

'What!' June was incensed. 'But it was his fault for not looking where he was going. Betty I think you were wrong to take the blame.'

'What's it showing you?' she countered.

'That I won't put up with second best and you both do,' June was unrepentant.

Betty shook her head. 'No that's not it.'

'What then?' I asked.

'I'm not sure,' she said. 'I suppose I thought something like, what have I damaged of someone else's, or where am I not looking where I am going? You see nothing happens that we haven't caused. So somewhere I must have earned the right to the damage.'

'Very good,' Stanley approved. 'You are on the right track Betty. All your responses have been in natural time.'

I decided to make a note of that.

Nothing happens that I haven't caused
I have earned the right to every situation

June looked at us both bewildered.

'I'm lost,' she said.

'Well, that's because you haven't been here for all the workshops,' Stanley told her.

'I haven't got time,' she said without thinking and we all collapsed with laughter, including Stanley.

'So, last scenario,' he pulled himself together and shook himself quickly like a dog shaking water from his coat.

'You have been invited to visit an ancient site, so far unknown. When you meet your escort you are told that the visit has been cancelled because they don't feel like going. What is your response?'

'I think I'd be upset and disappointed,' I said.

June turned her eyes towards the ceiling, considering. 'I'd ask them where it was and go by myself.'

I thought that was a good answer and wondered why I hadn't thought of it. June had more self confidence than me and was not afraid of asking for what she wanted. I resolved to be more like her. At least she wasn't stuck with second best and damaged goods. She was assertive and confident and didn't tolerate fools gladly. I realised that she loved herself more than I did and I had a lot to learn from her.

'Well there would have to be a reason why they cancelled,' Betty's voice interrupted my thoughts.

'Yes there was. They didn't feel like going,' June supplied.

'So, the question to ask yourself is, what is it you don't feel like seeing in yourself?'

June and I stared at her in surprise, that hadn't occurred to us.

'Is that the right answer?' I asked Stanley.

He smiled his irritating, enigmatic smile and gave me an equally annoying answer.

'Everything is the right answer, it just depends upon your point of view.'

'That's not helpful Stanley.'

'Oh isn't it?' he said carelessly looking unrepentant, 'but I'm giving you the right answer to your question.'

> *Everything is the right answer*
> *it just depends upon your point of view*

I wrote it down more to annoy him than anything and spoke to Betty, ignoring him.

'So they would have cancelled the trip because of our attitude?'

'Yes,' she confirmed. 'visiting an energy site will bring stuff up into our consciousness and if we don't feel like seeing it, then we can't go.'

'You're saying the timing is wrong?' June asked.

'Ah, our little friend Ti ming, he gets everywhere doesn't he?' Stanley beamed happily again.

'So, to clarify, a Timely Intervention is an event which happens at the right time. It is a divine learning process. It is divine protection.'

'How is it protection?' I wanted to know, writing it down:

> *A Timely Intervention is an event*
> *which happens at the right time*

It is a divine learning process
It is divine protection

'It stops the negative process and diverts from subconscious to conscious thought, – well, gives us the opportunity to do so anyway,' he added as an afterthought looking pointedly at me.

'Remember, there is no such thing as an accident, or fate, luck, chance or co-incidence. These are just names we give to events that we don't understand as yet. Nothing that happens in our life is a random occurrence. Everything happens for a reason and we should look beyond the surface of events and read the hidden message that the situation is giving us. We need to find out what it is showing us about us and be aware that everything happens at *exactly*, he emphasised this word, the right time. The questions we need to ask ourselves are:

What is the situation showing me about myself?

What is it that I need to learn from this situation?

Any questions?'

There was a stunned silence from June and I. Betty nodded in agreement.

He gave a bow.

'This then, ladies and gentlemen, concludes the Timely Intervention or Accidental Process workshop.'

I wrote hurriedly after he had finished before I forgot:

Everything happens for a reason
Look beyond the surface of events
Read the hidden messages

Ask the questions:

1. What is the situation showing me about myself?

2. What is it I need to learn from this situation?

146

Chapter 14

Now For Something
Completely Different

Day 5
Session 13

It was Wednesday, only two more days of workshops before we headed home. I lay in bed considering all that I had learned and feeling ashamed of my first reaction, that I would be bored listening to Stanley's twaddle. I also remembered that I had thought I was in for a relaxing time. Ha! That was a laugh, this was the most strenuous week of my life so far and it was not over yet. I headed for the bathroom.

'Morning,' Stanley greeted me with a smile when I finally emerged, dressed ready for the day. He had made himself tea and was sitting at the window in the living area drinking thoughtfully and staring out at the watery, early morning sunlight filtering through the trees.

I organised my breakfast and sat at the table in the dining area.

'What are we going to do today?' I asked him eagerly, breaking into the silence.

'Something completely different,' he answered with a sly grin.

'Good,' I said, 'we could do with a change.'

'This is the title of the next workshop.'

'Oh, I see, well that sounds exciting.'

'Doesn't it just?' Was all he would comment and avoided me by going outside until Betty arrived.

I relaxed and ate my breakfast, wondering what was in store for us. A dog barked making me jump. I looked out the window and saw a black labrador investigating Stanley, who was talking to it in low tones with his hand outstretched. The dog must have liked what he was saying, for he advanced and allowed himself to be patted.

The owner appeared to reclaim his pet just as Betty's car rounded the corner. Betty liked dogs as well, although she had never allowed her children to keep one as a pet. To her dogs were working farm animals and she didn't approve of them being indoors. She and Stanley exchanged pleasantries with the dog owner before heading my way.

'Morning Abby,' she greeted me enthusiastically with a hug, 'what a wonderful day, there was a bank of mist all over the moors, it was so magical, it reminds me of . . .'

Stanley followed her in and cut the conversation by clapping his hands for attention and put on a silly voice.

'Are we ready then for Now For Something Completely Different?'

Stanley, with you everything is always different, wouldn't you say so Abby? I wonder what he's got up his sleeve for us today?'

'It's the title of the workshop,' I informed her.

'Is it? Are you sure?' Betty looked at Stanley, hoping for confirmation, but he was silent.

'He told me earlier,' I said.

'Oh I see,' she looked somewhat disappointed as if she was hoping for a change from workshops.

I wrote down:

Now For Something Completely Different

'So, what kind of a week have you had so far?' he queried.

I relaxed, it was obviously some kind of feedback session.

'Interesting,' Betty commented. 'Not at all what I was expecting.'

'Oh, you were expecting to be bored were you?' Stanley laughed.

'No, but I have to admit I've attended many workshops where I have been bored, but your's have really kept me on my toes.'

'OK, so Abby, what about you, what kind of a week have you had?'

'Informative.'

'Glad to of been of help,' Stanley gave a mock bow. 'And may we enquire what you intend to do with this information you have acquired?'

I coloured. I knew he was getting at me. 'Put it into practice.'

'Put it into practice,' he repeated. 'We're so pleased to hear you say that.'

I noted the plural pronoun and concluded that Ti Ming had taken over again.

'Good. So to recap, Betty is on her toes and Abby is putting things into practice, or at least considering the idea, yes?'

We both nodded, wondering where he was going.

'OK,' he commenced marching, which I recognised by now meant that he was changing the energy in the room.

'Now I want you to consider six things that have gone wrong for you in the last month. Perhaps Abby you would be so good as to give Betty a sheet of paper so that she can write them down, and if you would write yours down as well please.'

'Six things?' Betty repeated as she rummaged in her bag for a pen. 'Do you mean six things that we have done, or six things that others have done?'

'Either, as long as you were involved in some way.'

We were quiet while we considered.

'Do you want big things or little things?' I enquired.

'Well, perhaps it would be as well to start off looking at the little things,' Stanley smiled at me, 'we can always progress to the bigger things later – if we get bored,' he said, with a dig at Betty and a grin in her direction.

She was oblivious however, already engrossed in thinking about her situations. I glanced at her sheet, there were already about four things on her list and I hadn't even started.

Small things. That shouldn't be too hard to think of, things were always going wrong in my life. My car was a major source of problems, together with my job and the children.

'OK what have we got?' Stanley enquired when we had put our pens down.

'Betty?'

'Well let me see, last week my Aga went out,' Betty said.

'And what did you do about that?' Stanley enquired.

'I phoned the plumber.'

'And what did you think or say?' Stanley enquired.

'I don't think it's repeatable,' Betty laughed rather sheepishly.

'I see. So it was negative?' Stanley enquired.

She nodded her confirmation.

'Very good. Bett, thank you for sharing that with us. Abby, have you something you wish to share?'

'Oh, I had a row with my daughter. She was looking through a catalogue and choosing things she couldn't afford, so I suggested she would be better off spending her time looking at the jobs pages of the paper and thinking about ways of earning money before she thought about ways of spending it. Needless to say, she was not amused and accused me of trying to live her life for her.'

'Oh dear,' Betty said sympathetically, 'and you were only trying to help her weren't you?'

'Well yes of course,' I said surprised at her tone, as if she doubted I had handled it in the best possible way.

'OK, thank you Abby.'

Stanley cut us short.

'Another situation from you please Bett.'

'Oh, aren't we going to discuss Abby's situation?' she asked surprised.

'Later,' he said soothingly. 'Just at the moment I want to find out what's been happening to you both.'

'Well, I had an argument with my friend Vicky.'

'You did?' Stanley sounded surprised, as if he thought Betty was above such behaviour.

'Yes, well she keeps phoning me up at inconvenient times and moans about all sorts of things, for hours on end. Her health, all about her aches and pains and the other people in her life and how they are upsetting her and I don't even know most of them. In the end I told her I was fed up with it and would she please only phone me when she had something nice to say.'

'What did she do?' I asked.

'She hung up,' Betty said, not looking in the least upset.

'Good. Thank you for that Bett,' Stanley cut in before I could comment.

'Next, Abby?'

'Oh, I cut my finger on a kitchen knife.'

'OK Betty?'

'I burnt a cake.'

'That's not like you Betty,' I said, 'your cakes are always delicious. It's me that burns everything.'

'Abby?' Stanley enquired.

'Oh, my car broke down.'

'Did it? You never said, when was this?' Betty wanted to know.

'Oh, the week before last, I had to get the breakdown people out.'

'Betty, your next disaster please.'

'Hmm, oh, my iron broke and I had to get a new one or they wouldn't have had shirts for the week. I iron about twenty at the weekends, and that's without everything else.

'You probably wore it out with all the ironing you do,' I laughed, I was always amazed at the amount of ironing Betty did, but with her family it was a necessity. She often ironed as we talked when I went round to see her.

'I hate ironing,' I said, shuddering at the thought of all the shirts Betty did each week.

'I'm sure you do, just as well you don't have to do Betty's load then isn't it? But what else have you got on your list? Stanley wanted to know.

I didn't think he sounded very sympathetic, but then I reflected, he had probably never ironed a shirt in his life.

'A friend, who shall be nameless, put a hot saucepan down on my new kitchen work surfaces,' I said.

'Oh no,' Betty gasped, 'did it do much damage?'

'Yes, it's burnt a nice saucepan shaped ring into the worktop as a reminder,' I said, still feeling upset when I thought about it.

'Betty?' Stanley moved us on without comment.

'My computer crashed and I couldn't get it going again. I wasted a load of money on help phone calls that weren't helpful and in the end my neighbour fixed it for me.'

'That's good,' I remarked, scared to say more in case I got told off.

'Your last one?' Stanley enquired, looking at me.

'Well, you know my fibre optic table,' I began.

Betty nodded. 'Yes, I think so, is it the one in the living room that changes colour?'

'Yes, that's right, well a visiting relative decided to stay up late one night and forgot to switch it off, so now it doesn't work, it's burnt out.'

'Oh what a shame, and it was so pretty,' Betty sympathised.

'I know and the annoying thing is the firm don't make them any more so I can't get a replacement.'

'Betty, your last disaster please.'

'Oh, well it's not really mine, it's just that Richard split up with his girlfriend and he has been very depressed lately.'

'Abby your last one?'

'A friend spilt paint all down my stairs.'

'But you've just had a new stair carpet haven't you?' Betty sounded horrified.

'Yes, I have,' I said, about to expand when Stanley interrupted me.

'Right then ladies, thank you for sharing your disasters with us this morning,' Stanley smiled gratefully at us. I was puzzled.

'I don't see how our disasters as you put it are something completely different, they're things that happen every day,' I said.

To my surprise he burst out laughing without giving me any explanation.

I looked at Betty.

'Well at least one of us finds it funny,' she commented.

'I wonder if he laughs at his own disasters so easily,' I remarked somewhat frustrated.

'I do try to,' he agreed, 'do you laugh at yours?'

'No,' I said getting annoyed. 'Most people don't Stanley.'

'OK so let us examine your reactions shall we?'

'Right Betty, your Aga wasn't it?' she nodded.

'So we know you phoned the plumber and presumably he fixed it?'

'Yes, he did, eventually, but it took him three days before he could find the fault and it caused complete disruption in the house with no heating or means of cooking and then of course it cost me a small fortune to have it repaired.'

'OK. So can you tell me please what were your reactions to all of this?'

'Well, obviously I was annoyed.'

'Whoa, stop right there please. Why do you find it obvious to be annoyed?'

'Well, anybody would be,' I said, rushing to her defence.

'Would they?' Stanley fixed his blue eyes on me. 'Are you telling me then that negativity is the obvious response to a negative situation?'

I was silent.

'What was your response Abby to having a row with your daughter? About a job wasn't it?'

'Not exactly, I was cross with her hinting for me to buy her things all the time and suggested she get a job and buy them for herself.'

'And would you say this was a negative response? Betty?'

'Well, no I don't think I would. After all, Abby was trying to get Samantha to take responsibility for herself and surely that has to be positive?' Betty replied.

'What do you think Abby? Were you being positive?' Stanley asked me.

I eyed him suspiciously, sensing a trap about to snap shut.

'Well, the motive might have been positive, but I was annoyed with her, for expecting me to be the Bank of England, so my feelings weren't positive,' I admitted.

'Ah, so you were annoyed were you?' he emphasised.

'Yes,' I agreed.

'Mmm, what do you think Bett, does being annoyed change the situation?'

She looked at me apologetically. 'Yes, I suppose it does.'

'Right, so your next one Betty, a row with your friend wasn't it? What do we think about this one, was Betty being positive or negative Abby?'

'Well,' I prevaricated, 'it depends whether you are going to class telling someone to stop being negative as being negative.'

'You tell me,' Betty retorted.

'I think so,' I said doubtfully, 'I'm not sure, what do you think Stan?'

'Well, at the moment I'm asking you Abby, what you think of Betty's actions, and what she thinks of yours and then when we have examined all the situations we will look into it further,' he replied mildly, refusing to be drawn.

'But that's making us do all the work,' Betty objected.

'That is the purpose of this workshop Betty, to enable you both to be able to deal with negative people and situations.'

'Oh I see.' Betty didn't look convinced.

'So can we move on now to Abby's cut finger? What happened Abby, how did you come to cut yourself?'

'I was chopping onions and the knife slipped,' I said. 'It was particularly painful because the onion juice got into the cut.'

'Ow,' Betty said sympathetically. 'I've done that myself and it's not pleasant.'

'So what were you thinking when you did it?' Stanley wanted to know.

'Thinking?' I looked at him surprised. 'I don't know, how would I remember that? Probably what an idiot I was to be so careless.'

'Oh, so you would tell yourself off would you?'

I thought about it. 'Well, I wouldn't say tell myself off, but I suppose I would be annoyed with myself yes.'

'OK, that's all I wanted to know at the moment.' Stanley shifted his gaze from me to Betty.

'Bett tell us about your burnt cake.'

'Well, it was a fruit cake.'

'Oh, that's alright then,' Stanley laughed, he didn't like fruit cake.

'Stanley,' I objected, 'that's not very nice, just because you don't like fruit cake, now whose being negative?'

153

'He's not being negative,' Betty cut in, 'he's just being playful, aren't you Stan?'

He shrugged by way of reply. 'The point is, were you being negative when you found out that you'd burnt it?' he asked Betty.

'Well, I suppose I wasn't too pleased,' she admitted, remembering. 'After all, I can't have let it go or I wouldn't be mentioning it now would I?'

'Good point,' he approved. 'So what was your first thought as you took it out of the oven?'

'Ummm, something like, oh no, it's useless, now what am I going to give them for tea?'

'So did you feel you were letting somebody down?' he asked.

'Well, yes I suppose I did,' Betty said thinking about it. 'I had to go out and buy a shop made one and they noticed the difference.'

'So you felt guilty?' Stanley said.

'Objection,' I cut in laughing, 'you're leading the witness.'

'Well now you mention it Stan, yes I did, but only after they complained and made me feel guilty.'

'Oh, so they made you did they?'

Betty looked surprised. 'Oh, so I took it on board? I see. Thank you Stanley.'

He gave a little bow. 'Always nice to be of service. Now Abby, tell us about your car.'

'Oh yes. I was late for work because it wouldn't start, my students were all hanging around, waiting for me to arrive and I felt totally incompetent.'

'You felt incompetent because the car wouldn't start?' Betty looked at me amazed. 'Why? It wasn't your fault was it?'

'Well no, I suppose not. I mean it wasn't anything I could have foreseen, but all the same I kept people waiting and inconvenienced everyone.'

'Did they say they'd been inconvenienced?' Stanley asked.

'Well no, but they must have been.'

'How do you know that?' Stanley pushed me further.

'Well, I suppose because I would have been in their situation.'

'Oh I see, you would have been, and everyone else is you are they?' Without waiting for my reply Stanley turned away from me and towards Betty.

'Bett, how about telling us about your iron?'

'Well, as I said, it broke and I had to go out and buy a new one.'

'And how did you feel about buying a new one?' Stanley enquired. 'Was it an excuse to update to something wonderful, that would make ironing all those shirts an enjoyable experience?'

'Shut up Stanley, ironing shirts is never an enjoyable experience,' I said.

'Well it is for me,' Betty contradicted, 'but as for the new iron, well, no, I preferred the old one. I was used to that and this new one just makes life harder while I get used to all the new settings and the steam isn't as good.'

'So it was a negative incident?' Stanley clarified.

'I suppose you could say so,' Betty heaved a huge sigh. 'Not doing very well are we Stanley?'

'That depends on what you mean,' he countered brightly. 'You're doing an excellent job at identifying all your negatives.'

'Oh, you always manage to turn everything around don't you?' Betty laughed.

'We do our best,' he agreed proudly.

'Now Abby, tell me about your burnt worktop.'

'Well, I can tell you now it's definitely a negative,' I said. 'I can't think of any way I could turn that to the positive. I mean, it's ruined the work surface and I'm reminded of it every time I look at it.'

'And do you think negatively every time you look at it?' Betty wanted to know.

'Well, yes, I suppose I do. Wouldn't anyone?'

'Shall we leave anyone and everyone out of this?' Stanley suggested. 'We are currently examining *your* reactions to events, not the world's in general. We are not blaming you for thinking negatively are we Bett?' He raised his eyebrows hopefully, 'because if we were then we would be thinking negatively ourselves wouldn't we?'

Betty hurriedly shook her head.

'No of course not.'

'You see?'

He smiled at me in such a way that I had to laugh. He certainly had a way with him.

'Let us proceed now to Betty's computer breaking down. What's the story about that Bett?'

'Well, I've been trying really hard to master the thing and justify all the money I've spent on it and just when I think I'm winning it goes and crashes on me. I phoned the help line they gave me and they were just useless. I couldn't follow their instructions and they were really patronising, asking me if I had switched it on. I mean really.'

I hadn't heard Betty so upset in a long time and I was surprised that a computer could have that effect on her.

'Your neighbour fixed it in the end you said?'

I recognised that Stanley wanted to move her on.

'Yes, Steve from next door but one came in and he was very good. He managed to find all my work that I thought I had lost.'

'So were you pleased.'

'Yes I was in the end, but I can't say I started out pleased.' Betty admitted.

'So you wouldn't say you dealt with the incident in a positive manner?' Stanley asked.

'No I wouldn't say that I did,' Betty admitted.

'Right ho then. Abby. What's your next one?'

I consulted my notes.

'My relative broke my fibre optic table.'

'And your response was?' he enquired.

'Negative of course,' I sighed resignedly.

'OK. Thank you for that Abby, Betty, your next one please.'

'My last one was about Richard and his girlfriend. She split up with him and he's devastated.'

'So how does that make you feel?' Stanley wanted to know.

'Well, sorry for him I suppose. I know you're going to say I shouldn't.'

'I am?' Stanley feigned surprise.

Betty ignored him. 'When you see someone you love unhappy, it's bound to make you miserable. After all I'm his mum and I worry about him, it's my job.'

'It is?' Stanley looked genuinely surprised this time.

'OK then Bett, but can I ask you, does your worrying about him help him?'

'I don't know. I suppose not,' she said. 'But it's natural isn't it?'

'Natural?' Stanley queried. 'Do you mean usual?'

'Oh don't split hairs Stanley. Natural, usual, whatever, they're the same aren't they?'

'Actually, no they're not,' he said quietly but very definitely. 'Usual is what you usually do and what other people usually do in a certain situation, but the natural response is the description of a balanced response, which is different from the positive response or the negative response.'

Betty stayed silent, thinking about what he had said, but she didn't look convinced. Stanley was on dangerous territory, challenging her reactions as a mother.

He must have sensed it, for he turned to me.

'Abby, will you please tell us your last disaster?'

'Yes, it was when a friend who was helping me decorate spilled paint all down the stairs onto my new carpet.'

'And you remained positive – yes?' Stanley grinned at me.

'Did I hell,' I retorted. 'I screamed blue murder at him.'

'Hmm, that would be a negative response then?' he enquired with mock thoughtfulness.

I threw a cushion at him.

'Beast. You try having your house ruined by someone and remaining positive.'

'Actually I have had my house – well flat, ruined by someone,' he surprised me by saying.

'But as for remaining positive with it, well, that I'm not so sure about.'

'You see!' I exclaimed triumphantly. 'You're not perfect after all.'

'Oh but I assure you I am,' he announced.

'Perfectly annoying,' Betty commented.

'Ah, but I didn't say perfectly what did I?' he dodged a second cushion I threw.

'Ah it seems ladies that you wish to change the energy. A good idea. I think it's time for a run round the caravan.'

'Oh no,' we groaned.

'Oh yes. Up you get,' he insisted, and reluctantly we obeyed.

'Now,' he continued once we had returned from running three times round the caravan. 'It is important to understand that every time we react in a negative way to situations we are using up about 5 minutes of our time.'

'What do you mean?' I asked.

'Negativity uses up time,' he clarified still further. 'Every time we have a negative thought or emotional reaction or express that reaction in anger, frustration, worry or guilt etc. we are using up about five minutes in addition to the time we are taking to deal with the situation. The more negative we are the less time we have available to us.'

My eyes widened like saucers and I gulped.

'Is that true?' I asked, knowing deep within me that it was.

'Yes, it's true,' he confirmed simply. 'We need therefore, I think you will agree, to learn how to stay positive in the face of negativity.'

'I think that would be very useful Stan yes,' Betty agreed.

'And the good news is . . .'

'You mean there is good news?' I interrupted.

'There is indeed. There is always good news, if you know how to recognise it. As I was saying, the good news is that every time you respond to a negative situation or person in a positive way you are reclaiming two minutes of your time. Always remember, negativity uses up time.'

'But what about the other three minutes?' I asked as I wrote:

Negativity takes away our time.

A negative response uses five minutes of our time.

A positive response adds to our time.

A positive response adds two minutes to our time.

'To reclaim the other three minutes you need to look at the actual negatives that have manifested. Firstly, don't make assumptions about other people's capabilities, Abby I think you are doing this by some of your examples, for instance, giving your friend too much responsibility in the kitchen and decorating department, and having unrealistic expectations of your daughter. Betty, watch your thinking for negativity, as demonstrated by your Aga and the computer.'

She nodded, and I wrote:

Don't make assumptions about other people's capabilities

'And Abby, try to think positively every time you look at your burnt work surface, because if you don't your negativity will be using up your time whenever you look at it. Ask yourself where you are leaving your mark on others.'

'Oh,' was my only comment.

'Get rid of blame, either of others or yourself, Betty specifically, thank your family for moaning about the shop cake because they are showing you that you are blaming yourself.'

'I don't think they'd understand that.'

'I don't mean literally thank them, you can do it in your mind. They will pick up the thought subconsciously.'

'Oh, right.'

Thank people (mentally) for their negative responses. They are enabling you to reclaim your time.

'And you Abby, were blaming yourself when your car broke down. It's negative thinking, stop it. You're using up your time. Blame is not required, whether of yourself or others. Situations occur because there is a reason for that situation. Look for the reason, which is a better reaction than to immediately respond with a negative. Remain centred in any situation.

Betty I'm thinking of your son and his girlfriend. You will not help them by being worried, in fact you have allowed yourself to be drawn into their negativity. The best way you can help is to remain centred. Realise that by indulging in worry you are losing your time. Recognise what you are doing.'

As I listened I wrote:

Stop Blaming yourself or others
Look for the Reason
Recognise what you are doing
Remember negativity uses up time

'Next, Abby, you keep getting interrupted, yes?'
'Yes,' I agreed.
'Well to deal with interruptions you need to keep your focus.'
'How do I do that?'
'Interrupt the interruption.'
This was a new idea for me, and I must have looked confused because he clarified without me having to ask.
'Are we talking about a visit or a phone call?' he wanted to know.
'Both,' I answered as I wrote:

Keep your focus.
Interrupt the interruption.

'Well, Betty perhaps you could explain to Abby how to deal with an unwanted visitor?'
'There are no unwanted visitors,' Betty said.
'Maybe not to you,' I retorted, 'but it happens to me all the time.'
'Now isn't that interesting?' Stanley drawled in a slow voice to bring my attention to the difference between us, but just in case it had escaped my notice he asked, 'Why do you think that might be Abby?'
'Because Betty's more tolerant than I am?' I suggested.
'No, I don't think I am, the people who call on me usually come just at the right time.'
'What always?' I asked incredulously.
'Well, usually.'
'Now why do you think that is?' Stanley asked.
'Because she is centred?'
Betty winked at me. Stanley smiled happily.
'Because she is centred,' he confirmed.

Remain centred

As I wrote the words I felt a tremendous burden lift from me, and I realised that I had been blaming my visitors for calling at inconvenient times when all along it was me who was out of harmony with myself.

'So are we clear on all of this?' Stanley enquired, scanning us anxiously as if he realised it had been a lot for us to take in.

'Well, I'm clear on it,' I said, 'but I'm just not sure I can do it all.'

'Ah,' he responded, 'I'm glad you said that, it leads me to my final point, claim your own power. Affirm I can and I will.'

'Now can you do it?' he asked us.

'Yes,' Betty nodded confidently.

'I can and I will,' I repeated obediently, and he smiled and put his hands together and bowed his head to us.

'This then is the end of the Now for Something Completely Different workshop. I thank you.'

I smiled at him and wrote:

Claim your power
Affirm:
I can and I will.

'I can and I will have coffee.' I affirmed and stood up.

'I can and I will have a biscuit,' Betty added, and we both laughed.

Chapter 15

Uncertainty in Time

After our coffee and biscuits Stanley moved us swiftly on.

'Right, so to continue. The title of the next workshop is Uncertainty in Time, can it be used? Any ideas?' he looked from one to the other of us with a hopeful expression.

Uncertainty in Time, can it be used?

'I know what you mean by uncertainty,' Betty replied, 'but I'm not clear on what you mean when you say it can be used.'

'OK, so let's stick with uncertainty for the time being,' he said. 'What is it?'

'Times when you have to make a decision, but you're not sure what the right decision would be,' I said.

'So, to Abby it's a decision making process, Bett what about you?'

'Well I'm not so sure,' she said.

'You mean you're uncertain?' he enquired laughing. 'Thank you Betty for demonstrating the principle to us so graphically.

'My pleasure I'm sure,' she gave a little incline of her head.

'Oh, so you're sure of your pleasure,' he countered.

She sighed, exasperated. There was no getting the better of Stanley.

'So what would make you uncertain Bett?'

Her expression changed as she paused for a moment, bringing her attention back and thinking seriously about the question.

'I suppose it would be about what action to take.'

'So, to Abby, uncertainty is about thinking and to you Betty, it's about action.'

We agreed that it was.

'So tell me Abby, when you feel uncertain, how do you make decisions?'

'Well,' I began, 'I look at the circumstances and come to a decision based on the facts.'

'OK.' He turned to Betty. 'So tell me Betty when you feel uncertain, how do you know what action to take?'

'I would follow my heart and go with the flow,' she replied without hesitation.

'So, by going with the flow, do you mean taking others into account as well as yourself?'

'Well of course. I would stay in harmony.' She smiled, pleased with her answer.

I waited to see what Stanley was going to say. I knew him well enough by now to be certain that it wasn't going to be that easy.

He marched for a moment on the spot while he considered us and (I presumed) waited for inspiration.

'OK, so you've both told me your strategies for dealing with uncertainty, but can you tell me please what *is* uncertainty?'

'It's a state of mind,' I suggested.

'Yes, but what state?'

'A state of confusion.' Betty came to my rescue.

'Good Betty. A state of confusion. Let's just look at that word for a moment. Fusion, and con-fusion the opposite, against fusion. Can anyone tell me what fusion means?'

'Well it's bringing all the parts together into one whole.'
I suggested.

'I agree,' Betty said.

'So confusion must be taking the one whole and separating it into parts?' Stanley asked.

Betty and I looked at each other and I shrugged. 'Yes, I guess. I hadn't really thought about it before.'

'So what do you think would bring about a state that is not whole?' he asked.

I knew the answer to that one at once.

'Negativity,' I said.

'Correct,' he agreed.

'Uncertainty is a negative time charge that has been created by your negative thinking. It is a final warning.'

He paused to allow us to digest the facts and to allow me to write them down:

Uncertainty is a negative time charge
It has been created by negative thinking
It is a final warning

'A final warning against what?' Betty wanted to know.

'Against a negative situation manifesting in your life,' was his answer.

I felt a shiver run through me as I realised that all the feelings of uncertainty I had experienced in the past had been warning me of events about to happen and I hadn't realised. I should have been listening, but instead I had just run headlong over the cliff edge.

'So when I said I use harmony as a basis for action, was that right?' Betty wanted to know.

'What do you think Bett?' was his inevitable question answer.

'I think so, but I'm not sure.'

'Well do the actions you take based on harmony get you the right outcomes?'

'Sometimes, but not always,' she admitted.

'So why not?'

'Abby, do you know?' he asked me.

'No,' I admitted.

'Well, would you say it depends on what you're harmonising with?' he asked.

We both nodded obediently.

He looked at us and laughed.

'The principle of harmony is generally a good basis for action, but you have to be careful what you're harmonising with.'

'What do you mean?' Betty asked curiously. 'Why would we have to be careful?'

'Well, is there such a thing as a negative person would you say?' he asked.

'Yes of course,' Betty agreed.

'So if you try to fit in with them what will happen?'

Light dawned on Betty's face. 'Oh I see. You mean I've harmonised with a negative.'

He smiled. 'Exactly. And if you do that, what will happen?'

'I'll get a negative outcome.'

'But it's alright to harmonise with a positive person,' I said.

'Is it?' he asked.

I was surprised. 'Isn't it?'

'That would depend,' he answered evasively.

I laughed. I could play this game.

'I bet it would.'

'No.' Betty interrupted me.

'He's being serious, aren't you Stan?'

'As always,' he grinned.

'Well why wouldn't it be right to harmonise with a positive person?'

'If you didn't want to,' he suggested.

'Oh.' I was taken aback. 'But we can't always do what we want to,' I objected.

'You see,' he explained, 'if you put the other person first because you are being unselfish, you might do what they want just because you think you should, but privately you don't want to. That would mean what?'

'That we were thinking negatively,' Betty supplied the answer.

'Precisely. So your action or decision would be based on a negative and that will not get you a positive outcome no matter how much you give in. If you don't say no when you want to you may feel resentment that your sacrifices go unnoticed, or develop a negative self image.'

'Why might you develop a negative self image?' I asked.

'*I* wouldn't.' He emphasised the I, grinning.

'Alright then why might *I* develop a negative self image?' I corrected.

'Because if you don't make your needs known then you would be ignored and might end up feeling that you didn't matter. Loss of identity equals loss of meaning and you could end up feeling very depressed, which isn't a very good basis for anything now is it?'

'No.' I had to admit, it explained a lot. I had forgotten to keep my notes and wrote hurriedly:

*Beware of harmonising
with the negative*

'You see wanting to keep the peace will not bring peace.'

'So what will?' Betty asked.

'Ah, good question Bett. Any ideas?'

'Following my feet.'

'Ah, you mean just doing it, and thinking about it afterwards?'

'Yes,' she agreed.

'OK, so let's look at that strategy. Do we think that just doing it will necessarily bring us a positive outcome?'

We were both silent.

He tried again to get a response from us.

'Well have either of you ever done that?'

'Yes,' Betty confessed. I merely nodded my affirmation.

'So you've both done it. What happened, were the outcomes positive or negative?'

'Sometimes one and sometimes the other,' I answered.

'Yes, the same for me,' Betty agreed.

'So, not a reliable way then of basing your actions, unless you are acting in Natural Time.'

'No,' we admitted. I made a note:

Just doing it is not a reliable method unless you are acting in Natural Time

'So what could we do when we're in a state of uncertainty and don't know what decision or action to take that would guarantee us a positive outcome?'

'Hand it up,' Betty replied promptly.

'Well done Bett, that's exactly what you need to do.'

'OK, so we hand up and then what?' I wanted to know. 'We still need to make a decision.'

'No. You hand up and the decision will be made for you. Of course if you need to take action then handing up is still essential before you use your will. Using your will can be a good basis for action providing it comes from a positive, resonant attitude, but using your will as a basis for action can be dangerous.'

'Why?' I enquired foolishly.

'Because you might just get your way,' he grinned at my bewilderment, and added, 'be careful what you want, you might just get it.'

I decided to make a note of that:

Using will as a basis for action
can be dangerous

Be careful what you want
you might just get it

'So what's the difference between using my will and handing up?' I wanted to know.

'Handing up is done by being in a state of resonance. A state of resonance can be obtained through meditation and/or prayer. Once you have attained this state you will know what action or decision to take. It is the only safe course of action when you are in a state of uncertainty.'

I wrote it down before we moved on. Stanley waited for me.

Handing up is the way to use Uncertainty

Handing up is done by being
in a state of resonance

This can be obtained through meditation
and/or prayer

'Right, so are we clear on the principle of Uncertainty, what it means when we are uncertain and what we can do about it? Abby, what is Uncertainty?'

I was ready for the question this time.

'It's a final warning that we have been thinking negatively and have created a negative time manifestation that is waiting to pounce on us if we don't do something.'

'Yes, I would say a negative charge that is waiting to earth. Now Betty, what is the something we should do in order to avoid manifesting the negative?'

'Hand up,' was her succinct reply.

'And how do we do this?' he wasn't going to let her get off so lightly.

'By finding the state of resonance.'

'Yes, and you know the next question we are going to ask you Abby, don't you?'

I noted the use of 'we' and acknowledged Ti Ming with a smile.

'How do we find the state of resonance?'

'Precisely. So enlighten us please,' he encouraged, waving his hand at me to continue.

'Through meditation and prayer.'

He gave a deep sigh and beamed at us.

'I think you've got it.'

He left nothing to chance however and decided to check our understanding with another question.

'What's the difference between resonance and using our will – Betty?' he pointed at her.

'God's will or ours,' she answered.

He frowned, still not happy. 'Hmm, try again please. I'm not saying it's wrong but it needs further clarification.'

Betty was never one to elaborate at length but she obliged.

'If we are in a state of resonance then there is no difference between our will and God's. God's will is the perfect win/win outcome for all concerned as only God has the God's eye view from the top of the mountain. From there all is known, the past, present and future consequences of our actions and those involved with us, but if we just use our own will we might be in resonance or we might not.

If we're not, we're at ground level and we can't see what's coming at us from the other side of the mountain, so we might manifest something that appears to be initially positive from where we are but may turn out to have negative consequences that we hadn't thought of because we don't have a God's eye view.'

'Thank you Betty. Well put. Now Abby, can you tell me why it might not be right to act in harmony with others?'

'Because we might be harmonising with the negative in ourselves or in others.'

'Very good and why might it be wrong to take decisions based on rational thought?'

'Because as Betty said, our minds don't have a God's eye view and we can be deceived.'

'But I thought you believed in the rational mind,' Betty sounded surprised.

'I do,' I agreed, 'but I can see the point that it's not the higher conscious and doesn't have all the facts, so it might make a decision that appears right based on the information available, but could turn out to be wrong in the light of further developments. It's rational to step aside and allow the professional to do the job. It would not be rational to insist on doing it yourself when you don't have the knowledge or expertise.'

Betty nodded, looking at me with some respect that I was willing to acknowledge a higher authority than my mind. I wrote as a reminder:

Don't rely on rational thought as our minds don't have a God's eye view

'What about asking for other people's opinions?' suggested Stanley.

'I do do that,' I admitted.

'And do you take their advice?'

'Rarely, but I do take what they say into consideration,' I added somewhat defensively.

'And you Betty, what do you do?'

'Well, I don't usually ask for other people's advice, but I do like to discuss the options with them.'

'So you are using them as a sounding board,' Stanley suggested.

'Yes, I suppose I am.'

'And is this a good basis for action?' he asked.

'Well, again, I suppose it will depend on where they're coming from,' she said.

'Will it?' he looked exaggeratedly puzzled. 'Why is that Bett?'

'Well, it will determine the advice they give.'

'But you said you didn't want their advice,' he objected.

She looked flustered. I was surprised. Betty didn't get flustered easily. Stanley just had a way about him that upset most people (in the nicest possible way) if they engaged with him.

'So what is it that they are doing for you?' he insisted.

She thought about the question, with a little frown.

'I suppose I'm using them as a mirror aren't I?'

He clapped silently.

'So they will just show me what I want to see and say what I want to hear.'

He nodded. 'Exactly, at least if you are positive they will, but if you are negative they will mirror the negative back to you. So as a help in taking the right action?'

'Useless,' she concluded.

'Mirrors can be useful if you recognise them as such,' he corrected, as they can clarify your thinking, and show you if you are being positive or negative, but yes they would be useless in giving the right action you should take.'

I wrote:

Asking other people's opinions is useless as a basis for action, because they are only a mirror of our own thoughts, but mirrors can clarify our thinking

'What about you Abby, if it feels right?'

I nodded and he cringed.

'Oh, no then,' I hastily corrected myself.

'Why not?'

'I've no idea,' I admitted carelessly. I was starting to think about food, it was past one fifteen and I was getting hungry.

He must have realised for he answered for me.

'This can be misleading as there could be subconscious negative attitudes influencing the feelings or past conditioning,' I wrote this down as he spoke:

Following our feelings can be misleading because we could be influenced by

(a) subconscious negative attitudes

(b) past conditioning

'Right. Got all that have we?' he peered down at my notes. 'Good, then I think you are now in a position to answer my original question, Uncertainty in Time, can it be Used?'

'Yes,' I answered immediately with some understanding and Betty confirmed.

'Yes,' she said.

He gave a bow. 'Then that, ladies, concludes the Uncertainty in Time workshop.

'Whew! They're quite intensive aren't they Stanley?' I said as I got up to get the lunch ready.

He smiled. 'We did warn you that six months would have been a more realistic timescale.'

'So what are we in for this afternoon?' Betty enquired.

'Ah well, this afternoon . . . are you sure you want to know?'

'Yes,' we both shouted together.

'OK then. This afternoon will be a fear encounter.'

I didn't like the sound of that at all.

'It just gets better, doesn't it?' I said.

He grinned. 'We aim to please.'

Chapter 16

Am I Controlled or Controller?

Day 5
Session 15

June joined us after lunch. She was wearing dark yellow trousers and a toning, pale lemon top which matched her blonde hair.

'It's my daffodil look,' she joked when we commented on how vibrant she was.

'I hope it's not going to be symbolic,' Betty remarked cryptically.

'What do you mean?' she asked.

'Well, Stanley tells us we're about to confront our fears.'

She still looked puzzled. 'So?'

'Yellow,' I interpreted.

She laughed suddenly. 'Oh I see. You think I might be a coward?'

'*I* wouldn't say so,' Betty emphasised.

'Do you think I'm a coward Stan?' she asked, looking slightly worried.

'The title of this workshop is, 'Am I Controlled or Controller?' Stanley smiled and bowed, deliberately ignoring the question, or maybe he hadn't heard it, as Ti Ming had now taken over.

I avoided her eyes as I didn't want to be drawn in. I wouldn't have classed June as a coward, she was far too impulsive for that, but the word made me uneasy as I wrote down the title:

Am I Controlled or Controller?

'What is the difference do you think?' he asked looking at each of us in turn.

'One is active and one is passive,' I answered.

'There's the dominated and dominator,' June replied.

'We are tools in the hand of God,' Betty said, 'we are being moulded. The Controller has achieved union with God and the Controlled hasn't.'

'Very good Betty,' Ti Ming approved. 'Now I have another question for you.'

She straightened as he addressed her specifically, listening attentively.

'What kind of orders would you be prepared to receive?'

'If I'm being employed to obey, then my employers,' she replied promptly, 'those which I'm capable of anyway.'

I wrote down the question.

What kind of orders would I be prepared to receive?

He watched me do it and waited to pounce.

'Abby?'

'Logical ones,' I was ready for him.

'And June?'

'Positive, intelligent ones,' June answered promptly.

'And what kind of orders would you give?' he addressed the question to Betty.

'Well, I hope I would give positive orders,' she replied.

What kind of orders would I give?

'Abby?'

'Necessary ones that would get the job done,' I answered.

'June?'

'Organising ones.'

'So would you all follow the kind of orders that you would give?' he clarified.

We nodded, wondering where this was leading.

'Another question. What kind of orders would you follow without question?'

'Without question?' Betty stopped to think about that one.

'Well I suppose it would depend on the person. Ones I agreed with I suppose. It would depend on whether it was coming from their ego.'

'How would you know that?' I asked, knowing I was interrupting, but genuinely wanting to know.

She glanced at me in surprise, as if it should have been obvious. 'Well, intuition of course. I always know if someone is coming from a clear space, or whether they are colouring what they are saying. I mean, sometimes you have to be careful what people are telling you to do, because they might have selfish motives.'

Stanley smiled.

'Indeed they might Bett, and June, what kind of orders would you follow without question?'

She sighed and thought about it before answering.

'Well, it's got to be orders in an emergency situation. I mean if there's a fire and someone yells, "Get the extinguisher!", you go, don't you? You wouldn't stop to question, or wonder where they were coming from. I think that's why the Army drill their soldiers and shout at them so much, because they have to be ready to follow orders without question in emergency situations.'

What kind of orders would I follow without question?

'OK,' Stanley nodded, 'and Abby?'

'As I said, I would follow logical ones.'

'So what kind of orders wouldn't you follow?'

'Well,' I answered, 'I wouldn't follow illogical ones, for instance, if someone said "pour petrol on the fire", then obviously I wouldn't,' I looked at Betty.

'I wouldn't follow orders coming from the ego,' she reiterated firmly.

'I bet that makes you popular with people,' Stanley grinned at her.

She smiled back conspiratorially.

174

'Well, they're not usually too pleased when I refuse to be drawn into their organising on my behalf. I usually say I'll check with upstairs and let you know.'

'Oh is that what you're doing?' I suddenly realised why Betty insisted on 'having it three times' before making any commitment to anything. It could sometimes be very frustrating when you wanted to know whether to include her in any arrangements.

She turned to me, as if she had read my thoughts.

'It's not necessarily that I'm checking their ego but I need to check my own, to see whether it's just me that wants to do something or whether the One wants me to.'

I was silent for a moment, while I considered her strategy. It had never occurred to me to check for ego.

'I just assume that if I want to do something then it's OK,' I said.

'Well you know what assuming does don't you?' Stanley enquired with a grin in my direction before focussing on June.

'June, what kind of orders wouldn't you follow?'

'Bossy ones,' she answered without hesitation.

'Right, so, last question, what kind of orders would you not give?'

'Well, isn't it the same as the ones I wouldn't tolerate?' Betty looked somewhat frustrated.

'Is it?' Stanley enquired, unrepentant.

'Yes,' she insisted. 'Ego based ones.'

What kind of orders wouldn't I follow?

'And mine is the same too, I wouldn't tolerate illogical orders.'

'Would you say they were the same?' Stanley asked.

'What, ego based ones and illogical ones?'

Stanley nodded.

I looked doubtful. 'I don't think so, because sometimes the ego can sound very logical.'

Betty added, 'By the same token, sometimes the One's orders can sound very illogical.'

'So you Abby, may find you are following the Ego's orders and ignoring the One's because you are following logic.'

'But surely the One isn't illogical?' I protested.

'No, but it may appear to be from our perspective,' Stanley marched a little before adding 'unless you consider you have a God's eye view of course,' he peered at me enquiringly.

I shook my head hurriedly and lowered my eyes.

'No of course not.'

'And Betty,' he added, just as she was looking pleased with herself, 'Ego based orders may also be correct. As June pointed out, in an emergency situation there may be no time to use your three times rule, and really does it matter? The ego is just as eager to survive as the higher part of you, and can give you good instructions that are worth following at times. It is best therefore to have no hard and fast rules about what you will and will not do.'

'So we should just decide in the moment?' June asked.

'Of course, there is only now, well done June,' June looked pleased, but suitably chastened. Betty and I sought refuge in our coffee mugs.

'What is the yardstick in our thinking by which we judge our orders, either given or received?' he asked.

'Awareness,' I answered.

'Good. What limits awareness?'

'Fear,' June answered.

'Pain,' Betty said.

'It is not pain itself that limits awareness, but the fear of pain is it not?'

Betty nodded. 'Yes, I suppose it is, I hadn't really thought about it before.'

'So,' he clapped his hands suddenly. 'I want you to do some writing.'

June and Betty looked startled, neither were keen on writing, they left that to me.

'Give them a sheet of paper each would you please Abby?'

I tore a few sheets off my pad to give them and handed out the pens. They eyed them somewhat suspiciously.

'Good. Consider now if you would, your fears. Make a list of them going down the page and number them please.

Then make three separate columns on the right hand side and label them Now, Past and Future. Now mark in each column whether you think the fear applies in the Past, Present or Future.

I wrote on the page:

What do I fear?

	Now	Past	Future
1. Lack of attention			
2. Lack of energy			
3. Negative thinking			
4. Being unable to accept total responsibility for me			
5. What other people think about me			
6. Others wellbeing			
7. Ignorance			
8. Being hurt			
9. Being thought stupid			
10. Frightening others			
11. Hurting others			
12. Ego			
13. Getting it wrong			
14. Being evil			
15. Karmic consequences			
16. Offending God			
17. Offending others			

	Now	*Past*	*Future*
18. *Making commitment*			
19. *Letting others down*			
20. *Surrender*			
21. *Unseen*			
22. *Destroying other peoples belief structures*			
23. *Aggression in others*			

Stanley watched while we all completed our sheets.

'OK. Next, add up how many of your future fears are manifesting now,' he instructed.

I did so and found five.

'Next, count how many past fears are manifesting now,' he waited while we did so.

'Now look at how many fears you have that you consider will be existing in the future.'

We completed this task while he marched up and down on the spot, watching us from his upside down viewpoint.

'OK. Now look at how many you have in all three columns.'

We counted up and when we had all finished the exercise we put our pens down and looked at him expectantly. He waited a few moments before continuing.

'Right. Now understand please that it is these fears which stop your energy and keep you in the conditioning of the past. It is these fears that are controlling your lives and subverting everything that you do.'

'So how can we break free?' June asked.

'I want each of you to look at the fears on your list and ask yourselves these questions.

If it's in the present, ask: Is this fear valid? If it's in the past, ask: Was this fear valid? If it's in the future ask: Will it be valid? Write yes or no in the appropriate columns.

I completed this task and then added to my notes:

Confronting our Fears

1. *If it's in the present, ask: Is this fear valid?*

2. *If it's in the past, ask: Was this fear valid?*

3. *If it's in the future ask: Will it be valid?*

4. *Write yes or no in the appropriate columns.*

'The fears that you have said are valid in the future are the fears you will need to confront in order to take control of your lives and remove the negative energy charges from the past.'

'How do we do that?' June wanted to know.

'We have covered the material in other workshops June. If you weren't present then I suggest you consult with the others at a later date. I'm sure Abby can provide you with copies of her notes.'

He looked at me and I nodded.

'Yes of course June. Which ones should I show her?' I wanted to know.

He sighed as if I shouldn't have needed to ask.

'Refer to Time Workshops Practical Time, Non-Practical Time and Natural Time. Use conscious will manifestations, regulators and passive pursuits to use up negative energy and change to positive, so that you can balance and surrender.'

'So, we should use the workshops we have done so far to eliminate our fears?' Betty suggested.

'It's a good idea wouldn't you say?' Stanley enquired, nodding at her eagerly.

'Remember, a fear that was valid in the past may not be valid today. We have hopefully grown as people in our understanding and maturity and that which we could not cope with in the past need hold no fears for us in the present. Any idea why not – June?'

'Because we have changed,' she answered.

'Yes, but in what way?' he wanted to know.

She looked worried, and didn't answer.

I came to her rescue.

'We have become more positive and have developed problem solving skills and coping strategies,' I answered promptly, looking somewhat smug. This was management speak with which I was familiar.

'OK. Oh, and that fear you have of offending God Abby, it's in the past, present and future is it not?'

He knew how to deflate my smugness, (or was it my ego)?

'Yes,' I reluctantly had to agree. So much for my trying to help June, the heat was on me now.

'Well, it is your duty to remove your fear of offending Him, as it is your fear of offending that He will find offensive. And your fear of letting others down.'

He looked down at my pad. 'This is karmic, do you now understand why others let you down?'

I nodded. 'Because I fear to let others down?'

'Yes, you must surrender and let go of your negative self image.'

'But that would trigger my fear of hurting others,' I protested.

'Let go and let God,' Betty suggested, 'God will act through you if you let Him and that will solve all your problems.'

'Yes, thanks Bett, but there's the problem of my fear of the unseen.'

'Use the knowledge of these workshops and change your viewpoint,' Stanley instructed.

'What's your other one?'

'Destroying other people's belief structures.'

'Ah, now that's a fear that comes from the ego. You are making a judgment about what you are saying being right or wrong. You need to let go and just allow. If you think it, follow through and say it and do it, trusting that you are being guided. After all, you don't know, maybe their belief structures need destroying, or yours do.'

'But that's not for me to do,' I protested.

'Quite right, it isn't,' he countered.

'But I don't understand,' I protested, 'you just said . . .'

'He means let God do it through you,' Betty said.

'Oh,' that shut me up.

'But how will I know when it is God doing it through me, or just me?' I needed to clarify this point as it was crucial to my understanding.

'You must trust,' it was Betty who answered me again.

'But what if I get it wrong?' I protested.

'Oh, you'll know soon enough by the consequences,' she assured me.

Ti Ming interrupted her at this point.

'Actually, you can't get it wrong. It's only by doing that you will learn.'

He studied my mournful face and laughed.

'It's fun,' he insisted.

I was not convinced. He clapped his hands together.

'Anybody else want to share?' he smiled encouragingly at June.

'I have a fear of pain,' June admitted.

'Past, present and future?' he enquired.

She nodded.

'OK. Are you in pain now?'

She shook her head.

'Right, so you can eliminate that fear, because it's not reality. You don't need to fear pain in the past because it's gone, – unless you like to relive it in your memory. Do you?' He asked as if he already knew the answer.

She shook her head hurriedly. 'No of course not.'

I suspected from her sudden flush that maybe she was guilty of this.

'The only fear of pain in the future is one of imagination, because we have not yet arrived in the future, and you can only experience sensations in the present. You have said that you have no pain in the present, so as long as that continues to be the case then pain is not an issue – is it?'

I could see June wanted to argue and yes, but. Worrying about pain was obviously important to her.

'Do you want to be controlled by this pain issue June?' he asked directly.

She shook her head once more. 'No, of course I don't.'

'So let it go.'

'Is it really that easy?' she looked dubious.

'It's really that easy,' he held her gaze for a long moment,

She sighed heavily, I could see her relax and then she smiled.

'Maybe it is,' she murmured.

'Bett?'

'I will take mine into the silence and meditate,' she answered quickly.

Hmm, I thought privately, perhaps Betty should have been wearing yellow as well. She obviously wasn't willing to just let go, but why would anyone want to hold onto pain? The thought immediately came to me 'Why would anyone want to hold onto fear?' I couldn't be sure that it was Stanley who had sent me the thought, but it seemed pretty likely. I fixed him with my scrutiny, but he merely smiled innocently back at me.

'Now are we all clear that holding onto a negative thought process is not a good idea, whether it is in the present, a memory from the past, or a projection into the future from our memory? Remember the Future Time workshop, we are creating our own future in the present, so to imagine pain for ourselves in the future will ensure that it will be there. To deny that we are creating our own future is not to take responsibility for our own energy.'

He gave a little bow. 'And that ladies, concludes the Am I Controlled or Controller workshop.'

There was a pause as we all looked at each other, feeling rather stunned. I wrote down:

To imagine pain for ourselves in the future will ensure that it will be there

To deny that we are creating our own future is not to take responsibility for our own energy

'Well thank you for that Stanley,' Betty acknowledged him. 'You've certainly given us a lot to think about,' Betty spoke for us all.

He smiled. 'I hope it's all positive.'

'Would it dare be anything else?' she countered.

'Are all the workshops you do as intensive as this?' June enquired.

'Pretty much,' I answered.

'Then I have to say I'm glad I only attend the one, I don't think I could cope with all of them,' she said as she rummaged in her bag for her car keys.

'Which is why you don't,' Stanley held out her jacket, 'we all have as much as we can cope with and no more.'

I hoped he was right about that. There have been times when I have doubted it, when problems have threatened to overwhelm me.

It was a lovely evening, although the wind made it chilly and when he suggested a walk after we had waved Betty and June goodbye I agreed.

'Just let me go back for my jacket.'

I was glad to earth the energy, my mind was racing and I needed time to assimilate all the new information I had taken on board that day.

'Are you enjoying it so far?' he enquired as we walked through the gate out of the campsite and up the hill to the site of the ancient church.

'I'm not sure enjoying is quite the right word,' I said, puffing slightly through the exertion of struggling uphill.

'You mean you're not enjoying it?' he made an exaggerated gesture of misery, hanging his head down on his chest.

'No it's not that, it's just that the word enjoyment makes me think more of entertainment, like TV or the cinema and the workshops are so much more than that. Yes, they're fun, but also challenging. They involve us too, we're not just the audience, or the spectator, and they change us, we're not the same afterwards.'

'Change you for the better I hope.'

'Yes of course,' I stopped to catch my breath and turned to look at him. 'You weren't having any doubts surely? I mean, that would be thinking negatively wouldn't it?'

'Of course it would and of course I wasn't. I mean, would I?'

He grinned at me and we carried on walking in silence.

Chapter 17

Time Motion

Day 6
Session 16

Thursday morning brought another sunny day. I was up before Stanley and thought I would take a walk up to the site on my own before breakfast. I fancied I was becoming athletic and made the site without stopping this time and carried on past it to the brow of the hill. There was a beautiful view from the top, I could see the caravan park with the hills of Welsh moor beyond and the marshes of Llanrhidian and the sea on the other side. The air was fresh up here and a bracing wind blew on my face. Once I had my breath back I started to feel chilly and hungry and the thought of the caravan and breakfast called me back.

As I unlatched the gate into the campsite I could see Stanley leaning against my car, breakfasting al fresco with a cigarette in one hand and a mug of tea in the other. I waved and received a nod of his head in reply. I hurried inside to make my breakfast and he remained where he was until Betty arrived 20 minutes later.

She filled the tiny space with her presence, although she didn't say much more than Hello, as instructed. She hugged us both and divested herself of a blue woollen cape and orange scarf, then squeezed in beside me on the little bench seat in the dining area. Stanley watched in silence until we had settled ourselves.

'Good morning ladies,' he began with a bow as if we were strangers. Ti Ming loved to be formal.

'Todays workshop is entitled 'Time Motion.'

I wrote the heading on my notepad, which I had placed in readiness.

Time Motion

'Now what would you suppose this workshop is about?' he asked.

I stared at the title on my pad without any clue at all.

'Energy?' Betty suggested.

'Excellent,' he beamed at her. 'You're on top form today aren't you Bett.'

I felt a little surge of annoyance flare in me at the praise and then quickly dispelled it, recognising the child mode with some amusement. How quickly it was ready to respond, a left over from my school days, but now I had the tools to recognise it and dispel it as inappropriate. I was not about to allow the Past to affect the Present and hey, now I was the Controller and not the Controlled. Pleasure replaced the annoyance as I realised I was using the workshops to consciously change my reactions.

'What kind of energy would you say Abby?'

'Unbalanced energy?' I guessed quickly, from looking at the title in front of me.

'Hmmm,' was the only reply I received, and I realised that he knew I was not concentrating.

'Now this workshop will enable you to identify the positive and negative energies around you.'

'Interesting,' Betty commented.

'And useful,' I added.

'But are we talking about places or people?' Betty wanted to know.

'A good question Bett. There is a distinction. Today we are considering the negative energies of other people that we encounter, their effect on us and what we can do about it. Now can you tell me if you have ever felt a draining effect by being in someone's company?'

'Well yes, I definitely have,' Betty said. 'It happens to me quite a lot. In fact, sometimes it's so bad that I get a migraine that knocks me out for a couple of days.'

'Oh is that what it is Bett?' I said excitedly as the light dawned. 'I hadn't connected the headaches I get with being drained by other people.'

'So you would both agree that others can have a draining effect on you?'

'Yes,' we both acknowledged.

'So what do you do about it?' he enquired.

'Well, I usually surround myself in white light,' Betty said, 'and sometimes I hold a crystal for protection, or to recharge myself.'

So that explained why Betty had such a collection of crystals. I had thought they were only ornaments.

'Surrounding yourself in white light is not a very good idea Bett.'

'Isn't it?' she looked surprised.

'Why not?'

'Because if someone is draining you they will be taking the Light from around you and leaving you with your negative. You would be better surrounding yourself with black clouds and keep the sunlight within, then they can drain off the black clouds and leave you with your positive.'

'Oh. I see.'

'And also it's a beacon.'

'What do you mean a beacon?'

'Well, a Light in the darkness. Anyone can see it for miles around and will head straight for you.'

'But isn't that a good thing?' she asked.

'It depends. Do you really want all those in darkness to surround you?'

'No,' she said thoughtfully. 'Thank you Stanley, that explains a lot.'

'Abby what do you do?' he asked me.

I felt rather foolish as I admitted. 'I don't do anything. I didn't realise any of this. I only knew that sometimes I felt terrible after seeing someone, or talking to them on the phone.'

'But you remember to close down afterwards?' Stanley asked me with an enquiring smile, knowing very well that I didn't.

'I didn't know I was supposed to,' I said in my defence.

'Always cut the link when you have been interacting with someone,' he said. 'Whoever they are, positive or negative, as you need to rebalance.'

Always cut the link
after you have finished interacting with someone

Remember to rebalance your energy

'I always do that,' Betty remarked, pleased with herself.

'Do you?' I said. 'I didn't know that, do you do it when I have been round?'

'Well yes of course, I do it with everyone,' she seemed surprised that I didn't know.

I felt vaguely upset that she did it after seeing me, as if it made me unclean in some way.

'It's just a way of rebalancing your energy,' Stanley explained, attempting to soothe my unexpressed concern.

'You always need to do it to realign yourself, ready for the next interaction, otherwise you are mixing energies and everything can get very muddy.'

His explanation made me feel better, I could see the need for recentering after an interaction with someone.

'But how do you do it?' I wanted to know.

'Abby really, day six and you still don't know,' To my surprise Betty admonished me before Stanley could say anything.

'Remember regulators?' Stanley asked, giving me a clue.

I looked vague. I could remember the word, but not what it was or what to do.

'Was it something to do with cushions and pens?' I asked.

'Try looking at your notes for day two, the Non-Practical Time workshop,' he hinted.

'Not now,' he chided, as I was about to flip back through my pad.

'There's also running round the caravan,' he suggested wickedly, laughing at our worried faces. 'That's always a good way to rebalance your energy wouldn't you say?'

'Yes,' I agreed and hurriedly added, 'but I don't feel drained at the moment, in fact I feel very balanced, don't you Betty?'

'Oh, extremely balanced,' she agreed.

He laughed again.

'OK relax, I know you've had your walk for this morning Abby, and we're not about to drain you here. But remember, you should always close after an energy interaction with someone.'

'I always clap my hands and shake off the energy,' Betty said.

I looked at her in surprise. It had never occurred to me to do anything like that.

Clap your hands and shake off the energy to close

'Very good Bett. So you've told me some of the things you can do to cut the energy and to rebalance after you've been drained, but what do you do to stop someone from draining you in the first place?'

'Well I didn't know you could stop them,' Betty said. 'I've always just put up with it, but I'd certainly be very interested to know how to stop them.'

Stanley looked at me. 'There's no point in asking you is there, as you didn't know you were being drained.'

'No,' I agreed humbly.

He continued briskly.

'Well you can be drained physically or mentally, emotionally or spiritually. All of them are energy resources that can be drained by others either consciously or unconsciously.

For instance, physical draining is done by people touching you on your right side, which is the side you give out energy. You take in with the left and give out with the right.'

You take in energy with your left hand
You give out energy with your right hand

'Is that why we shake hands with our right hand?' I interrupted excitedly.

'Yes,' he agreed. 'It's so you can sense each other's energy.'

'I always thought it was because that was your gun hand, and you were showing that you didn't have a weapon,' Betty said.

He laughed. 'Well maybe so Bett in the Wild West, but we don't need to do that now do we? In any case you could show you are defenceless without touching each other. You touch hands so that you make an energy connection when you meet a stranger for the first time.'

'Oh I see,' she said thoughtfully.

'But doesn't that drain you?' I asked.

'No, because you are both using your right hands,' he said, 'but if someone took your right hand in their left, then they would be draining you. Could you both stand up. Come over here.'

He indicated the living room area on the other side of the table where there was more room.

'OK, now Bett, hold out your right hand as if you were going to shake hands with me,' she did so and Stanley took hold of her hand in his left, putting his right hand around her shoulders in a seemingly friendly hug.

'Hello Bett, lovely to see you, how are you?' he released her.

'Now you Abby,' I held out my hand and he did the same with me. It felt quite natural and I would not have been at all suspicious.

'OK, here's another way,' he linked his left arm through my right and walked me around the caravan.

'Now let me take you over here, I just want to show you something,' he walked me to the kitchen.

'What?' I asked innocently, half expecting him to point out something. He released me and laughed. 'You see how easily it's done?'

'You mean you were draining me?' I asked ingenuously.

'If I had kept it up, yes,' he agreed.

'Now how would you counteract these moves to stop yourself from being drained?'

'I could just push you away,' Betty replied.

'You could, but it wouldn't be very friendly would it?'

'You could shout at them or just tell them to stop,' I suggested.

'You could, but remembering that much of what they do is subconscious, they wouldn't know what you were talking about, and they'd be very upset if you suddenly shouted at them for no reason they could see. They'd either be offended or think you'd gone mad, and they would deny they were doing any such thing.'

'You mean they're not aware of what they're doing?' I asked incredulously.

'Mostly not,' he agreed. 'And if you pushed them off, would it be a positive reaction or a negative on your part?'

'Negative,' Betty admitted.

'Correct. Understandable perhaps, but negative all the same.

'So what can we do?' I wanted to know.

'Well, as always we can choose to react negatively, positively or naturally in any situation. As we have said, the negative reaction is to recognise what they are doing and respond with a flash of anger and either shout at them or push them off. The positive response – any ideas either of you?'

'Take counter measures?' Betty suggested.

Take counter measures
if being drained

Stanley watched me write it down.

'Yes. Very good, any idea of what counter measures?'

We were both silent at that point.

'Shake them off and grab them?' I suggested eventually.

He shook his head.

'OK, let's do it again. Abby, try to take my hand in your left and put your arm around me, like I did with you,' He extended his right hand in greeting towards me.

'Nice to see you again.'

'You too,' I countered and advanced taking his right hand in my left, but as I attempted to put my arm around his shoulders he twisted away from me and placed his left hand over my right.

'And how are you keeping?' he enquired, smiling as he executed the manoeuvre.

He broke away from me. 'Were you offended by what I just did?' he enquired.

'No,' I had to admit. 'I don't think I would have noticed anything unusual if I hadn't been deliberately trying to manipulate you.'

'And if you had?' Betty wanted to know.

'If I had been trying to drain you I wouldn't have succeeded and I would know that you were on to me so I wouldn't try it again,' I said.

'So, mission accomplished,' Stanley said.

'Can I try that now?' Betty asked.

'Of course you can my darling.'

He extended his right hand to her and she took it with her left and attempted to put her arm around him, but as with me, he skilfully evaded her manoeuvre, sidestepping deftly to his left and placing his left arm around her shoulders.

'You see, you couldn't possibly be offended with me while I'm being so affectionate now could you?' With that he squeezed her to him in a hug.

'Look how friendly I am.' He released her and she shook herself suddenly as if to shake off his energy.

'I don't like this Stanley, it all feels very contrived,' she objected.

'OK, well take a seat again ladies and we will look at the natural ways of dealing with others who drain our energy.'

I eased myself back between the bench seat and the table and Betty arranged herself beside me as before.

'So what do we think the natural response would be?' Stanley enquired.

'Back off, make an excuse and leave?' I suggested.

'And how is that natural?' he cocked his head to one side, in an exaggerated gesture as if listening intently for my response.

'Well, you wouldn't want to be around people like that would you, so if you leave you won't have them in your space and you won't have to deal with them.'

'Interesting,' was his only answer. 'Bett, what do you think?'

'Look to see what it's showing me?'

He gave a mock clap. 'Well done. Yes indeed, the natural is always to acknowledge that we are the cause of all our experiences. So we would need to look at where we have drained them or someone else in the past.'

Look to see what it's showing you

'But I've never done that,' I objected as I wrote it down.

'Not knowingly,' he corrected.

'But that's ridiculous,' my voice rose as I became indignant.

'How can we be on the receiving end of something that we created entirely unknowingly.'

'The majority of the people on the planet are in exactly that situation,' he replied solemnly.

'We can only change things once we become conscious of what we are doing, otherwise, as you point out, we are at the mercy of our own subconscious creations.'

I was silent, thinking about what he had said.

I picked up my pen and wrote:

We are at the mercy of our own subconscious creations until we become conscious of them

'How will I know what I have created if it's subconscious?' I wanted to know.

'It's a good question. How will she know Bett?'

'By using the Natural Mirror,' she answered promptly, as if she had anticipated the question.

I frowned in puzzlement, trying to figure out how that might work.

Stanley as usual knew what I was thinking, or trying to think.

'Whenever somebody does something that annoys or puzzles you the first response should always be, what's it showing me about me, because other people are unconsciously mirroring us as we are unconsciously mirroring them.'

'But what if someone tries draining me and I've never met them before, how could I have drained them?'

'It doesn't have to be the same person,' Stanley explained. 'In fact it usually isn't, and it may not be at the same level.'

'What do you mean?' I asked.

'Well, maybe you don't drain people physically, but perhaps you might drain them mentally, emotionally or spiritually,' he suggested.

'Oh,' I was quiet then, considering.

'I know that I can get the bit between my teeth sometimes when I am talking about something that excites me, perhaps I bore people.'

'That wouldn't necessarily do it,' Stanley said, 'it would be the negative dumping you should look at, the moaning, blaming or criticising. Not that I'm suggesting that you do any of those,' he added hurriedly, with mock horror.

'Only that if you should happen to indulge in any of them, then it will come back to you in one form or another.'

'Oh I see,' I cringed inwardly because I knew very well that I often used Betty as a dumping ground for moaning about my life and I often criticised Stanley about his bad habits of smoking and eating junk food, the way he dressed, the way he patronised people and well, just about everything really.

Betty patted my arm comfortingly.

'Don't worry about it Abby.'

Don't worry. I was distraught. ·

'But I do, now I realise how much I have dumped on you in the past.'

'Well I didn't like to say, but I often get a headache after you've been round,' Betty admitted.

I felt even worse.

'Oh Betty I'm so sorry. I didn't realise. It's the last thing I would want to do to you, you're such a good friend to me.'

'Good, so now that's cleared up we can move on,' said Stanley briskly. He waited until I had made some notes.

Negative Dumping includes:

(a) Moaning
(b) Blaming
(c) Criticising

This drains others and will come back to you

'Other forms of draining include sympathy bids, or attempts to draw us into their negative reference frame.'

'How would giving someone sympathy drain us?' Betty asked.

'Because you have joined them in the illusion that they are victims in their life, rather than affirming the truth, that they are the Creators of their life,' he answered.

'Oh, I see. That's another reason then, why I get drained,' Betty said. 'I'm always being sympathetic to people.'

'Yes, you are too passive and allow yourself to be drawn into other people's reality, rather than remaining linked to upstairs. You are careful not to let your own ego dominate you but you allow other people's ego's to dictate to you and draw you into their reference frame. Refer to the Time Manifestation workshop.'

Betty looked at me and I nodded. Just as well I had taken notes or none of us would have remembered all of this.

'I'll let you have a copy when I've typed it up,' I said, and then wrote:

Giving sympathy can drain us
Resist the temptation and remain centred

'How would someone draw us into their negative reference frame?' I wanted to know.

'Well, they could tell us bad things about others, and try making us wary or suspicious of them. Negative people are always anxious to get others to join them in their negativity. You can always spot a negative person trying to draw physical energy, because they make exaggerated movements.'

'What kind of movements?' I was curious.

'Oh you'll know when you are looking for it. Often they stretch, yawn or sigh excessively.'

'Oh, that's why they do it,' I said, light suddenly dawning. 'I know a few people who are always doing that. It struck me as odd.'

'Oh do you?' said Stanley grimly. 'Well, from now on you can be aware of what is happening, can't you?'

'Yes,' I said gratefully. 'Thank you Stanley.'

'You're welcome,' he smiled, thanks from me was rare indeed.

'Stay awake and you will find that they always give themselves away. Right, so let us consider how to deal with specific people and situations. With a false jovial person for instance, close your energy field into your body and restrict their access to your aura by raising your hand to your head on the side nearest to them.'

'I hadn't realised a false jovial person was negative,' Betty remarked. 'I always thought they were just putting it on to try and be positive.'

'Oh no,' Stanley shook his head. 'They're a good example of thinking one thing and doing another.'

'I'd better look to see where I do that then,' Betty murmured, rather subdued.

'You're never falsely jovial,' I reassured her.

'Maybe not, but perhaps they are showing me that I think one thing and do another.'

Stanley ignored her, neither confirming nor denying.

'Now a depressed person. What will you do with them? Betty?'

He was obviously trying to keep her focussed in the present.

'Well, normally I would give them sympathy, but now I know not to do that, so I don't know.'

'Abby?'

I just shrugged by way of reply.

'OK, there are three things you can do. Firstly you can take them to a third person who will act as a neutral to you, or, if there are only the two of you, sit them down with a cup of tea and take over the conversation getting them to make yes statements.'

'But what if they burst into tears?' I asked, playing devil's advocate.

'Well let's try it shall we? Pretend to burst into tears.'

'Boo hoo,' I said unconvincingly.

'There now, don't you feel better now you've had a good cry? Would you like a tissue? It always makes you feel better to get it off your chest doesn't it? You see the kind of the thing, say whatever you can to get them to say yes to you. Saying yes changes their state.'

'Clever,' I remarked. I knew it was an NLP technique.

'Isn't it?' he agreed.

'Thirdly, accept that they are returning your own negative energy and mentally thank them while sending it up.'

Ways to deal with a depressed person:

(a) Take them to a third neutral party

(b) Make tea/coffee, chat and get them to say yes

(c) Mentally thank them and hand it up

'Got that?'

I nodded.

'Right then, what do you do if you are being drained?'

'Ask them to leave,' I suggested.

'We've already covered that one,' he said.

'Look at what it's showing you?' Betty said confidently.

'Well, yes, but that's only afterwards, what steps do you take at the time? Come on, what do they do?'

'Oh,' I said startled. 'Yawn, stretch and sigh. Make exaggerated movements.'

'Yes. Move. Change the energy. Block them. Turn it around, put your negativity on the outside, ask for help from upstairs and then Betty,' he smiled at her, 'when they've gone you can consider what it's showing you.'

What to do if you are being drained:

(a) Move
(b) Change the energy (regulators)
(c) Block them
(d) Ask for Help
(e) Rebalance
(f) Look at what it's showing you

'But suppose they don't want to leave?' I objected.

'Believe me, when they realise they can't get your positive energy they will want to leave, and especially if you succeed in blocking their negatives. In fact it will surprise you just how quickly they will go.'

'It's horrible,' I said. 'It sounds like vampires, they are only coming to feed off us.'

'Yes you could say that, it's exactly what they are, energy vampires,' Stanley agreed. 'Only remember, until we are conscious of what we are doing, we can't choose to stop.'

I shuddered involuntarily as I wrote:

Beware the energy vampires

'So what do we do about group draining?' was his next question.

'Group draining?' I was startled.

'Yes, it can happen, especially if you are giving a talk or in charge of a group, and if that happens it will ruin the dynamic. You need to know how to manage a group's energies. Any ideas?'

'Stay centred,' Betty contributed immediately.

'Yes, indeed, a good idea if you can manage it, and take precautions from the start, but if you don't realise it and find your energy is going, you may not have sufficient strength to rebalance.'

'So what do we do?' I asked exasperatedly as he stayed silent.

'I thought you'd never ask,' he grinned.

'Well, it's easy to spot them, they are needing energy so they play games. It might be the Drama Queen, who wants all the attention of the group or the Life and Soul of the Party type, always telling jokes and diverting the focus back to them. Others may make sarcastic comments in an attempt to wind people up.'

'But surely they will only succeed in annoying everyone,' I said.

'Correct, but the energy vampires are quite happy to drain your negative energy as well as your positive. To them it's all energy. As long as they get your attention they're happy, attention equals energy.'

'So that's why children will play up if they can't get your attention any other way,' Betty remarked. 'And that's why it makes us so angry, because we know subconsciously they are draining us.'

'Yes,' Stanley agreed.

'Other ways to spot an energy vampire, they may draw attention to themselves by playing the deep and mysterious type and refusing to join in with anything. They are wanting you or the others to cajole and coax them and give them your energy that way. On the other hand they may be giving you energy if they are a wizard.'

'Why would they do that?'

'To take you into Natural Time.'

'This is all very depressing stuff Stanley,' Betty remarked. 'I never realised that all this was going on.

'That's the problem not realising,' he agreed.

'So how do we deal with it?' I asked

'Be aware of what is going on and hand the situation up and ask for the negative energy to be transmuted to the positive which can be used, while taking intuitive action – make them move or use a regulator.'

He marched on the spot for a moment looking at us.

'Time for a run round the caravan I think. And that ladies, concludes the Time Motion workshop. I thank you.' He gave his usual closing bow. 'Now up with you.'

'Let me just write this down,' I pleaded, and he granted me a concession until I had finished.

Group Draining includes:

(a) Be aware of what is happening

(b) Use a regulator

(c) Move (get them to move)

(d) Hand the situation up and ask for the negative energy to be transmuted

'Right finished?' he enquired, watching me and amid protestations, he herded us out into the sunshine. We had to admit that after a few laps we felt better.

'There we are,' he said as we sat down afterwards with a well deserved coffee and biscuit, 'I told you it was fun.'

Chapter 18

The Natural Mirror

Day 6
Session 17

I was still slightly dazed after the last session. To think that there was so much going on outside of my awareness came as a shock to me, even though I had experienced the effects of being drained by others and had complained about it, but to have it confirmed made it feel more real. Of course I realised it would feel more real, now it was in my conscious awareness.

I wondered what the next session would bring and was half dreading it.

As usual he answered my unspoken thought.

'Ah, next we will be joining Alice in the Looking Glass,' he answered somewhat mysteriously,

'What do you mean by that?' I enquired suspiciously, but he wouldn't be drawn any further.

'Well I must say you're in top form today Stanley,' Betty remarked. She sounded more amused than worried which reassured me. Betty was my rock. If we were going on a journey through the looking glass, there was no one I would rather have by my side.

Stanley watched as we settled ourselves.

'Good morning,' he greeted us formally with a little bow as if he hadn't seen us before. Ti Ming had arrived.

'Now it's time for an investigation of the Mirror.'

We waited and looked around for a mirror. There wasn't one in the caravan's living space, only in the bathroom and bedroom. He watched us, waiting for our understanding. When none came he informed us with a slight smile playing around the corners of his mouth.

'That is the title of this workshop, the Natural Mirror.'

'Oh I see,' I said, feeling mystified and not seeing at all, but I dutifully wrote down:

'I want you to tell me about one day last week,' he requested
'Which day?' I asked.
'Any day will do, perhaps we'll say last Wednesday.'
I had to think. Last Wednesday. I was at work.
'I want to know what things went wrong and what you did about them.'
'We've done this before,' I objected.
'Yes, I know we've looked at problems before,' Stanley agreed, 'but this is in a different way.'
'I can't think of anything,' I said unhelpfully.
'My washing line broke,' Betty volunteered. 'I had towels and sheets to put out and it just decided to collapse under the weight.'
'Oh no,' I sympathised. 'Did you manage to stop them falling on the ground and getting dirty again?'
'Fortunately yes.'
'Oh that was something anyway.'
'Ahem,' Stanley interrupted.
'So what were your first thoughts Betty when this happened?' he asked.
She winced. 'Negative I'm afraid. Something like, Oh no, now what am I going to do?'
'And what did you do?' he asked.
'I brought them all in and dried them on the clothes horse in the kitchen,' she said. 'But it was horrible, having wet sheets all over the place and getting in the way of everyone.'
'Did you stop to consider at all why this might have happened?'
'Well, I realised that the load was too heavy for the line.'
'The load was too heavy,' he repeated thoughtfully.
'Oh I see,' Betty stopped.
'What do you see?' I asked, looking from one to the other of them.
'Well, the load was too heavy,' she repeated.
'Yes, I heard that – so?'
'So he means that the load I am carrying is too heavy, don't you Stanley?' she looked up at him quickly to check that she was right.
He smiled and nodded.
'Yes Bett, you are right. The line breaking was a warning to you that you are trying to take on too much and something will have to give if you carry on the way you have been.'

'Oh I see, you're interpreting events in a symbolic way aren't you?' I said, light dawning as I listened to them, 'but maybe it was just an old line that was going to break anyway, why does it have to be a warning?'

'Because it broke then,' Betty answered mysteriously.

I still didn't get it. 'What do you mean, it broke then? So? If it was getting worn it would have broken at some time wouldn't it?'

'Well, yes it was an old line, and yes, it had to break sometime, but the point is that it chose to break at that particular moment when I was overloading it is significant.'

'But why is it?' I objected. 'It's obviously going to break when it's overloaded. It's not going to break if there's only one sock on it is it?'

Stanley laughed. 'You never know, one sock might be enough to sock it to you.'

Betty joined in his laughter and I felt very much left out.

I put my pen down and considered what they were saying.

'OK let me get this straight. Stanley are you seriously saying that Betty's washing line broke at that precise moment in order to warn her to take things easy?'

'I am,' he confirmed.

'And he's right,' Betty agreed. 'I saw the Doctor the next day and he said I was overdoing it because my blood pressure has gone sky high and he started me on medication.'

'Oh,' I was startled.

'You see,' Stanley remarked. 'A warning.'

That was certainly something to think about, although I still couldn't see how it worked. How did the washing line know Betty had high blood pressure? I didn't dare ask and risk being ridiculed.

Stanley allowed me a few minutes silence before asking,

'Have you had time yet to think what went wrong for you Abby?'

I sighed, remembering. 'Well nothing dramatic, my son forgot to feed Heidi that's all and she kept pestering me for food which I thought she'd had, so I shouted at her.'

'OK, and what did you do as regards your son?'

'I shouted at him as well.'

'I see, and then what happened?' he asked, an amused smirk appearing at the corners of his mouth.

'My daughter shouted at me for shouting at him,' I replied.

'So what did you do then?' Betty was curious now.

'I shouted at her for shouting at me.'

'Oh, so fun was had by all,' Stanley grinned.

'Sounds like a typical morning in my house,' Betty sympathised. 'It's all very well for you Stanley, but you don't have children.'

'Now there's an assumption Bett.'

She coloured, embarrassed. Stanley was a single man.

'Oh, well, I mean, I didn't think you had any children Stanley.'

'You kept that quiet,' I remarked.

'Actually, I have very many children,' he smiled at our shocked faces. 'They are all my spiritual children.'

We relaxed, smiling at his attempt to wind us up, and realising he had succeeded.

'So these two examples you have provided, give us an opportunity to respond in any of three ways, as all events do. Negatively, Positively or Naturally. Betty, you have said you chose the negative reaction when your washing line broke, can you tell us what would have been the positive reaction?'

'Well, to have brought them in cheerfully without moaning to myself I suppose,' she answered.

'OK, and the Natural?'

'What you said about showing me the overload.'

'Right,' he agreed. 'Good. Abby, what about you, and your responses?'

'Well, I was being negative wasn't I?'

'I think so,' he agreed. 'It sounded like a lot of shouting. What other action could you have taken when you found out that your son had forgotten to feed the dog?'

'Asked him again.'

'Without shouting at him,' Betty reminded me.

'Who, her son or the dog?' Stanley asked laughing. 'Come on tell us, which one did you shout at Abby?'

As if he didn't know. 'Both,' I admitted shamefaced.

'Oh yes, and your daughter. So can you tell us please what would have been the positive way of dealing with the situation?'

'I could have reminded my son to feed the dog without shouting at him,' I suggested.

'You could indeed, and what would you have been thinking while you were reminding him?' he enquired peering at me suspiciously.

I felt cornered.

'If I was really honest I suppose I would still have been thinking things,' I admitted.

'What kind of things?' Stanley had no intention of letting me get away with anything.

I answered him somewhat reluctantly,

'Oh something like, why can't he do anything I ask without having to be told a dozen times.'

'And this is *positive*?' Stanley asked with exaggerated emphasis.

'Oh. So you mean I've not only got to *act* positive, I've got to *think* positive as well?' I wanted clarification on this point.

'Oh it's even worse than that,' he lowered his voice to a whisper and leaned over the table to put his mouth near my ear and muttered in a phony conspiratorial voice.

'You've also got to *feel* positive.'

My face must have been a picture, because both he and Betty burst out laughing at the same time. I wrote it down while protesting.

Remember to think, feel and act positive in all situations

'It's all very well laughing, but how am I going to manage to do all that?'

'By remembering not to shoot the messenger,' Betty replied.

'What do you mean Betty?'

'Well have you ever forgotten to do something?' she asked.

'All the time.'

'Well there you are then, don't blame your son when he does it, he's only enabling you to be on the receiving end of your own actions.'

'And the natural response?' Stanley cut in quickly before I could think of an answer.

There was a pause while Betty and Stanley both waited for me to answer.

'Look at what it's showing me?' I ventured. To my surprise Stanley agreed.

'Yes, that's always a good thing to do.'

'But isn't that what I just said? It's about forgetting something isn't it?' Betty protested.

'Well there's looking at forgetting yes, but there's something else as well isn't there?'

'Is there?'

'Who fed the dog?' Stanley generously gave us a clue.

'My son did. Oh I see. I could have fed the dog myself, you mean?' Stanley gave a mock clap.

'You could indeed.'

'But wasn't it her son's responsibility?' Betty enquired. 'After all, if Abby always feeds the dog, then how will her son ever learn to take responsibility and do the chores assigned to him?'

Stanley was silent and marched up and down on the spot, waiting for us to find our own answer.

We watched him, wondering what we had missed.

'Oh,' Betty gave an exclamation. She must have seen it, for she looked quickly at me and then folded her arms, looking at Stanley and waiting for me to catch on.

'What?' I looked from one to the other of them in exasperation.

I knew they were waiting for me to see something, but I didn't know what.

'I need to take responsibility for the chores assigned to me?' I hazarded a guess.

'That is correct, you do, but which chores specifically?' Stanley asked gently. I felt as if I were blindfold, being led along a path. As long as it wasn't up the garden path I thought, and then immediately chastised myself for thinking negatively.

'I don't know. I have so many. Household chores?'

'What about feeding the hungry?' Stanley asked, realising I had lost the plot.

'My children never go hungry,' I felt offended by his remark.

'No, not that kind of hungry,' Betty intervened quickly, obviously deciding to interpret on Stanley's behalf lest I attack him. 'He means spiritual hunger Abby.'

'Not spiritual Bett,' Stanley contradicted her.

'Oh,' I looked from one to the other, I still didn't understand.

Stanley took over from Betty. They had joined forces and were running a double act.

'Your son was showing you that you are forgetting to feed your animal nature.'

'How do you arrive at that conclusion?' Betty asked rather sharply.

'It was an animal he forgot to feed was it not?'

'Oh I see,' she said.

'But what do you mean by my animal nature?' I enquired.

He raised his eyebrows at me and gave me a suggestive wink.

'Oh you know, your animal passions.'

'Oh I see,' I coloured in embarrasment, my private life was of no concern to them. How did we get here I wondered.

'So are you saying that just because I'm not in a relationship at the moment my son is justified in forgetting to feed the dog?'

I was somewhat incredulous.

'Well yes. It's an example of the Natural Mirror in operation. It's exactly what is happening around us all the time only we are not aware of it. This world is a mirror of the other worlds around us.'

'What other worlds?' I wanted to know.

'What indeed? It's a good question. Bett, can you tell Abby?'

'Well, there's the Spiritual world, the Intellectual world, the Emotional world and the Physical world,' she informed me.

'Thank you Bett,' Stanley looked satisfied and seemed to think that was all the information I needed.

'So what's the animal nature? In which world?'

'In the Physical world I should imagine,' Betty replied, looking somewhat embarrassed. She didn't agree with sexual relationships, despite being married and having six children, (or perhaps it was because she'd had six children) she often insisted that people should keep their energy above the throat centre and abstain from sex altogether, relating only on the higher levels.

'So you are saying that Betty's washing line broke to demonstrate to her that her blood pressure was too high and my son forgot to feed the dog because he was demonstrating to me that I am forgetting to feed my animal nature?'

'Well, yes, but it's not so much a demonstration as a reflection.' Stanley corrected.

'What's the difference?' I asked, now completely confused.

'Well a demonstration is something that someone else shows you, whereas a reflection is merely a mirror image of yourself.'

'Well alright, I can just about see how my son might be a reflection of me, but how can Betty's washing line be a reflection of her? It's not even alive,' I protested.

They both laughed.

'Everything is a reflection of us,' he insisted, 'and everything is alive.'

'But does that mean that I'm a reflection of them?'

'Yes it does,' he nodded to emphasise the point.

I thought about it, my head spinning. I needed to recap.

'So in every situation, there are three possible reactions.'

'Go on,' he encouraged me.

'Positive, negative and natural.'

'Yes. Very good,' he clapped his hands in genuine pleasure that I had grasped the point. I wrote down:

In every situation, there are three possible reactions:

1. Positive

2. Negative

3. Natural

'I suppose there's more than three reactions really,' I reflected, 'but they could be categorised under those headings.'

'Yes that's right. You are using the Natural Mirror when you are looking at events and attempting to see what they are reflecting back to you.'

The Natural Mirror uses events to reflect yourself back to you Or uses you to reflect events back to others

'How do I know if I'm being used to reflect back to others?' I wanted to know.

'Oh, you'll soon know, because they'll blame you or criticise you for something that you know wasn't your fault.'

Stanley laughed, although I didn't really see the funny side of it.

Looking at my face, he changed the subject abruptly.

'Remember there are four worlds,' he recapped for us.

You can have positive, negative or natural reactions on the spiritual plane, which is our energy, the intellectual plane, which is our thoughts, the emotional plane, which is our feelings and the physical plane which is our actions. So we always need to be aware of our energy, our thinking, our feelings and our actions as well as those of the people around us and look at what they're showing us.'

'In every situation?' I was incredulous.

'In every situation,' Stanley confirmed. 'That should keep you on your toes.'

'It certainly will,' Betty agreed.

I wrote the four worlds down and considered what I wrote:

The spiritual plane is our energy

The intellectual plane is our thoughts

The emotional plane is our feelings

The physical plane is our actions

'But I still don't understand,' I protested, conscious that they were both looking at me. 'How does the Natural Mirror work? How did my son know he had to forget to feed the dog in order to show me that I wasn't feeding my animal nature?'

Betty laughed, Stanley shook his head.

'Yes well, it's a good question Bett.'

'I'm glad you're answering this and not me,' she giggled.

'Thanks,' he retorted playfully.

'So what's the answer?' I repeated impatiently, looking from one to the other.

Stanley took a deep breath before replying to me.

'The answer is he didn't.'

I was more puzzled than ever.

'But if he didn't know, why would he do it?'

'He did it unconsciously. People do things all the time in response to others learning needs or their own without being aware that they are doing so.'

I was amazed.

'So are you saying that I could be doing things in response to other people's learning needs and not know that I am doing it?'

Stanley nodded.

'Exactly. Fun isn't it?'

'Fun! I don't think I'd call it that.'

'Oh but you will once you get used to the idea. You just need to remember that the Natural Mirror comes straight from the unconscious but that it needs higher conscious awareness in order to read it.'

'So are all problems we encounter showing us something?' I wanted to know.'

Betty nodded and Stanley confirmed.

'In a word – yes.'

I wrote down on my pad as a reminder:

The Natural Mirror uses the unconscious mind of others

It needs our higher conscious awareness to read it

Remember:

All our problems are showing us something

Stanley hovered over me, watching while I wrote it down and then asked,

'Now are you both clear about the four worlds?'

Betty nodded. I felt like the backward child of the class.

'No,' I admitted.

He explained carefully.

'Well, whenever someone annoys you or ruffles your feathers in some way, there's something for you to see. Sometimes you may not be ruffled, it may just be that you wish to know the answer to a problem and the One will give it to you via the actions of those around you, if you will just pay attention.

'How will I recognise the answer?'

'Very often you won't. We miss answers all the time because we are just not aware that we can get one.'

'So how do we know?'

'By repetition,' Stanley laughed. 'Most of us miss it the first time around, but if something happens twice we start to notice and usually comment on it and by the third time something happens we are starting to think that something unusual is going on and start asking questions and mentioning it to our friends. Just remember there is no such thing as a co-incidence, so if something keeps on happening then look to see what it's showing you.'

Betty agreed. 'Our friends in spirit must get very frustrated when they can't get through to us.'

'Oh they'll get through to us eventually,' Stanley assured her. 'You see the mirror magnifies.'

'What do you mean?' I asked.

'Gets bigger,' he winked at me. 'The situation will get so ridiculous that we will wonder if we are going mad.'

'Is that to punish us because we're not seeing it?' Betty asked.

'Not at all. It's merely that we haven't earthed the negative charge, and like a rolling stone gathering moss, the situation will gather energy, and express in a more dramatic way.'

'Oh I see,' I was impressed with the explanation.

'I could have done with that information years ago Stanley.'

'You only had to ask,' he bowed slightly. 'We are always at your service.'

I wrote:

Repeated situations are indications of answers
Look to see what they're showing you
The mirror magnifies

'Remember also that the Natural Mirror speaks in symbols,' Stanley reminded me.

I was suddenly very excited remembering the first day that Betty gave me a lift home in her car. An incident that had puzzled me fell into place. I wanted to confirm with her that I had got it right.

'Betty, do you remember the first time you gave me a lift home and when you parked the car outside that lamp post you damaged the door trying to get out?'

She smiled. 'As if I could forget.'

'I was so shocked when you tried to close it and couldn't because it had buckled so much. All you said was – a door has been opened that will never close again.'

'That's right,' she nodded.

'I was upset because I knew it was Tony's car and he would be mad at you, but you weren't in the least bothered, and I couldn't understand your reaction at the time. But now I think I understand, you were reading the Natural Mirror weren't you?'

'I was,' she confirmed.

'And the door that had been opened and would never close again' – I hesitated before continuing, 'was that us?'

'It was,' she leaned over and gave me a hug.

Emotion welled in me, Betty was such a special person in my life and had taught me so much.

The Natural Mirror speaks in symbols

Stanley marched in front of me watching for a few moments before announcing, 'And that ladies, concludes the Natural Mirror workshop.' He gave his usual little bow, and then departed for a cigarette.

Instead of thinking negatively (as I usually did) that it was a bad habit for him to have, I reflected this time that he probably needed to go outside to earth the energy and regain his balance in order to keep the workshops on track. He returned smiling, without comment, and accepted the tea and sandwiches we offered.

Chapter 19

Time Energy

Day 6
Session 18

June arrived in time for the afternoon session, her usual cheerful self, which lifted my spirits. I wondered briefly if I was taking her energy and then snapped myself out of it. I had to trust myself and the higher consciousness that all was well, or I would go mad with self doubt.

'Have I missed anything?' she enquired.

'June you have no idea,' I replied.

It must have been a somewhat mournful response on my part, because both Betty and Stanley laughed.

She looked from one to the other in surprise.

'Well, obviously something's been going on.'

'Well I should hope so,' Stanley said briskly, cutting through her curiosity, 'and what's going on now June is the next workshop. There was a pause while he tuned in. Then he gave a bow. 'This workshop ladies is entitled Time Energy.'

I wrote it down, waiting for the explanation:

Time Energy

I should have known better.

'So what do we think this is ladies?' Ti Ming enquired with an encouraging smile.

'The energy generated by time?' June volunteered. She was fresh to the fray.

'It's a good answer June,' he approved.

'Anyone else?'

June looked pleased and settled back in her seat to wait for our offerings.

211

'The difference in energy created by the past, the present and the future?' I suggested cautiously.

'Thank you for that Abby. Again, a good answer. Betty?'

He swivelled his gaze to Betty and she shifted slightly in her seat as if she were uncomfortable.

'Balanced time?' she sounded unsure for once.

'Indeed it is, very good. Balanced time.' He smiled happily and surveyed us, marching for a moment on the spot.

'So, you all are right in your own way. Time energy is an energy created by time. It is also balanced time and the time generated by the past, the present and the future. In this workshop we are asking you to consider time as energy and to look at what kind of energy you are creating for yourselves in your life.'

I noted:

Time is Energy
What kind of energy are we creating in our lives?

'Do you mean positive, negative or balanced?' I enquired, looking up.

He smiled at me without answering and addressed the group as if I had not spoken.

'Let me ask you a question, do you use Thought in Time or Time in Thought?'

'What?' we asked in unison.

'Thought in Time or Time in Thought,' Betty repeated helpfully while I wrote it down:

Thought in Time or Time in Thought?

'What's the difference?' June had a habit of getting to the crux of the matter.

'Well, let's take them one at a time shall we?' Ti Ming smiled.

'What about Thought in Time?'

I looked at Betty. 'You go first,' I invited.

'Thanks, very generous of you,' she said grimacing.

'I suppose it's about taking your time to think things through,'

'June?' he questioned, without responding to Betty.

She looked flustered. 'Me? Oh well, I agree with Betty, it's thinking things through.'

'Abby?'

It was my turn to be in the spotlight.

I squirmed a bit and tapped my pen on the table. Regulating the energy, I told myself, but actually I was just buying time. Buying time, now there was an interesting expression.

'In your own time,' I jumped as Stanley's remark re-focussed my mind on the question.

'Well, I don't think I can add to Betty or June's definition. Thought in Time must be about thinking, but maybe it's about thinking about the past – more remembering perhaps?' I was pleased with my sudden flash of inspiration.

'Hmmm,' was all I got from Stanley. He obviously wasn't impressed.

'OK then ladies, now let us consider Time in Thought. What are your ideas about this?'

We all looked at one another hopefully.

'Is there a difference?' June enquired doubtfully.

Stanley smiled at her. 'Oh yes June, I can promise you there is a great deal of difference.'

'Well, if Thought in Time is thinking about the past, as I suggested, maybe Time in Thought is thinking about the present.' I offered.

Betty looked excited. 'Or the future,' she put in.

Stanley sighed. 'Ladies, we are getting somewhat carried away are we not?'

'Well you asked us,' June protested on our behalf.

'Stanley we don't know, we're just guessing,' I informed him, in case he didn't know.

He nodded. 'Yes, I had gathered that.'

'So why don't you just tell us?' I asked him totally exasperated.

He observed us for a moment, marching as he did so. He must have decided that we had tried our best, so he took pity on us.

'Alright then. Thought in Time is thinking and the reaction to the thought.'

'I said that.' Betty was triumphant.

'And me,' June chimed in, wanting to claim some of the glory.

'Not thinking in the past then?' I queried gloomily.

'In a way yes,' he answered, surprising me.

'That's just the point. But not remembering though.'

'I don't understand,' I said.

'Nor me,' said June.

'Well, it's in the present, but it's thinking about a course of action, what you are planning to do, whereas Time in Thought is about spontaneous action. You act first and think about it afterwards.'

'Oh I see,' Betty remarked slowly. 'You mean follow your feet?'

'Exactly,' Stanley looked pleased that she had understood him.

'So what's the problem with thinking about it first?' I wanted to know. 'You know what they say in Management?'

'No,' he said patiently, as if I were a child with an elephant joke, 'what do they say in Management?'

'If you fail to plan, you plan to fail.'

'Do they indeed?'

'Yes, they do,' I confirmed, pleased with myself. Let him get out of that one.

'And what does planning consist of?' he threw back at me.

'Having an outcome in mind and taking all the known factors into account to plot a course of action that will take you where you want to be, at the time you have set,' I was pleased with my definition.

'Ah, taking the known factors into account.'

'Well, yes, obviously, you couldn't take the unknown ones into account, could you, because you wouldn't know what they were.'

I knew he was trying to wriggle out of it, and I was determined I wasn't going to let him.

'I'm referring you to the Uncertainty in Time workshop where we considered the God's eye view from the top of the mountain. Do you remember what we said?'

'I wasn't there, so I don't,' June reminded us.

'We said that the rational mind wasn't in possession of all the facts, June, and so it is better to let go and let God,' Betty informed her much to my chagrin.

Teach me to think I could get the better of Ti Ming.

'Do you now understand why direct action is better than thought?' Ti Ming asked me gently.

I nodded. 'Because the higher conscious is in possession of all the facts, and ego consiousness isn't.'

He, and/or Stanley smiled in agreement and clarified.

'It's not that there has been a failure to plan, but rather that the plans have already been made at a higher level.'

He surveyed us (probably sampling our energy) I thought.

'Now are we all clear on this – June?' he enquired.

She looked doubtful. 'I think so. Thought in Time is thinking and planning what to do before you do it, and Time in Thought is acting first and thinking about it afterwards?'

'Wonderful. I think she's got it. Everyone else clear?'

We nodded.

'Thank you June,' I said, 'you put that really well. I'm going to write it down.'

She looked pleased as she watched me writing:

Thought in Time is
Thinking and planning what to do
before you do it

Time in Thought is
Acting first and thinking about it afterwards

Stanley waited until I had finished.

'OK then, next question, what is Word in Time?'

'Thinking about what you're going to say before you say it?' I answered quick as a flash.

He grinned at me. 'Well done Abby. Not right, but well done. Anyone else?'

I was disappointed. I was sure I had been on the right tack.

Betty looked amused, but didn't say anything.

June fiddled with her handbag, searching its depths.

'I'm sure I've got a tissue in here somewhere.'

'Who else can tell me what is Word in Time. June?'

'What? Oh me? I'm just looking for a tissue Stan.'

'I can see that,' he commented, and produced one from his pocket.

'Oh thank you,' she took it and closed her bag reluctantly.

'Word in Time?' she repeated thoughtfully.

'Talking about the past?' she hazarded a guess.

Stanley clapped making us all jump. 'Well done June. Memory yes. Anything to add Bett?'

June had a pleased expression as she wiped her nose with the tissue Stanley had given her. We both stared at Betty.

'Well, I suppose memory is from the past and so if what we say is based on past memories we are going to colour what is happening in the present.'

I was impressed.

'Very good,' Stanley agreed. 'And what will happen June if we do that?'

She wasn't expecting the question and was perceptibly startled.

'Me? Oh, um, well, I suppose it might not be appropriate, because we're talking about what we're remembering happened back then instead of what's happening now.'

'Exactly. Thank you June. Now do you all understand June's point? Word in Time is memory, and if we speak from our experiences based on the past we are not in the moment and what we say may not be relevant or appropriate.'

Word in Time is memory it may not be relevant or appropriate

'So, to continue, what is Time in Word?'

'I guess it must be the opposite of Word in Time,' Betty suggested.

'Which is?'

He made a gesture with his hand as if to indicate for her to say more. He wasn't going to let her off that easily.

'Speaking without thinking?'

'Yes, and what happens when you speak without thinking?' he asked.

'You put your foot in it?' June laughed. 'At least I always do.'

'I think you just did again June,' he said, laughing.

'Did I?' she enquired innocently. 'How?'

I laughed this time and she looked at me puzzled. I decided to come to her rescue.

'I think June means that we speak spontaneously, while linked to our Higher Self, don't you June?'

'Do I?' she said sounding doubtful.

'Yes you do,' Betty joined in with the game.

'OK then I do,' June finally agreed.

'Perhaps you could also tell June what happens when we speak spontaneously while linked to the Higher Self?' Stanley enquired of me, with a tilt of his elfin face to the right.

I looked stricken. He'd caught me out.

He smiled at me sweetly in his pleasure.

'Come on Abby,' prompted Betty, trying to rally the troops.

'I don't know. You say if you do,' I replied, somewhat petulantly.

'Would it be that you invoke the Power of the Spoken Word?' Betty asked, speaking for us all.

'It would indeed,' Stanley nodded, 'and what happens when you use the power of the spoken word? Anyone?'

'Things change,' Betty answered.

'They do indeed,' he agreed. 'In what way do they change?'

'For the better?' she didn't sound too sure.

'Yes, for the better, how does that work?' he was trying to make sure that we understood the process I realised, rather than just being annoying.

'It cuts through negative thinking,' I said.

'That's what I wanted to hear. Yes, it's the sword that cuts both ways, Time in Word. The power of the Spoken Word, the two edged sword of Truth. That's what you are wielding when you use Time in Word. The power of the Spoken Word.'

Time in Word is

The power of the Spoken Word.

The two edged sword of Truth

'Oh,' I needed a moment to digest the information as I wrote it down and peered at what I had written. It was a powerful tool that Stanley had given us. The magical tool of voice command.

'Now consider please if you will what is Time in Action?'

His voice cut through my thinking. There was to be no respite, the workshops carried us ever onwards.

'Haven't we done this?' June asked.

'No, June, why would you think that?' he asked.

'Well, it's acting without thinking isn't it?'

'Ah, you are thinking of Time in Thought June.'

'Yes that's right.'

'Now we are considering the action rather than the thought.'

'I don't understand the difference,' she objected.

'We agreed that it is better to act first and think afterwards, yes?'

'Yes,' she agreed.

'Now we are considering the action rather than the thinking.'

'Oh,' was all she said, but still looked confused.

I felt the same.

Fortunately Betty was on the ball.

'Time in Action comes from the past, which must be your experiences,' she concluded.

'Well done Bett. You are correct. It is your experiences,' Stanley confirmed.

Oh. Somehow I had been expecting it to be more difficult. I noted:

*Time in Action is acting
from your experiences*

'So perhaps you could also tell us what is Action in Time?'

'Ah, now there you've got me,' she laughed and sat back, expecting us to answer.

I looked at June and her eyes widened and rolled, in a grimace of I haven't got a clue.

My brain had gone woolly. I think I was getting tired.

'Sorry Stanley, we don't know,' I admitted.

His response was to march as if somehow the marching would inspire us.

I waited to see what would happen. He couldn't march for ever.

'Action in Time is acting spontaneously from a greater understanding,' he announced.

Of course it was. Silly me. I had come to the point of not caring. But I wrote it down for future reference.

Action in Time is acting spontaneously from a greater understanding

'I think at this point you need a run round the caravan,' he announced.

'Oh Stanley no, I'm too tired,' I complained.

'Exactly why you need some fresh air,' he walked over to the door and flung it wide.

'Come on off you go.'

Grumbling, we obeyed. It could hardly be described as a run, but I plodded round feeling lethargic and trailing behind Betty and June who seemed to find a new lease of life once they were outside. I observed Stanley having a cigarette and wondered about his motives for dragging us outside. Was this a negative thought I wondered idly. However, I had to admit that by the time I sat down again my mind was more alert.

Betty and June were laughing breathlessly from their exertions.

'OK, now for the last part. What is Time in Being?' he enquired. 'Who can tell me?'

I avoided his eyes by writing:

Time in Being

'Getting old,' Betty answered.

Stanley looked surprised. 'Not really. Why would you think that Betty?'

'Well, you know, Being, that is me, and Time, well me in time and time is passing, so it's me getting old.'

'Interesting,' was his only comment.

'Anyone else?'

I followed Betty's train of thought. 'Me in Time, that would be my life wouldn't it?'

Stanley nodded. 'Yes, it would.'

'Is that the right answer?' I wanted to know.

'Oh, the right answer,' he laughed. 'You do like to have the *right* answer don't you Abby?'

'Well there's no point in getting it wrong is there?' I looked puzzled. I was a teacher after all, and I had been trained that it was important to get your facts right.

'I thought we had established that the answer comes from your point of view?'

'So what is the right point of view?' I was relentless.

'That depends upon what state of consciousness you are in,' he threw back, 'whether you are living the past in the present or you are living the future in the present.' He smiled.

'So are you saying that Time in Being is when we are reliving the past in our heads?' I asked.

'Yes,' he confirmed, 'or living in the future.'

'Do you mean imagining it?' Betty asked.

'Well it's more than imagining, it's living it in your head as if it were real,' he said.

I wrote:

Time in Being is Living the Past or the Future in the Present

'Let us consider Being in Time shall we?'

'Oh no,' was my reaction, 'how many more of these are there Stanley?'

'Are you staying positive?' Betty enquired.

June quickly put her arm around me.

'It's OK, I love you.'

'Thanks June,' I smiled at her and pulled a face at Betty.

Betty laughed.

'Being in Time anyone?' Stanley's little voice insisted. It was beginning to feel like dripping tap torture.

'Two please with chocolate sprinkles,' I quipped. I was getting hungry and going random.

'Being in Time is the flow of past, present and future isn't it?' Betty suggested.

Stanley clapped. He was probably as pleased as I was that she had got it.

'Well done Bett. It is the past, present and future.'

I wrote it down as my contribution:

Being in Time is Past, Present and Future

'Now if you could please pay attention, because a lifeline is being thrown in this workshop.'

His words had the desired effect. We all sat up straighter to listen.

'Our concept of a lifetime has to go.'

'I don't understand,' June interrupted.

'By Being in Time rather than using Time in Being,' he explained.

'When things go wrong Create, use Conscious Will, don't fall back on old understandings. Remain open to whatever is occurring. Time Energy is living in the Now. How can we do this?'

'By being spontaneous, act now think about it later,' Betty suggested.

'Yes,' he agreed. 'By using Time in Thought but not Thought in Time. What about our words?'

I sneaked a look at my notes.

'Use the power of the spoken word, the two edged Sword of Truth,' I said.

'Yes. Use Time in Word, but not Word in Time. And what about actions June?'

'Me? Oh, act spontaneously, not from past experiences,' she said.

'Yes. Thank you June. Use Time in Action but not Action in Time. When you do this you will be totally responsible for yourselves without blame or judgment.'

There was a pause and I dared to ask, 'How can we be totally responsible?'

'Come on Abby, you should know this. Be aware of the mirrors. In the past you have avoided taking responsibility by denying your subconscious.'

'How did I do that? Surely if it was subconscious I wouldn't have been aware of it?' I objected.

'Exactly. So stay awake. Be aware of yourself and what you do, stop saying things like, 'it wasn't my fault, I didn't do that, I didn't know,' and stop denying your spirit by saying things like, "I was directed to do it, or it wasn't anything to do with me." When things go wrong, remember, Create, Use conscious Will, Remain open to experience and take total responsibility for yourself.'

When things go wrong, remember:

(a) Create

(b) Use conscious Will

(c) Remain open to experience

(d) Take total responsibility for yourself

He watched while I wrote it down and then gave a little bow.

'And that ladies, ends the Time Energy workshop. I thank you.'

I watched as Ti Ming departed.

'Whew,' June remarked. 'I don't think I'll be able to sleep tonight with all of this sloshing around in my head.'

'I'm sure you are conscious of being able to have a good night's sleep,' Stanley corrected her negative, 'and be able to integrate the information you have been given and put it into *practice*,' he added for emphasis.

'Yes of course, thank you Stan,' she replied, getting up in a hurry and putting on her coat. 'See you tomorrow then.' She seemed anxious to get out as quickly as possible.

Betty rose as well. 'The last day tomorrow. I'm going to miss this you know.'

Stanley smiled. 'So long as you don't miss it while it's happening Bett,' he put his arm around her shoulders and escorted her to the door.

'And you know, I've a feeling it's going to stay with you longer than you think.'

Chapter 20

No Time

I woke early the next morning aware that it was the final day of the workshops. There was so much whirling in my mind, concepts and their consequences. I had never realised how negative I had been. I had always thought I was quite a positive person before I went into detail with Stanley. Now it was rising to the surface enabling me to see what I had been doing all these years. It was scary when I realised that I had been creating all the problems in my life without even knowing that I had.

And now I thought, it can all change. I am capable of understanding all these new ideas and putting them into practice so that I can turn my life around. I was aware that I was deliberately using conscious will affirmations – and before breakfast! I was quite proud of myself.

Reluctantly I stirred. I could hear the rain on the roof and hoped we wouldn't have to run around the caravan today. I would resolve to stay as positive as possible. I smiled to myself, amazing what the thought of getting wet would do. Maybe if someone threw a bucket of water over us every time we were negative the world would change consciousness overnight.

'Morning,' Stanley greeted me with a nod as I emerged into the kitchen. 'And did we sleep well?'

'We did,' I agreed. 'And what about you?'

'As always.'

'What have you got in store for us today then Stanley?'

'Ah, now that would be telling wouldn't it?' he grinned at me conspiratorially while he sipped his tea.

Betty arrived in good time and divested herself of her wet garments. She gladly accepted a mug of coffee before settling into the little bench seat beside me.

'Whew, it's a blustery day out there,' she announced.

'Did the rain keep you awake?'

'No, I slept very well thank you,' I replied.

'Good,' Stanley commenced marching in front of us.

'Now that we have established that you are able to sleep through the rainstorm Abby, perhaps we can suggest that you are able to stay awake for today's workshop, which is entitled No Time.'

No Time

'That sounds familiar,' I said, looking at what I had written, 'haven't we done that?'

'No we have not, although we have mentioned it in other workshops.'

'Yes, I thought I knew something about it too,' Betty said.

'Oh good,' Stanley grinned. 'In that case Bett you can tell us what it is.'

'Something about Negative No Time,' she said vaguely.

'And I remember Positive No Time,' I said. 'We did it when we talked about the dog on the path.'

'Oh yes that's right,' Betty agreed excitedly, 'I remember now, the dog was in the way of the path or was the path in the way of the dog?'

'Very good,' Stanley said gravely, 'and is this the extent of your knowledge?'

'Negative Time doesn't change,' I said, 'and Positive Time is always changing.'

'Oh yes, you're right Abby, it's coming to me now, it was in the workshop Does Time Affect Reality wasn't it?' Betty looked pleased with her contribution.

'OK. Good,' Stanley marched for a while observing us. I knew he was doing something, but I was not sure what. Maybe he was waiting for Ti Ming to arrive, or sampling our energy or tuning in to us. Whatever it was he suddenly came to life.

'When we are creating reality or destroying it, we are in No Time,' he announced.

'I don't understand,' I immediately protested.

'You referred to the workshop Does Time Affect Reality,' he said, 'but there are other workshops that are relevant here also, do you remember the Natural Time workshop?'

'Wasn't it about being balanced?' I glanced out of the window for inspiration.

'Yes, that's right,' Betty agreed with me, 'I remember a balanced spiritual state.'

'Oh yes, and a balanced mental and emotional state,' Betty as usual had been my inspiration.

'Good,' Stanley nodded. 'I'm glad you remember because a state of No Time can only occur through having accumulated enough Natural Time. Can we all remember how to accumulate Natural Time?'

'By being positive?'

Stanley smiled at me in appreciation.

'Exactly, and can you tell me what Positive No Time is called?'

'Positive No Time?' I queried.

'Yes Abby, there is a Positive No Time, and it is called Constant No Time.'

'So are there two types of No Time?' I wanted to know.

'No, there's only one.'

'But didn't you say there was a Negative No Time?'

I was confused.

'Yes. I did,' he confirmed. 'It's called Static No Time.'

'But how can there be only one type of No Time if there's a positive and a negative?'

'Well, it's easy enough,' Stanley began in his slow drawl.

'Easy for you I daresay,' I interrupted, shaking back my hair from my face in a cross kind of way.

Stanley continued as if I had not spoken.

'It just depends on your viewpoint.'

'On whether you are positive or negative?' Betty cut in, wanting to check her insight.

Stanley smiled at her for having got him off the hook.

'That's right Bett.'

I relaxed, suddenly understanding.

'Oh I see. You mean No Time is not anything, but we make it one or the other by our state?'

Stanley nodded looking relieved. 'Well put.'

Betty laughed. 'Well I suppose it wouldn't be anything would it, after all it is No Time.'

'It's a very interesting state,' Stanley commented, 'and it can only be accessed by having accumulated enough Natural Time, which as we

225

know,' here he paused and looked at both of us intently, making sure that we did know, 'can only be accessed by being positive. That's why being positive is so important.'

I wrote while he was talking, which I knew he didn't like, but I needed to take notes as we went along or I would forget.

No Time can be experienced as either
Positive or Negative
Positive = Constant No Time
Negative = Static No Time

'We can aid this process by walking in the country, using the Natural Mirror and Meditation. A strange thing can happen if we go deep enough into meditation. Any ideas – Abby?'

Aids to accumulating Natural Time:

(a) Walking in the country
(b) Using the Natural Mirror
(c) Meditation

He paused and looked pointedly at me just as I looked up from writing the word meditation.

My brain seized and all I could do was stare at my pen like an imbecile. I shook my head in answer to his question.

He smiled and continued.

'You won't be there. Some people experience it as an infinite moment.'

'Wait a minute,' I interrupted. At this he froze and exaggeratedly looked at his watch.

'Oh, sorry, I mean cancel.'

He smilingly continued to stare at his watch and Betty and I looked at each other helplessly until he resumed normal service.

'Right. One minute exactly. So, what did you want to say Abby?'

I was mortified.

'I'm sorry Stanley, I forgot, I didn't mean to put a time lock on you.'

'No problem,' he bowed his head to me.

'Does that mean she will have to pay that minute back?' Betty wanted to know.

'Unless she chooses to put it into No Time.'

That galvanised me. 'Oh yes, that's what I wanted to say Stanley, would that go into Static No Time?'

'It would indeed,' he confirmed.

'And you said Static No Time is Negative, so that would be Non-Practical Time is that correct?'

'Yes.'

I could see he was starting to wonder where I was going with my line of enquiry. It made a change for me to be asking the questions for once. And it felt good.

'You also said that No Time can only be accessed from the Natural State.'

'I did.'

I wrote quickly while still talking:

No Time can only be accessed from the Natural State

'But I don't understand how a negative state can be accessed through the positive? I'm confused Stanley, it's not logical.'

He didn't answer me, but commenced marching, so I waited, knowing he was waiting for Spirit (or his intuition) to give him the answer.

'I'm sorry to confuse you even more, but it's Static No Time that creates your negative state.'

'What!' Now I was really confused.

'I thought it was our negative state that created Static No Time, not the other way around.'

227

Stanley was silent, observing my reaction.

'I think I've lost you both,' Betty looked from one to the other of us in a worried kind of way.

'I think that's both of us lost,' I said.

'No. You're ahead of me,' she contradicted, 'because I don't understand your objection.'

'Well, Stanley has said that in order to get into a state of No Time we have to go through Negative Non-Practical Time into Positive Practical Time and then into Natural Balanced Time?'

'Yes,' She agreed. 'Negative, Positive then Natural.'

'Well, just now he said that I could put my negative state into Static No Time without going through the Practical or Natural and now he's saying that it's not us who creates the Static No Time but that it's the Static No Time that creates the negative state.'

'Ah, I can see why you are confused,' Betty nodded thoughtfully.

Stanley just waited, watching our interchange.

'Well spotted Abby. You have realised that in order to put your negative on hold in Static No Time you have to have at least one positive thought.'

'Like what?' I asked.

'Like Stop,' he suggested, 'Or, I've had enough of this to last me a lifetime.'

I laughed, although it wasn't really funny.

'Time for a run round the caravan I think,' he announced, picking up on my mood.

'What in the rain?' Betty sounded surprised, but I for once agreed with him, my brain needed Time Out before it fried, besides, I realised, that I must have manifested a run in the rain that morning when I thought 'I hope he doesn't send us out in the rain,' I didn't confess to Betty however.

We donned our jackets and pulled up the hoods and headed out into the drizzle. I could feel my brain almost heaving a sigh of relief as the energy shifted down into my body. The cold started to seep into me, even though I was moving and I was glad when we were back in the caravan. My brain was clearer I was pleased to find and noted on my pad:

Static No Time creates the negative state

I stared at the sentence trying to understand. Stanley or Ti Ming had said that we can only access No Time through Natural Time and yet it was also the case that No Time could create our negative learning experiences. How could this be? Light started to dawn. Something from my Psychology studies came into my head.

There are four stages in learning. The first is unconscious incompetence, we don't know that we don't know. Then there is conscious incompetence, where we realise what it is that we don't know. Then comes stage three, conscious competence where we are learning and having to concentrate and focus our attention in order to gain the skills and finally when we have mastered the task we become unconsciously competent, we don't have to think about what we are doing, the skills are automatic.

Before you learn to drive and are just a passenger in a car you aren't aware of the skills needed to drive, you just look out of the window and admire the scenery. Once you decide to learn how to drive you start to notice the gear lever and the clutch and on your first lesson you realise all the things you don't know. Then you learn how to do it, how to change gear how to park, etc. but you have to think about what you're doing. Then you pass your test and after a while you don't have to think about driving, it becomes automatic.

Could this model also apply to No Time?

'Stanley, if we are not aware that No Time exists, then we are unconsciously incompetent, is that correct?'

'It is,' he confirmed with a little bow. I felt I was talking to Ti Ming and that I was on the right tack.

'So in this state of awareness, or lack of it I should say, would our subconscious mind create our learning experiences for us?'

'It would indeed,' he commenced marching, hopefully, I thought to assist my thinking processes, I was on a roll.'

'Where are you going with this?' Betty enquired.

'I'm just trying to understand what has been said Betty. I know there are four stages to learning.'

'Learning what?'

'Well anything you care to name.'

'OK, say driving.'

'Funny you should mention that,' I said.

'Could we keep the focus on No Time please?' Ti Ming chided gently.

'Right, so the first stage is that we are unconsciously incompetent.'

'What does that mean?' Betty wanted to know.

'Well it means for instance that we don't know anything about No Time or even that it exists, let alone things we should be learning about it.'

'Right. I see. Yes, I'm with you so far,' Betty nodded.

I wrote it on my pad:

The first stage is where we are unconsciously incompetent

We don't know that we don't know

'So when we start to realise that there is such a thing as No Time and things we should be learning about it, we know that we don't know and this is the consciously incompetent stage.'

'About where I am,' Betty laughed.

'Me too,' I agreed.

The second stage is where we are consciously incompetent

We know we don't know

'Go on,' Ti Ming encouraged, still marching.

I sighed. 'Well, the next stage would be the learning about it, which is what we're doing now isn't it?'

Ti Ming nodded.

'So this is the consciously competent stage.'

'And how long does that last?' Betty looked from me to Ti Ming, but neither of us answered.

I merely shrugged as I wrote it down before answering her:

The third stage is where we are consciously competent

We know that we know

'Who knows, as long as it takes I suppose, until we don't have to think about it any more. When one day we suddenly realise that we've been doing it without thinking, that's when we realise we've become unconsciously competent.'

The fourth stage is where we become unconsciously competent

We just do it

'Very good,' Ti Ming bowed to me, 'and can you now apply this to No Time?'

'Well I'm just thinking that maybe it's the process of accessing our own subconscious through the Conscious, which is Positive or Practical Time and then the Higher Conscious through Natural Time. When we do this we would have the ability to manipulate Time, but until we gain this competence, we are doing it all unconsciously and it feels like we are being used by it. Is that right Stanley?'

I received a bow by way of reply and took it to mean yes.

'It's the only way I can make sense out of the information we've been given.

'So you're saying that once we've got it, we just act from intuition?' Betty wanted clarification.

Stanley (or Ti Ming) took over.

'That is correct. Remember that No Time is made up of Constant No Time and Static No Time, it can be positive or negative.'

No Time is made up of
Constant No Time and Static No Time

'But why would we choose to manifest a negative experience for ourself?' I wanted to know. 'That doesn't make sense.'

'Oh but it does,' Stanley insisted.

'But what's the reason? There has to be one,' I insisted.

'Does everything have to have a reason?'

Betty's question took me by surprise. It felt like she was on Stanley's side.

'Yes. I think it does,' I insisted.

'Abby is correct,' Stanley cut across my defensiveness. 'There is a reason. Can either of you ladies tell me what that might be?'

He had cleverly brought us back onto the same side to consider the question.

'Why would we choose to manifest a negative experience for ourself?' he repeated. 'Any ideas?'

'To learn something,' Betty said thoughtfully.

'Yes,' he looked delighted. 'To learn something.'

'But why does it have to be negative, couldn't we learn from a positive experience?' I asked.

He shook his head.

'But why not?'

I couldn't see the point of having to learn through suffering. I realised that most people did, (if they learned at all) but I was not personally comfortable with the glorification of suffering. It was a particularly Christian ethic and one that I had always questioned.

'Can you tell us why not Betty?' he enquired. 'What happens when you're happy?'

'Because when we're happy we just enjoy ourselves. We don't question things and we don't make judgments about others, so we don't set any wheels in motion to generate learning experiences.'

Stanley nodded. 'Exactly. Thanks Bett, well put. Do you see the point now Abby? We create our learning consciously in Natural Time. Natural Time consists of both positive and negative. Remember, it is the balanced state where you experience Unity, but you can only grow and learn through No Time. You use No Time to teach yourself or others to balance and join you in this unifying state.'

I understood what he was saying, but I was still not satisfied, it went against my principles. I would think about it later.

In the balanced state you experience Unity But can only learn through No Time

'What you are failing to take into account,' Stanley informed me, watching my reaction as I wrote, 'is that when you consciously create your learning experience for yourself, you understand what is happening and it becomes fun.'

'Fun?' I stared at him in disbelief. 'You are telling me that negative experiences are fun?'

'Yes,' he grinned happily. 'You learn to see the funny side of everything.'

'Even disasters?'

'Well yes. It's just like watching a disaster movie, you find it entertaining.'

I was not convinced.

'Yes, but a film is different,' I objected.

'Of course it is,' he agreed. 'When you are watching a film you are merely the passive spectator. You don't get to write the script, play the part and direct it do you? In 'real' life you do. Fun isn't it?'

In spite of myself I started to be amused as I wrote:

Negative experiences can be fun We write our own script

If what he said was true it changed everything. To actually be conscious of what you created in your life was power indeed.

I found myself starting to feel excited.

'So are you saying then Stanley that we can use No Time to create reality or to destroy it?'

'Well we're doing that anyway all the time, it's just that we are not doing it consciously, we don't know that we are the scriptwriter.'

He was completely calm and blasé about the information, as if it were nothing new. It obviously wasn't to him, but to me it was mind blowing.

We can use No Time to create reality or to destroy it.

'Well ladies, now that you are consciously aware of what kind of time you are creating, perhaps while you are involved in your learning experiences, you will come to understand that it is fun.

'Things to guard against, he held up his left hand with the fingers spread wide and proceeded to count things off as he spoke, starting with the little finger.

We can become too negative by thinking negatively, visiting a negative energy site, meeting a negative person or existing in a state of Non Practical Time plus an accumulation from past negatives.'

He then swapped hands and held up his right hand.

We may have become too positive, by thinking positively, visiting a positive energy site, meeting a positive person or existing in a state of Practical Time plus an accumulation from past positives.'

'But I thought it was OK to be positive,' I interrupted.

'Where there is imbalance in Natural Time, stress occurs in the No Time fabric and causes psychic phenomena,' was his surprising reply, 'this happens because we have created a field around ourselves by not linking with all of the six elements, Earth, Air, Fire, Water, the creative/destructive force and Spirit, but have excluded one or more.'

Betty was excited. 'That explains a lot, thank you Stanley.'

He gave a little bow of acknowledgement.

I can't say I understood it.

'When we are in No Time and we encounter someone who is unbalanced either positively or negatively, we can use either our positive or negative charge, whichever is opposite to theirs, to lift the excess off them.'

'Why would we do that?' Betty looked rather disapproving.

'Well, to help them to rebalance.'

'Oh I see,' she relaxed again, smiling. 'Helping others was something Betty liked to do.

'But they would have to change their habits in order not to repeat the situation in future. If our experience of No Time becomes too negative we will develop feelings of unreality which could lead to an accident, suicide or insanity. These are jolts to the Spirit, to try and wake it up.'

'That's interesting,' Betty nodded to herself, lost in her private thoughts.

If we become too negative we will develop feelings of unreality.

This could lead to accidents, suicide or insanity.

These are Jolts to the Spirit to wake it up.

'We may need jolts to the Spirit if we lose track of our Spiritual purpose.'

'How could we lose track?' I wanted to know.

'Well, we might become so absorbed in our everyday life that we lose track, or we might allow our offering to God to become our God.'

'I don't understand what you mean by the last bit,' Betty said.

'Well supposing your offering to God was service to humanity.'

'Yes,' she nodded.

'Well, if you were a healer for instance, you might identify with the label of healer and that would become your God.'

'I don't understand,' She said.

'Any labels that we adopt can stand in the way of our free flowing energy and bind us in our own limited conceptions, or those of others.'

'So the images we have of ourself, or the images others have of us can bind us?' I asked, needing clarification.

'Yes, that's right,' Stanley nodded. 'If we take them on board.'

'Supposing we have, what can we do about it?' I was worried that I had allowed the images of myself as a Manager to become my God, and the images that others had of me I may have taken on board also.

'Betty? Any ideas?' Stanley lapsed into non answering mode.

'Ask Spirit for help?' she suggested.

He clapped his hands together.

'Yes indeed. Ask Spirit for help.'

I should have known that. I was penitent.

'Why is it wrong to be too positive?' Betty wanted to know.

'Ah, now that's a good question,' Stanley smiled.

'Anyone?'

What did he mean by anyone? There was only Betty and myself there, and it was Betty who had asked the question.

He marched a little and waited before answering.

'Well, if someone was too positive they would be creating reality at a faster and faster rate and the speed of the change occurring around them could confuse their ego minds which might lead to insanity or destroy those around them who are less positive.'

I was surprised.

'It never occurred to me that you could be too positive.'

'But it's not balanced is it?' Stanley pointed out gently. 'Anything that is not balanced will incur an equal and opposite reaction.'

'Oh I see,' I was thoughtful as I made my notes:

If we become too positive we could become confused and no longer sane because of the speed of change around us

'Is there anything we could do to help?' Betty enquired.

'We can lift the excess off them and put it into Positive No Time where the energy can be prepared and held for future use. It can be stored as in a storage battery and used to counteract future negativity.

Of course, if we met someone else immediately afterwards,' Stanley continued, 'we would not have the resources left to help them and so we would have to reach outside ourselves for help.'

'Do you mean to Nature?' Betty asked.

'Yes,' he confirmed, 'or to Spirit. It is this reaching out process that causes psychic phenomena.'

'Does psychic phenomena occur in Natural Time?' I asked.

'No. It only occurs in No Time. It is the gifts of the Spirit that come through the psyche in No Time.'

Psychic Phenomena only occur in No Time

'Which particular gifts of the Spirit?' Betty enquired, looking wary once again.

'Well, they are many, but could include, Clairvoyance, Telepathy, Clairaudience, Teleportation, Invisibility and Apports.'

Gifts of the Spirit include:

(a) Clairvoyance

(b) Telepathy

(c) Clairaudience

(d) Teleportation

(e) Invisibility

(f) Apports

'Whew, quite a list,' I commented, as I wrote them down.

'Those are only some of them,' Stanley reminded me.

'It's quite enough to be going on with thank you,' I said.

'What happens when psychic phenomena occur when we are alone?' Betty wanted to know.

'That could be because you were on some kind of energy site, either positive or negative,' Stanley replied.

'These sites are useful to allow you to balance your energy. Always remember, No Time can be either Positive or Negative and it is wise to avoid being unbalanced in either if we wish to avoid the consequences of an unbalanced state. Of course you may not have been as alone as you thought and the phenomena is being caused to attract your attention.'

He brought his hands together and gave a little bow. 'This is the end of the No Time workshop. I thank you.'

There was a pause as Ti Ming departed.

Betty and I were quiet, considering the implications of what had been said.

Chapter 21

Spirit Time

Day 7
Session 20

Betty and I looked at each other somewhat dazed after the last workshop.

'Coffee?' Betty suggested, and I nodded. She was nearest to the stove, so she filled the kettle.

'I hope after that, you've got a nice easy one in store for us,' I laughed.

'Whether it's easy or not will depend on you,' he retorted immediately.

'When will you learn, you'll never get the better of Stanley?'

Betty winked at him, but he didn't acknowledge it.

We lapsed into silence until the whistle of the kettle. Then he just accepted his tea from Betty and stepped outside into the rain without a jacket.

She watched his receding back and sighed. 'Oh well, I expect he needs some space to himself before the next workshop.'

'He'll get wet,' I observed.

'Since when did that ever bother Stanley?'

I had to agree. Weather wasn't a thing that preoccupied him.

He re-appeared just before eleven thirty, smiling and composed, his fair hair looking dark with rain and hanging in dripping strands over his face. He ran his fingers through it and pushed the wet fringe to one side. That was Stanley's idea of grooming. Betty handed him a towel to dry his face.

'Right then ladies are we ready to begin the next workshop?' he smiled at us eagerly from underneath the towel.

We confirmed that we were.

'This one is entitled Spirit Time.'

I wrote it down:

Spirit Time

'This workshop encompasses all the others, so I hope we've been paying attention this past week.'

He smiled at us. 'Of course you have, haven't you?'

I stared at him wide eyed, not daring to speak in case I dropped myself in it. I knew full well that if I said no he would be most upset and if I said yes, he would ask me an awkward question.

Betty managed a compromise.

'We've tried our best Stanley – or is it Ti Ming?'

He gave a little bow in confirmation.

'Well, we must just hope your best is good enough to be able to grasp the principles. Has either of you any idea of what Spirit Time might be?'

He asked the question as if he was asking for the Theory of Relativity from a five year old. Come to think of it, it was probably a fairly accurate analogy I thought ruefully.

I suddenly felt sorry for Ti Ming, for having such an onerous task as having to teach us – well, me anyway. Betty was much more intuitive as she now proved by answering.

'Would it be when we link with Spirit?'

Ti Ming smiled at her. 'It would indeed, and how do we do that? Do you have any idea?'

Betty puffed up, sitting taller and straighter and looking somewhat offended that he should question her ability to link with Spirit.

'By letting go of the ego and handing up,' she replied rather stiffly.

'Very good,' Ti Ming was equally formal and bowed slightly to her.

I relaxed and started to feel somewhat amused, watching the exchange. I wondered who would win in a confrontation between Betty and Ti Ming. I had lost to him, but I thought that Betty might do rather better.

'Let us consider the Time Wheel if you please. You remember the Time Wheel from the Does Future Time relate to Present Time Workshop of course?'

He didn't wait for confirmation but hurriedly continued.

'Think of a point in the infinity of space, a point named 'I'.

Betty and I complied.

'Now consider a second point in space, some distance from the first, and this second point call 'the Finder.'

'Can I write this down?' I interrupted.

'If you must.'

'Well I'm getting lost without a pen,' I pulled my pad towards me. Could you say that again please.'

'Consider a point in the infinity of space, a point named 'I.'

'OK. What next?'
'A second point named the Finder.'
'Whereabouts?
'Wherever you like. Now draw a line joining the two.'
I drew:

'Can I write this down as well?' Betty indicated for me to pass her a sheet of paper.
Betty's diagram was different from mine.
Betty's Diagram:

Ti Ming observed our progress.
'Now draw a second line from the Finder stretching out into the space around it, and enclose this space by a ring of straight edges.'
My diagram – Time:

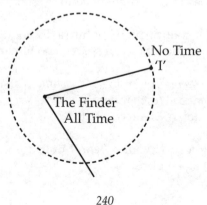

240

'Is this right?' I enquired dubiously, looking at Betty's and realising that they were very different diagrams.

'You are back to your right again. Could we forget right for a moment and concentrate on the procedure?' Ti Ming chided me.

'Yes, but,' I protested, 'if I'm doing it wrong it won't work will it?'

Ti Ming sighed, ignored my remarks and continued with his instructions. I had to assume I was doing it right.

'That which the Finder needs to find is in one of the straight edges of the ring and the point 'I' determines where it is found.'

'Is this the Lore of the Ring of Time you mentioned before?' I asked excitedly.

Betty's Diagram – Time:

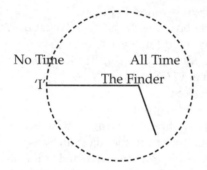

'It is,' he confirmed. 'Now, to continue, the point 'I' we will call No Time and the point Finder we will call All Time. Now what is the difference between the Finder and I?' he asked.

Betty and I stared at our diagrams. We looked at each other and shrugged.

Ti Ming paused to allow us to be struck by the lightning of inspiration, but as it obviously wasn't about to happen in the immediate future he answered.

'The Finder is the point of manifestation, and the 'I' is the point of non-manifestation. Every straight edge on your ring represents an 'I'. We will call each one of these an object of your desires. The whole picture we will call Time.'

I went back and labelled my diagram Time, and Betty did the same.

'Now decide what you would like to find and picture where the object is on the ring. You, the point I, move along the line to you the point of

241

Finder, then move to the end of the line from Finder to where the object is.'

'But I can't,' I objected. 'My point is outside of the ring.'

Ti Ming looked at my diagram.

'This shows that what you are attempting to find is in the unmanifest world, but you have not yet made it a desire. You are attempting to find it before you require it. You are ahead of yourself.'

'Mine is inside the ring,' Betty commented, and turned her diagram around for Ti Ming's inspection.

'Ah, this shows that what you need to find is already in manifest existence at the moment. You already have that which you are attempting to find but have not recognised it. This diagram shows whether you are a Seeker or a Finder.'

'Which am I?' Betty wanted to know.

'It's a good question,' was the answer. 'What do you think Betty?'

'Well, I've always said I'm a Seeker.'

'That is correct. You are a Seeker,' Ti Ming confirmed.

'And me? What am I?' I asked.

'You too are a Seeker.'

'I thought so,' I said happily.

He surveyed my smiling face without humour for once.

'How can you tell that from the diagram?' I was curious.

'Because neither you nor Betty connected to the object that you sought to find on the outer ring. If you were a Finder then it would be one of the 'I's that is represented by the dashes.'

'What's the difference between a Seeker and a Finder?' Betty looked as confused as me.

'A Finder finds things, a Seeker merely looks.' Ti Ming's/Stanley's expression was still serious. 'Stop Seeking, become a Finder.' His voice was urgent.

It sort of made sense, at least it sounded right, but I still hadn't grasped the concept.

'I don't understand,' I complained, looking at what I had written.

Stop Seeking,
become a Finder

242

'Why are the I's represented by dashes? And why do we need to become Finders not Seekers?'

'Look at the diagram,' Ti Ming instructed.

'I have said the 'I' is the point of No Time and the Finder is the point of All Time. What is the difference between the two?'

'No Time is either positive or negative,' I said. 'There's Static No Time and Constant No Time which is always moving.'

'So what is likely to happen if you were in Static No Time?' Ti Ming asked.

'Nothing,' I replied.

'Correct.' His smile returned. 'And what about if you were in Constant No Time?'

I paused considering before I answered, thinking about it.

'Constant No Time creates reality and change, it can only be accessed through Practical Time.'

'No, Natural Time,' Betty corrected. 'You have to go through Practical Time to reach Natural Time.'

'Oh yes, that's right,' I agreed.

'So in which state would you be most likely to find that which you require?' Ti Ming asked.

'In Constant No Time,' Betty answered before I had the chance.

'Yes, in Constant No Time. And can you tell me Betty, why you would need to become the Finder in order to find that which you required?'

'So you would find it?' she guessed.

He laughed. 'Well, yes, but why would you find it?'

He looked at me. I looked down at my diagram swiftly in order to avoid the question.

'OK. You need to become the Finder in order to find something, because the Finder is the point of All Time and what does All Time create?'

We both looked worried, we had no idea and we knew we should.

'I refer you to the Workshop 'Does Time Affect Reality?' where we established that All Time creates the Experience.'

'Oh yes,' I said, relieved that he had given us the answer. Of course, I remembered now that he had said it.

All Time creates the Experience

'So, if you are wanting to find something, you create the experience of you finding it. See. Simple really isn't it?'

He smiled happily and we both stared at him. I thought he had to be joking, but then realised maybe he wasn't. Perhaps to him it really was that simple. I gazed at the man (if that's what he was) in awe.

I needed to get this straight in my head.

'So are you saying that if we want to find something then we have to be positive in order to create the experience of finding it?'

'Yes,' he nodded, 'but not quite. It's not just a matter of being positive, you also have to be in Natural Time, a balanced state in order to centre in No Time. From No Time you create the Finder, who then finds the experience. If you're not balanced, you the Finder could find things you were trying to avoid.'

'What does that mean exactly, find things we are trying to avoid?' I asked him. It didn't sound too good.

'Well, all the negatives you have put out there.'

'Have I?' I asked uncertainly.

'Haven't you?' he countered. 'You mean you have never had a worrying thought, a what if, kind of thought, or considered a worse case scenario?'

'Oh I see.'

'I'm glad you do,' he said. 'So you know that when you are the Seeker you are looking through things that have already been manifested, which is why you can't find what you are looking for, because it's not there. Of course we all know from previous workshops that you create your own reality.'

Here he paused and looked at us to check that we were nodding our agreement. Satisfied that we both were, he continued.

'If a thing disappears from your reality where has it gone?'

The question came at us unexpected as ever. We just stared at him. It was an answer I was keen to have as I was forever losing the children's socks and there was no way they were just misplaced. I just kept buying more and even invented a story called Mr. Nobody, who came into people's homes and helped himself to whatever he fancied, hair slides, shoes, hats, gloves. Everyone I spoke to had the same problem. It was an ongoing mystery, and Stanley was about to solve it. I leaned forward in anticipation. I was not disappointed with the reply.

'It's become unmanifest, so you use the Finder to manifest it and the object reappears. Lo and Behold! It's Magic!' He threw his arms wide in an excited gesture.

'But why did it become unmanifest?' Betty asked, looking puzzled.

'It's a good question Bett. Anyone?' he looked at me. I picked up my pen and looked down. He sighed. He had to be joking I thought, there's no way he could expect me to know the answer.

If a thing disappears it's become unmanifest

'It's become unmanifest because you've used No Time to destroy that reality and if you are the Seeker you're not going to find it. The Seeker searches in that which is already manifest, and therefore it cannot find what you've unmanifested. Only the Finder can do that. Now have you all got that?'

Find it in the unmanifest
and it reappears

He sounded as if were addressing a large auditorium and I wondered briefly how many spirit people were listening in. Quite a few I imagined.

'You still haven't told us about all the 'I's on the edge of the circle,' I said, 'what are they doing there?'

'Whatever they like,' he laughed. 'Or should I say whatever you like?'

'Stanley,' I complained, 'you're being difficult again.'

'I am aren't I?' he agreed grinning cheekily.

'The I's on the circle. OK. Bett, any ideas?'

'Well they're all me,' she looked thoughtfully down at her diagram.

'They are indeed,' Stanley agreed. 'But Abby wants to know what they're doing there.'

She looked up at him with a smile. 'I want to know what they're doing there as well.'

He paused and marched for a moment before answering.

'Well, each one of those I's is an order that you have placed in the unmanifest, and it's waiting to manifest.'

'Oh,' I was startled. 'Do you mean like a child's Christmas letter to Santa Claus?'

He laughed, 'Yes, something like that.'

Each one of the I's is an order in the unmanifest — waiting to manifest

'But I haven't asked for anything,' Betty objected.

'So you've never thought, I wonder, I don't understand, I would like, why can't I have, or I want it Now?'

'Oh I see,' Betty was silent for a moment, digesting the information.

I wonder

I don't understand

I would like

Why can't I have

I want it Now

'So it doesn't have to be conscious ordering?' I said.

'That would be nice but mostly it isn't,' he agreed.

'So could it be negative?' It was a worrying thought that had just occurred to me.

'It could indeed,' he confirmed.

'This is why we are constantly stressing the importance of remaining positive,' Ti Ming put in.

'So how will we know what we have been creating for ourselves?' I wanted to know.

'Oh you'll soon know when it manifests,' Stanley laughed.

'Thanks,' I said rather huffily.

'You're welcome,' he replied.

'The point is to be careful in the future,' Betty contributed.

'Oh the *Future*,' Stanley laughed.

'I mean the present,' Betty corrected herself hurriedly.

'You see most people have surrounded themselves with their un-manifested desires and amongst that little lot will be the thing that you're trying to find.'

'A bit like searching in the attic,' I commented.

'Yes,' he agreed, 'very much like that. And remember, everything that is in that attic is taking up your time.'

'On both levels,' I said.

'What do you mean?' Betty asked.

'Well, there's the actual attic full of things, you remember, he said that everything we've got is taking up our time either positively or nega-tively?'

Betty nodded.

'Well obviously, this little lot,' I indicated the circle of dashes with the 'I's in my diagram, 'is also taking up our time. Isn't that right Stanley?'

He just nodded.

'Oh I see,' Betty was quiet for a moment. Then she rallied. 'I think I feel a spring clean coming on, on all levels.'

'That would be a good idea,' Stanley agreed. 'Now the point 'I'.' He looked at my diagram. 'Your 'I' should be in the centre.'

'You didn't say that,' I complained.

'Well, aren't you the centre of your world?'

'No I wouldn't say I am,' I said somewhat bitterly. 'It's mostly every-body else.'

'Me too,' Betty agreed. 'It comes from being a wife and mother.'

Stanley did some marching while he observed us silently.

I would suggest ladies that you consider making yourselves the centre of your world, otherwise you will never achieve the balanced state.'

'But isn't that being selfish?' Betty said. 'I mean if I am the centre of my world that would make me self centred wouldn't it?'

'Ah but it depends upon which self we are talking about doesn't it?'

'Oh, so you're not talking about the ego self then?' I asked.

'We are talking about the Spirit Self, as this is the Spirit Time work-shop. Make the Spirit Self the centre of your world and I refer you back to the Time Manifestation workshop.'

I wrote it down quickly. It was something I needed to remember.

Make the Spirit Self the centre of your world

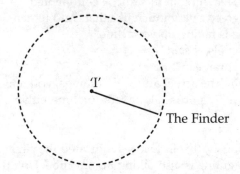

'And that ladies,' he looked around the caravan and addressed the area behind him, 'and gentlemen, concludes the Spirit Time workshop. I thank you.' He bowed and grinned at us as he observed our stunned faces.

'Come on, up with you. Time for a run around the caravan.'

We did not object for once.

Chapter 22

Time Games

Upon returning, I made lunch while Betty and Stanley feasted on their sandwiches. I felt much better after I had eaten, less stressed and more relaxed. Ready for the last workshop.

June arrived in plenty of time and joined us in coffee before we started.

'Have I missed anything important?' she enquired, resplendent in green.

'June, you've no idea,' I was about to elaborate when Stanley interrupted.

'Right ladies, are we ready?'

'Yes Stanley, we're ready,' we intoned in unison.

'I think you'll like this one. Not a lot, but you'll like it.'

I winced, and wished he'd get on with it. Then I realized I was being negative.

He beamed happily at me as if he could read my thought processes, which he probably could.

I looked down at my notebook, pen poised to receive the title of the workshop.

'This workshop is called Time Games,' he announced with a bow, and there was a pause while Ti Ming arrived.

Time Games

'That sounds interesting,' June remarked.

'Yes, it is,' he agreed, 'interesting and fun.'

'That's good. I like fun.'

'As you like fun so much June, you can be the first one to start the ball rolling.'

'Oooh, what have I let myself in for?' she giggled excitedly like a schoolgirl.

I reflected that her head wasn't full of No Time and Spirit Time. She had missed so much, how could she be expected to do this workshop?

However, Stanley or Ti Ming had confidence in her.

'OK June, choose a time.'

'What, like four thirty do you mean?'

He shook his head.

'No, a time, like yesterday, the distant past, the future, ten years ago, the present, anything.'

'Oh I see, well, can I have Ancient Egypt?'

'You can have anything you want Angel. I was going to suggest that the place was chosen by someone else, but if everyone is happy with Ancient Egypt?'

Betty and I nodded our agreement.

Stanley started marching.

'Right, everyone up. Come round here please ladies.'

We obediently trooped around the table to the living area of the caravan and settled ourselves more comfortably on the bench seats.

'OK. So now you're in Ancient Egypt. Abby, pick a person you'd like to be in Ancient Egypt.'

'Oh, it would have to be a priestess. I've always known I was a priestess in Ancient Egypt.'

'Your name?' he enquired.

I thought about it. I was starting to enjoy myself, this was a change from the hard work we had been doing. I supposed that because it was the last workshop he had decided to allow us to have time out and play.

A name came to me. 'Ramuna.'

'Good,' he approved. 'Betty what about you, who are you in Ancient Egypt?'

'Me? Oh I don't really know.'

'Come on Bett, play the game. You can be whoever you want to be,' he encouraged her.

'Oh, alright then, I'll be the king,' she decided.

'The King? That would be Amun Ra.' June seemed to know her Egyptology. I was impressed.

'Of course you realise Bett that you are now a God?' Stanley informed her.

'Am I? Oh, there we are then.' She appeared unimpressed. Typical Betty I thought, unruffled no matter what.

'And June, what about you? Who are you going to be?' Stanley enquired.

'I think I'll be a priestess too. My name is Celene.' June looked at me. 'Only I serve the Sun God Ra. We were always rivals you and I.'

I nodded. I could believe it. Somehow it was starting to feel familiar to me. Strange though, because I always liked June.

'And what are you going to be?' Betty asked him.

'Me? Oh I set the scene, I am the story teller.'

'The manipulator more like,' I said under my breath.

'So, you are all in Ancient Egypt, the sky is blue and the sun is shining.'

We all laughed at that point.

'No, seriously, it could have been the rainy season,' he insisted.

'Stan, you're on your own,' June informed him.

He bowed his head.

'That is one thing I never am,' he told her, 'even though it may often appear to be otherwise.' He clapped his hands suddenly making us jump.

'So, priestesses, you are standing on either shore of the Nile. You Ramuna are standing alongside your King. Amun Ra, what is it you require of your priestess?'

Betty warmed to her role, and announced in a very convincing regal tone.

'I require Ramuna, that you fetch the golden rod from the centre of the Nile river and bring it to me, as it is the symbol of my power and it has been stolen from me. I have reason to believe it was a priest of Ra who dropped it in the Nile as he was escaping in his boat.'

'His feluka do you mean?' I asked Betty.

'What's a feluka?' June wanted to know.

'It's a native boat that I think they would have had in those days, I went on one last year on holiday. Anyway, I'm not speaking to you,' I suddenly informed her, dropping into role, 'you're Celene, my enemy, and you're trying to steal my King's power.'

'Right, off you go,' Stanley directed.

'You are diving into the Nile just as Celene is doing on the other side, she wants the rod of power for her God. Who gets there first?'

'I do,' I said, imagining myself diving down through the clear waters. It was as if I could see the golden rod, lying there in the silt at the bottom. I picked it up and rose triumphantly to the surface.

Stanley handed me a spoon, and I waved it above my head.

Celene grabbed at it.

'I am claiming it,' she announced, 'and now I'm going to drown you.'

I struggled with her, somewhat halfheartedly as I was conscious that it was only a game and I didn't want to hurt her. June however had no such reservations and put her whole energy into the fight and managed to wrest it from me.

'Why are you doing this?' I asked. 'I was the stronger swimmer, I dived for it and won the contest fairly. Besides it was never yours in the first place. Give it back and acknowledge Amun Ra as your rightful King and He will accept you as one of his priestesses.'

'Never,' She shook her head. 'The symbol of power belongs to whoever can hold it, as does the power itself,' June proclaimed with the authority of her Celene voice.

'And now you Ramuna must die.'

'I have a knife and I've just slit her throat,' June informed us.

I was shocked. 'You can't do that,' I protested.

'I think she just did,' Stanley laughed.

She then presented the spoon to Betty who accepted it gravely.

'Thank you Celene. You are now my new priestess.'

Celene bowed her head to her new king.

I was bewildered at the turn of events.

'Betty you can't do that, she's just killed me, aren't you going to punish her for killing your priestess?'

Betty shook her head. 'No. All I wanted was the rod of power back. Now I have it and the allegiance of the priestess of my enemy which puts me in an even stronger position as she will know the weakness of my rival and help me to work magic against him, so I can take over his kingdom as well as my own and bring the people to the true faith.'

I was genuinely upset and felt betrayed by both of them.

Stanley smiled at me.

'Fun isn't it?' he enquired.

I was silent. I felt thoroughly ruffled.

'It's only a game,' Betty consoled me and June tried to put her arm around me. I shook it off.

'Don't. You just killed me.'

They all laughed. I didn't find it funny.

'So Abby, would you say you're state at this moment is positive, negative or natural?' Stanley enquired, endeavouring to pull me out of it.

'Negative,' I mumbled crossly. Of course it was. I had just been murdered and betrayed by my king. It also felt as if Betty and June didn't care about me, or Stanley either come to that.

For the first time since the workshops began I wanted to go home. I was so glad that this was the last one. I just wanted to get out of there and never see any of them again. It might sound strange, but it really did feel as though it was more than just a game.

'And what about your state during the game?' he enquired.

'Positive,' I said.

'Well no, actually it was natural. What were you thinking about while you were swimming and diving?'

'I wasn't thinking anything,' I said surprised.

'Exactly. Natural,' he confirmed. 'And the outcome was natural.'

'What to be murdered?'

'To die and be reborn. Of course if you started thinking and went into blame you would have become negative. Is that what you did?'

I shrugged and said nothing and wrote down rather sulkily,

If you go into blame
you become negative

'OK. So we'll take it that you were Natural. And June, what about your state during the game?'

'I think mine was positive,' she said.

'How can you say that?' I protested. 'You killed me, surely that has to be negative?'

'Not necessarily,' Stanley said.

'What!' I was furious.

'Well, she achieved her goal,' he explained. 'So it wasn't a negative outcome and you can't get a positive outcome from a negative state can you?'

'So you're saying all the murderers in society are positive?' I was scathing but I wrote:

You can't get a positive outcome from a negative state

'No, because they normally end up in prison,' he replied.

'Oh, so if they're not caught, it's OK is it?'

'What we do comes back on us even if we're not caught,' he said gently. 'There is only us, remember?'

'And what about Betty, are you going to say she was positive?'

'I'm not going to say anything. Betty, would you say your behaviour in that game was positive?'

'Yes,' she nodded confidently. 'I would say so. I got what I wanted, in fact, more than I wanted, because I had Celene then to work with me to unite the kingdom.'

'But Betty, didn't it bother you that she murdered me?' I pleaded, feeling totally betrayed.

'No, because your death was a sacrifice that was made to the God who is me and which enabled me to be stronger and gain in power.'

Stanley nodded. 'That was always the Priestess's ultimate role, to serve God and be sacrificed when needed.'

'But that's awful,' I cried.

'No,' He said calmly, ignoring my anguish, 'Remember the Priestess would then become One with the God Amun Ra, which is the ultimate goal for a spiritual being. She achieved unity and a higher level of existence, so she was the one who really won in the end.'

Betty and June looked put out by this interpretation, as if I had checkmated them unexpectedly.

'So tell me Abby, is betrayal and sacrifice a programme that you often run in your life?'

I looked at him in surprise. It wasn't a question I had ever asked myself.

'It sounds very messianic when you put it like that,' Betty remarked.

'So are you trying to emulate the Christ?' Stanley enquired.

I was horrified. 'No. Not at all. In fact I have an issue with Christianity. I abhor the concept of a sacrificial lamb.'

Stanley nodded. 'I can see why you would.'

He stood up and clapped his hands.

'Right. Game over. Next. Betty, you can choose the time you want to be in.'

'I think I'll stay in the present,' she decided.

'OK. Choose, Land, Sea, or Air,' Stanley instructed me.

'Air,' I said.

'June, choose a vehicle in the present that's to do with the air.'

'Well, it's got to be a plane hasn't it?' she said.

'Right, so we're in a plane in the present day. June you can be a passenger, Abby a stewardess and Betty, you are the pilot.'

'Where are we going?' Betty wanted to know.

'Wherever you like,' Stanley replied.

'Let's go to Peru,' June suggested, 'I've always wanted to see the Inca Pyramids.'

'Good idea,' I said, emerging from the dark blanket that had enfolded me from the previous game. This sounded a lot more fun.

'How am I supposed to fly this plane?' Betty complained. 'I don't know the first thing about flying Stanley, couldn't you be the pilot?'

'No. I don't participate in the games, I merely observe.'

'That's the story of your life,' I muttered.

'When's lunch?' June enquired, looking at me. I stared at her blankly for a moment before I realised she was already in role.

'Oh, it's half an hour yet Madam, can I get you a drink while you wait.'

'Yes please a coffee. Does that mean I really get a coffee?' June enquired with a giggle.'

Stanley shook his head.

'But it would make it more real,' she protested.

'I agree,' I said, getting up to put the kettle on.

'No,' Stanley indicated for me to stay where I was.

'You can't make coffee, and anyway the plane is in trouble.'

'Is it?' Betty looked surprised. 'What kind of trouble? Engine failure?'

'Yes,' Stanley agreed. 'You're going to have to crash land the plane Betty.'

'Right,' she suddenly became business like.

'Abby, tell everyone to fasten their seat belts and adopt the crash position. Reassure them and tell them it's just a diversion, and that as soon as we get the plane fixed we will resume our destination.'

'What does she mean, just a diversion?' June looked worried. 'A diversion straight into the sea?'

'No, mountains actually,' I joked.

'Abby. Is that something you would have said as a stewardess?' Stanley queried, looking disapproving.

I felt rebuked, and meekly adopted my role.

'You will be fine Madam, I just need you to fasten your seat belt and adopt the crash position as a cautionary measure. Our pilot is very experienced and will land us safely.'

'I'm glad somebody has confidence in me,' Betty muttered. 'It's more than I have in myself.'

'Ah but who can you have confidence in?' Stanley questioned.

'The One,' Betty replied automatically.

'Good,' Stanley looked pleased with her reply.

'You can't say that,' I objected, 'you're not in the plane Stanley.'

'Oh, aren't I? I'm very sorry. I'll tell you what, I'll be another passenger, after all we wouldn't want to leave June all on her own in a plane that's about to crash now would we?' He sat down beside June on the bench opposite me.

'Is it about to crash?' June looked nervous. 'You said it wouldn't,' she accused me with something very much like fear in her eyes.

I thought it very odd she was taking it all so seriously.

'Don't worry June,' Betty called across to her, 'I'll crash the plane and we'll all go into a higher dimension in Natural Time and that will be the end of the Workshops won't it Stan?'

Stanley said nothing, he stood up and started to march. We all watched him and waited for him to speak.

'OK. You have managed to land the plane without too much damage Betty, but your instruments are out and you are miles from anywhere, all you can see is distant hills. You don't even know what country you are in, but you were almost there, so you could be in Peru.'

'Whew. I'm glad we're down,' June said.

'Yes, but what are we going to do now?' I said. 'It looks like we've got a long walk ahead of us.'

'Walk?' June looked startled. 'Oh, I don't think we should leave the plane do you Betty?'.

'No. I think they're bound to come looking for us,' Betty said. 'And we've food and shelter if we stay on board.'

'But your instruments are down,' I objected. 'We won't be able to call for help.'

'I'll use my mobile,' June said.

'There's no signal, I've already tried,' I said. 'It must be the mountains that are blocking the signal.'

'That's if we can get one in Peru,' Betty said. 'Anyone know?' We shrugged.

'I still think that we should walk to the nearest town or village,' I said.

'But we might not be in Peru at all,' June looked thoughtful, 'I mean we could be somewhere else.'

'Where?' I asked. 'What's near Peru?'

Betty and June just stared at me blankly. 'Geography was never my strong point,' June said. 'Come on Betty you should know, you're the pilot,' Betty just made a face and didn't say anything.

'Abby's the one who should know.'

'Well, we're talking South America,' I said briskly, 'so we could be in Bolivia or Columbia I guess, if we're not in Peru.'

'What with the drug barons?' June said. 'All the more reason for staying in the plane I think.'

'I agree,' Betty said.

'Well, I'll go on my own then,' I replied. 'I'll pack some food and water and if I can raise the alarm I'll send them looking for you.

'But what if you get kidnapped or you don't make it?' June asked, looking worried.

'Well, if as you say the alarm will be raised back at home because the plane has disappeared then you will be found, so you can send them looking for me.

'But you could be killed,' Betty objected, 'and you don't speak the language.'

'I'm sure I'll be fine,' I said, 'and I'll manage.'

'But how can you tell anyone what's happened, even if you do find them?' June asked.

'I don't know, I'll mime.' I spread my arms out, tilting them to indicate a plane and just missed knocking Betty's glasses off her nose.

She grabbed at them laughing.

Stanley clapped his hands and made us jump.

'Right then. So Abby goes to find rescuers and sets off with her back pack. Some of the other passengers go with her. They come across a village and the natives take them by llama to the nearest town where they radio for help and rescue Betty and June and the other survivors.'

'You didn't say anything about anyone else on the plane,' June protested.

'It doesn't matter June does it? What matters is how you dealt with the situation. How did you feel you dealt with it?'

'I think I did the right thing,' June answered, looking smug.

'Well of course you would,' Stanley agreed, 'that's why you did it. Don't we all do what we think is the right thing?'

'Mostly,' Betty agreed.

'Well why wouldn't you?' I said, curious.

'Well, if you stood to gain. For instance, criminals don't care about doing the right thing, because they want to get something without paying for it.'

'Ah now, interestingly I have worked with criminals,' I said, 'and they do think they are doing the right thing.'

'But how can they?' June looked surprised.

'They must know they are breaking the law.'

'Yes, of course they do, but they think the law is just an obstacle that stands in the way of them getting what they want. They think it's OK to use any means to get what you want in life.'

'And you all wanted to be rescued, and did what you thought would get you what you wanted,' Stanley said, 'but you chose different courses of action to achieving that end.'

'So are you saying,' I said thoughtfully, 'that if we want something, say a new car, some of us choose to work to get money to buy it, and some of us choose to steal one?'

'I didn't say that, you did, but yes, you are correct, it is a question of choice, but it's also about outcomes. What you need to ask yourself is, do the choices I make give me the outcomes I want?'

Do the choices I make give me the outcomes I want?

'But where do ethics come into that?' Although I wrote it down, I was shocked at what I found to be his complaisant reply.

'They don't,' he confirmed my worst fears. 'Ethics only come into something if you want them to. For instance was it ethical for Betty and June to let you go alone into the wilderness?'

'But she wasn't alone.' Betty said.

'Ah, but you only knew that after I had told you,' Stanley smiled. He liked making up the rules as he went along. 'You made the decision thinking that she might come to harm, and you were prepared to let her.'

'I knew I'd be fine,' I said.

'But June didn't, she thought you might not make it, or be kidnapped,' Stanley corrected me, 'but thinking that, she still agreed for you to go.'

'I feel terrible now,' June confessed.

'I don't know why,' I said. 'You didn't feel terrible last time when you killed me.'

'But that was different.'

'I don't see how, in fact it was worse.'

'Ladies,' Stanley interrupted hurriedly, 'can we please hold the focus? We are considering what kind of energies you used when confronting a crisis situation. Betty and June chose to remain negatively passive. Now what do we know about being negatively passive?'

'It creates Static No Time,' I said.

'Correct,' he smiled at me, looking pleased. 'Very good Abby, I'm glad you remembered.'

I made a note of it. It was worth reminding myself.

Negative Passivity creates Static No Time

'So are you saying that we were wrong to do nothing?' Betty queried.

'Ah, we are back to right and wrong again. Can we just say that we are attempting to decipher which course of action creates which kind of time. What does being positive create?'

'Constant no time,' I answered.

Being positive creates Constant No Time

'Correct again,' Stanley nodded at me.

'But we were being positive,' Betty objected.

'Were you?' Stanley asked. 'You said you thought Abby could be killed and mentioned that she didn't speak the language. She managed to overcome all your negative fears for her.'

'But we didn't want anything to happen to her,' Betty said.

'So you could have given her positive affirmations for her journey.'

'Like what?' June asked. (It was obvious that she had missed many of the workshops.)

'Like trusting that she would be alright,' Stanley suggested.

'We were trusting that we would be rescued,' she said.

'And so you were, – by Abby,' Stanley winked at her.

'I would say there ladies, that you Betty and you June were both neg-ative, and Abby was positive. Interesting isn't it that in the water ele-ment Abby was natural and June and Betty were positive, but in the air element Abby was positive and Betty and June were negative.'

'What do you mean by the water element and the air element?' June asked.

'Well, water is the emotions, the element of the feeling realm and the air is the mind, the element of the mental realm. Time is also an impor-tant element which needs to be taken into account, for instance, this game was set in the present time, so I would suggest June that you have a fear of flying, is this the case?'

June was taken unawares by the question.

'Actually, I have,' she said. 'But how would you know that Stan?'

'Because you accused Abby of not telling you that the plane might crash. It suggests that plane crashes are in your reality when you fly.'

'You're right Stan they are.'

'Do you think that by holding this reality it will ensure that you have a safe flight?' he asked.

She looked down at the table and hung her head.

'No, I suppose it won't.'

Holding onto past negative realities can affect your present reality

'And what did I do?' Betty asked.

'You mean you don't know?' Stanley threw back at her.

'Well, I asked for help from upstairs and trusted that we would be rescued, wasn't that positive? In fact, no, I would say that it was natu-ral.' She looked confident with her assessment.

'Would you indeed?' Stanley marched for a moment before continu-ing.

'You are correct, it was, but unfortunately you failed to recognise the instrument of the help when it was offered.'

'What, Abby you mean?'

He nodded.

'But Abby's not God,' she protested.

'But she was His instrument in this situation,' Stanley insisted, 'God has to have an instrument to work through. In the physical world, a physical instrument is required, you surely didn't expect to be invisibly transported back to the Airport without physical aid did you?' he queried, looking rather amused.

I wrote down:

God has to have an instrument to work through

'No of course not,' she said crossly.

'So what were you expecting?'

'Someone other than Abby.'

'Oh I *see*,' he exaggerated, 'you wanted a stranger. A stranger is always to be preferred to someone we know as an instrument of God aren't they? Why do you think that is?'

'Because someone we know, we know all their faults and we know they're not perfect,' June suggested.

'Oh, so you can't be an instrument of God unless you're perfect?' Stanley enquired.

'You mean, I'm not perfect?' I enquired with false petulance.

'Of course you are,' Stanley comforted me, and then added, 'everyone is,' which rather took away the compliment I thought.

'You see Bett, would you agree that this is a strategy you often adopt?'

'I don't understand what you mean,' she said.

'That although you hand things up and ask for help, you don't always recognise the help that comes, especially if it's from someone you know, as being from the divine source and so you reject it.'

Betty was quiet at that. I knew it was something that she often did, but knew better than to say so. I wrote down however, trying to be discrete and not let her see what I was writing:

Divine help can come from any source, family, friends or strangers

'You see ladies, that although we are only playing games here, who we are is always revealed in what we say, how we think and what actions we take. In this way the games are a useful tool for ascertaining our strategies without actually having to experience the consequences of our actions which would be the case if we were in real life situations.'

Who we are is always revealed in what we say, how we think and what actions we take

'So do you mean Stanley, that I've been rejecting my family and friends as potential channels for divine help?' Betty looked thoughtful.

'I don't know, have you?' he enquired, looking at her and marching.

She nodded slowly. 'I think I may have.'

'You see Bett, it's likely that divine help will come from someone we know as obviously they are the ones already in contact with us. The One can use anyone as a channel, strangers or friends, whichever way is the fastest route to get the help or the information to us. Right,' he clapped his hands.

'Ready for another game?' And without waiting for an answer he continued, 'Abby you choose the time.'

'Well, we've had the past and the present, so I suppose we might as well have the future.'

'OK the future. Betty, land, sea or air?'

'Well, as Abby says, we might as well go with what we haven't done yet, so I'll choose land.'

'Wasn't the first one land?' June asked.

'It didn't feel like it to me,' I said somewhat mournfully, and they all laughed. I didn't see what was funny about drowning.

'Situation, June?'

'Oh Stan, I've no idea, the future? Maybe a car that runs on water?'

'OK. A car that runs on water. You're all in the desert and you're short of water, what do you do, drink the water or use it as fuel?'

Betty laughed. I was pleased to note she had managed to shake off the last game.

'Trust you to put us in a dilemma Stan.'

'Abby you're the driver, Betty you have the map and June you're in charge of the water.'

I started the ball rolling.

'I think we're lost,' I said.

'Betty, it's your map reading,' June accused.

'There's nothing wrong with my map reading, we're not lost we'll be fine.'

'How can we be fine when we haven't got enough water to get wherever it is we are going. Where are we going anyway?' June wanted to know, looking at Stanley.

'We're in Morocco, heading for Marrekesh,' I suggested.

'No,' he contradicted, 'you're in Birmingham, heading for London.'

'What! What are you talking about?' I said somewhat crossly.

'Global warming,' he smiled grimly. 'It's the future, remember?'

We suddenly went quiet. The fun went for a moment. Surely he wasn't serious?

'Come on,' he rallied us, 'it doesn't really matter where you are, does it, it's a game remember? The point is, you're nearly out of water, what are you going to do?'

'Put it in the car,' I was certain it was the only course of action.

'That's no good if we're dead before we get there,' June said.

'Well how about putting half in the car and drinking half?' Betty suggested.

'That's just halving our chances,' I objected.

'Well let's drink it then,' June put in.

'It's because we've been drinking it we're in this mess,' I said.

'You should have been rationing us June, you're in charge of the water supplies.'

'Don't blame me, you're the one who's been driving in circles, we had enough water to get us there if you'd been driving properly.'

'There's nothing wrong with my driving, it's the directions I've been getting that's wrong,' I said.

'Oh thanks,' Betty said, 'just blame me. I've told you what to do but you don't listen.'

Stanley held up his hand.

'Ok ladies, now everyone has blamed someone else, perhaps you might like to consider what strategies you can employ to resolve the situation?'

We stopped, looked at each other and laughed.

'Let's work together on this,' I suggested.

'Do we know where we are Betty?'

'No idea,' she admitted. 'The map is out of date.'

'Somewhere between Birmingham and London,' June laughed.

'OK. So let's abandon London and try for somewhere nearer.'

'Nearer to where?' Betty asked.

'Good question,' I admitted. 'Well, all we can do is think how long the car will run if it takes all the water. How much have we got left June?'

She shrugged. 'About two litres.'

'Two litres, is that all?'

'I don't know how far that will get us, but suppose we head West, maybe we can come out of the desert as we get nearer the coast. Perhaps it was the motorways that became deserts first, because there's not much in the way of trees along motorways is there?'

'Not that I've noticed,' admitted Betty.

'So if we put all the water in the car we have a chance, we're not going to die of thirst in the next couple of hours, but we might if we have to start walking. Do you agree?' I looked round at them. They shrugged.

'Well, what do you want to do?' I asked.

'I don't know,' June said, we might as well do what you say.'

'Betty?' I looked at her.

'Go on then.'

'Right. Game over,' Stanley held up his hand.

'Did we make it?' June wanted to know.

'Yes, you made it,' Stanley reassured us. 'There was a village only half an hour away.'

'Whew,' June commented. 'Well that was all right then.'

I smiled. 'Now that's what I call team work.'

'Yes,' agreed Betty.

'Really?' Stanley looked amused. 'From where I was standing there was no teamwork to be seen.'

'What do you mean?' June protested. 'We made it didn't we?'

'You did,' he conceded. 'But only by the grace of God.'

'I think that means him,' Betty whispered rather loudly.

He merely grinned. 'Exactly. If it had been real circumstances you would not have made it.'

'Why not?' June turned to peer at him.

'Because you were all negative and what outcomes do you get from negative input?'

'Negative,' I muttered reluctantly. I had to agree, and wrote down:

Negative input creates negative outcomes

Betty didn't. 'I wasn't negative,' she protested.

'Well, you certainly weren't positive,' he retorted.

'Well, what should we have done?' June wanted to know.

'Oh, what *should* you have done?' he mimicked.

'He doesn't know,' I teased.

'Well he *does* know so there,' he countered.

'What then?' Betty challenged him.

'Time for a run around the caravan,' was his reply.

'Cop out,' I couldn't resist saying.

'No, I'll tell you when you get back,' he said, 'and I'll put the kettle on.'

'In that case, how could we refuse?' Betty laughed and rose to her feet, June followed and I scribbled frantically a last message to myself:

Remember to earth your energy and clear your head

Running was good. It did earth my energy and clear my head. It was the end of the workshops I realised and felt somehow bereft. I had grown used to being here and now it was all over. It had been an adventure. I didn't regret for one moment giving up my holiday. It had been the holiday of a lifetime, one that I would never forget. In fact, I realised, as I panted round the last bend, they had been holy-days that would change my life for ever.

Good as his word, he had made the coffee.

We arranged ourselves breathlessly around the table.

'So come on tell us what we should have done,' June demanded. 'You promised.'

'I did didn't I?' he said laughing. 'Well, the first thing you should have done on setting out was to make sure that someone was expecting you. Then you hand up and check your progress regularly. You ration your drinking water and make conscious will affirmations.'

'Like what?' June wanted to know.

'Like, I am capable of completing this journey. Did any of you do this?'

We were silent.

'And what did you do pray?'

'We blamed each other,' I admitted.

'You did. And did blaming each other draw you closer together as a team?'

'No of course not,' Betty said.

'And did it help you achieve your goal?'

'No.'

'It is disappointing is it not that now we are at the end of the workshops and you have all the tools of awareness at your disposal and the ability to create your own reality consciously, you are still using the old ways of negativity to sabotage yourselves.'

'They've become a habit,' I said, by way of explanation.

'And is this a habit you wish to keep?'

I had the feeling Ti Ming had taken over here.

'No. It's a habit I wish to break,' I answered.

'I see. And how do you intend to go about this?' he asked.

I paused for a moment thinking.

'Affirm I am capable of remaining consciously aware of my state,' Betty suggested.

'Yes, but how about I am capable of remaining consciously in a balanced state?' Ti Ming suggested.

I decided to write it down:

I am capable of remaining consciously in a balanced state

Ti Ming watched me.

'Good,' he approved. 'Now all you have to do is live it. And that ladies and gentlemen,' he turned around, 'is the end of this workshop Time Games and also the conclusion of the Time Workshops. I thank you.' Stanley smiled at us.

'As requested these are the very basic principles of how to be a Time Master. As you use the knowledge you will find it will continue to grow and expand your awareness. You now have the keys to Modern Wizardry and over the next weeks, months and years you will continue to progress and yet remain the same. Anyone want to ask why?'

He looked at our blank faces.

'No? Oh well I guess you will find out in Time.' He chuckled to himself and inclined his head as if listening to someone (perhaps Ti Ming?). 'Yes, you *will* find out in Time.'

He gave a little bow and there was silence apart from a bird singing outside the window.

Appendix

Talks and Workshops giving further
clarification on this book are available.

Please contact Abrielle Jones
via Timeslip Books for details.